Cosmopolitanisms

Also by Robert J. Holton

Global Networks
Making Globalization
Globalization and the Nation-State

Cosmopolitanisms
New Thinking and New Directions

Robert J. Holton

Emeritus Professor and Fellow, Trinity College, Dublin, Ireland

First published 2009 by
PALGRAVE MACMILLAN

Palgrave Macmillan in the UK is an imprint of Macmillan Publishers Limited, registered in England, company number 785998, of Houndmills, Basingstoke, Hampshire RG21 6XS.

Palgrave Macmillan in the US is a division of St Martin's Press LLC, 175 Fifth Avenue, New York, NY 10010.

Palgrave Macmillan is the global academic imprint of the above companies and has companies and representatives throughout the world.

Palgrave® and Macmillan® are registered trademarks in the United States, the United Kingdom, Europe and other countries

ISBN-13: 978-0-230-22866-5   hardback
ISBN-10: 0-230-22866-6   hardback
ISBN-13: 978-0-230-22867-2   paperback
ISBN-10: 0-230-22867-4   paperback

This book is printed on paper suitable for recycling and made from fully managed and sustained forest sources. Logging, pulping and manufacturing processes are expected to conform to the environmental regulations of the country of origin.

A catalogue record for this book is available from the British Library.

A catalogue record for this book is available from the Library of Congress.

10   9   8   7   6   5   4   3   2   1
18 17 16 15 14 13 12 11 10 09

Printed and bound in Great Britain by
CPI Antony Rowe, Chippenham and Eastbourne

Contents

List of Tables

Preface and Acknowledgements

This book represents my fourth book on issues relating to global-ization. It was written at various locations in Australia, Ireland and England. These multiple locations reflect the cross-border nature of academic life and might be taken to indicate the choice of a cosmopol-itan lifestyle. Yet they equally reflect the attraction of particular places and the particular people who inhabit them. On a personal level, this study may be read as an attempt to make sense of this dialectic between mobility and place, as well as being an exploration of the feasibility of a more peaceful and just cosmopolitan world order.

Underlying this work, I wish to acknowledge the generous financial support of the Irish Research Council for the Humanities and Social Sciences, who awarded me a Senior Research Fellowship in 2007–8 so that I could bring it to fruition.

Many individuals have contributed directly or indirectly to my think-ing on cosmopolitanism. I owe a particular debt to Roland Robertson, Chris Rumford, Sandra Holton, Supriya Singh, John Braithwaite, Zlatko Skrbis, Rosemary Byrne and Tony McGrew in this respect, as well as to previous generations of my postgraduate research students at Trinity College, including Aisling Heath, Christian Gheorghiu and Martha van der Blij. The intellectual hospitality of Anthony Elliott and his colleagues at Flinders University of South Australia was also much appreciated during my time in Australia.

Papers upon which parts of the argument in this book are based were delivered at the Royal Melbourne Institute of Technology University and the Universities of Ghent and Nijmegen. I am grateful for the insights of others at these meetings into issues with which I was struggling. I am also very appreciative of the comments of the two anonymous referees of the book manuscript, and of the unfailingly constructive and thoughtful role played by Emily Salz, senior editor at Palgrave, in the publication of this book.

The hospitality and gastronomic excellence of George and Anthony, together with their tolerance of my idiosyncratic writing habits, was crucial in the early stages of writing, together with the good cheer and delicious produce provided by Flora. The music of Amy Winehouse, Beethoven, John Coltrane and Thelonious Monk also played a part in getting this written. To Sandra I owe the most for keeping me from

vii

going completely 'nuts' during the frantic pace of work I set myself, reminding me to keep breathing, and encouraging walks around the Port Elliot shoreline or on the Somerset Levels at crucial moments.

ROBERT HOLTON
South Horrington

1

Introduction

Many people today feel the world is in a state of disarray and uncertainty. Globalization, war, inequality, environmental crisis, banking collapse, volatile markets, terrorism and ethnic cleansing have created an enormous pessimism. Some diagnose an impending 'war of civilizations' in which conflicts between the West and radical Islam play a major part. Another aspect of this sense of disarray is the seemingly inexorable process of global warming and doubts as to the willingness of governments and peoples to take action to minimize its destructive consequences. In this mood of uncertainty and doubt, it is not difficult to create a long list of global crises, social problems and popular anxieties about the capacity of markets, governments or communities to resolve the fundamental problems of the age. Many are sceptical about capitalism and socialism as adequate models for the future, while 'third ways' between the two are often regarded as flabby and ineffectual. Fundamentalist religious revival in some places has not undermined secularization elsewhere, while for populations in abject poverty and suffering, simply surviving with some sense of dignity from day to day is the immediate pre-occupation.

In the face of this tally sheet of major challenges facing individuals, communities and governments, it may seem perverse or simple-minded to believe any longer in solutions or at least in responses that offer a secure or satisfactory future. To take an optimistic stance may seem both unrealistic and insensitive to crises and problems all around us. It is often thought that it is only 'the haves' – those with wealth, education, and social networks – who have this capacity, privilege or luxury – a viewpoint that has some force but tends to be blind to responses from below. There are nonetheless an array of ways of life, moral principles, political ideologies and forms of governance that claim to offer or represent not simply strategies for survival but also improvement in the human condition and the creation of a better world. One of these, cosmopolitanism, is the subject of this book.

Cosmopolitanism at its simplest joins together two ideas, that of the *cosmos* or the world as a whole with *polis*, or political community. Put together, the two refer to ideas of a global politics involving citizens of the world. However the terms cosmopolitan and cosmopolitanism have come to take on far broader meanings, to do with being at home in a world of mobility and travel, involving contact between peoples and cultures. In this way, cosmopolitanism has recently become seen as a way of life as much as a sense of political or ethical obligation to the world as a whole.

In the process it has been associated with many different activities, values and institutions. Some of these are typically regarded in a positive way, such as connections between cosmopolitanism and the search for peace, an end to war, promotion of human rights over tyranny and racism, and tolerance of or curiosity about other cultures and ways of life. Other estimations are more negative, such as those that see cosmopolitanism as the privilege of the wealthy and powerful, as a rootless search for new experience that undermines community, or as a fruitless dream of global unity that flies in the face of local and national allegiances. Such estimations are both *moral or normative* – relating to views about how social life and politics should be organized – as well as *empirical* – pertaining to the reality of social processes and human endeavours. Political activists and lawyers, migrants and religious communities, internet users and tourists, workers, corporate managers and diplomats are all implicated in cosmopolitanism, for better or worse.

One reason for writing this book is to analyse why there has been a revival of interest in cosmopolitanism over the last twenty years, involving the worlds of practical politics, law, business, urban life and the media, as well as among scholars from a range of disciplines. It is important to analyse how and why this is so. What is it that is interesting, significant, and possibly inescapable about cosmopolitanism? And what are its strengths and limitations? How far can it really contribute to the resolution of the challenges and uncertainties of the age?

A second reason for the book is to draw attention to the way cosmopolitanism has been radically rethought in scholarship. This has involved prising the topic away from the grasp of philosophers and bringing it into a broader relationship with sociological, anthropological scholars, as well as political scientists, geographers, literary theorists and practitioners of cultural studies. What matters here is as much to do with analysis of what cosmopolitanism is, where and how it takes root and becomes built into enduring institutions, or fades away, as much as whether one should support cosmopolitanism as a political or ethical doctrine.

Scholarship in cosmopolitanism is at an exciting but often frustrating stage. Researchers have identified dozens of types of cosmopolitanism across space and time, deploying many new theories and concepts dealing with different facets of a topic. These have not so far been brought together in one place, but left to proliferate. The study of cosmopolitanism threatens to become over-burdened with so many disparate elements and implications that it will become incoherent chaos. This book is therefore designed as an intellectual mapping of an important but difficult and seemingly intractable terrain. This requires a surer grasp of definitions and concepts, as well as a more realistic sense of what evidence about cosmopolitanism has been assembled and analysed across multiple fields. This exercise is in turn important not only for an understanding of issues like globalization and social change and the prospects for a more just and democratic world, but also because evidence sheds light on the feasibility of cosmopolitanism and the challenges facing those who would seek to promote it.

A final reason for this book is personal in the sense that I am myself part of the phenomena in question, living and writing in three different countries. This creates not only puzzling difficulties for my identity – can I be simultaneously Australian, British and Irish? – but also awareness of the manner in which cultural, as well as economic and political processes, take a cross-border form. Few cultures stop or start at territorial boundaries, and it may be that few ever did. The world of ideas has never done so, while migrants and those connected with them have always faced challenges as to how the various claims and ties of place(s) of origin and destination are to be approached. As a writer, migrant, and traveller, I puzzle too about why it is that particular places, people and moments still matter so much for those that enjoy mobility and dislocation, but equally wonder whether forced mobility, poverty and higher-risk processes of cross-border mobility necessarily create obstacles and impediments to cosmopolitanism. The paradoxes of simultaneously global and local ways of life and affiliations have been a spur to writing this volume, as has a political interest in how cosmopolitan democracy might or may already be working in practice as distinct from mere rhetorical celebration of cosmopolitan values.

The Multiple Legacies of Cosmopolitanism

In one form or another, cosmopolitanism has a long history stretching back over 2,000 years to ancient Greece and Rome (Nussbaum, 1997; Inglis and Robertson, 2004, 2005). The word derives linguistically from two terms, *cosmos*, or the world as a whole, and *polis*, referring to the idea of a self-governing political community. Put together these represent the idea that citizenship can and ought to be founded on a worldwide community, composed of citizens of the world, or cosmopolitans. In this world-view we all have a duty to help each other or at least to be sensitive towards our respective values and ways of life, regardless of political borders and cultural differences. As a *moral or ethical doctrine*, the cosmopolitan legacy to the contemporary world urges that universal or global commitments to all should, in some sense, override though not necessarily deny or negate local and particular loyalties of kinship, place and nation. Moral universalism takes precedence over moral particularism.

From its historic origins amongst philosophers, historians, empire builders and those who have held political office (Inglis and Robertson, 2005), ideas of this kind have surfaced and been reformulated in a range of settings across time and space, involving religion, the arts and popular culture, business and law. Cosmopolitanism is evident for example in early Christianity and medieval literature (Edwards, 2001), the 18th century Enlightenment, and more recent global movements for cosmopolitan law based on human rights, environmental sustainability and greater global democracy (Held, 1995).

Multiple and often inter-connected legacies have fed into cosmopolitan thought and action. It has also been linked, for example, with specific forms of cultural identity and daily activities in a globalizing world. Here the ways of life of social groups such as professionals, migrants, travellers and tourists also cross borders and require attention to the challenges of 'living with strangers' (Appiah, 2006). Alongside the historical connection with the very general and abstract values and obligations of world citizenship, the idea of cosmopolitanism as a varied array of inter-cultural ways of life has recently become far more significant. What matters here is not moral universalism able to transcend any particular social context, but the ways in which cosmopolitan impulses and ways of life emerge in specific contexts and carry with them particular traditions, meanings and social practices that are somehow brought into more general inter-cultural engagements with others.

In addition to prominent individuals over the ages who have been associated with cosmopolitanism, such as Socrates, Cicero, the Roman Emperor Marcus Aurelius, St Augustine, Geoffrey Chaucer, Immanuel Kant and Mother Teresa, there are many more unnamed and unsung cosmopolitans who should be added to the reckoning. These include millions of pilgrims who see themselves as part of a single worldwide religious community, whether Christian or Islamic, as well as those who are physically mobile across borders and who actively engage with and learn from cultural difference. It also comprises those with a cosmopolitan imagination that crosses borders and seeks to create moral, cultural and political linkages, sympathies and solidarities, as well as movements of practical change. A striking example of this is contemporary environmentalism which has arisen as a response to environmental challenges that cannot be resolved on a national basis within single countries, and which draws emotional power from images of Planet Earth under imminent threat of ecological crisis.

Paradoxically, the idea of cosmopolitanism has now expanded in so many different ways that it cannot be easily identified with an explicit philosophical outlook or political theory enshrined in a set of formal principles to which adherents must sign up or commit. Cosmopolitan principles have certainly been enunciated (Kant, 1991 [1784]), and cosmopolitan manifestoes have emerged (Beck, 1998), but the term has also been extended in a more sociological and anthropological direction. Such extensions have seen cosmopolitanism presented as a leading principle of contemporary social life (Beck, 2006). As part of this process, 'ordinary' or 'vernacular' cosmopolitanism has been identified among many who may not explicitly think of themselves as political activists and who have not read the ancient philosophers, but whose thoughts and actions exhibit key features of cosmopolitanism as sketched above. Quite how many of such unwitting cosmopolitans there are, and in what social circumstances such views and practices emerge, is an interesting and complex question, which we shall return to at a number of points in this book.

For the moment we simply note the vast proliferation of settings within which cosmopolitanism has been identified. This includes a diversity of social groups (corporate, upper class, working class, migrant), cultural constellations (Black, Christian, Islamic, South Asian), types of social function (anti-colonial, democratic, emancipatory, exclusionary, Romantic) and forms of expression (aesthetic, ethical, institutional, normative-political, symbolic, and visceral). [Detailed citations for this body of work are available in Chapter 2 and in Appendix 1.] Meanwhile, a sense of the thematic range and disciplinary breadth of this body of research and commentary can usefully be gained from the following three examples.

The first is Mica Nava's (2002) study of cosmopolitanism as a 'structure of feeling' in certain aspects of consumer behaviour in the highly mobile cross-cultural setting of early 20th century London. This structure arises through a powerful intersection between the promotion of modernist fashion and décor in Selfridges department store and the arts more generally, on the one side, and the desires and imagination of women consumers attracted by the symbolic and erotic allure of cultural difference in fashion, dance and theatre. Particular examples included the Oriental style in Russian ballet and the tango coupled with exoticized Latin lovers (e.g. Rudolf Valentino) in film. This is a long way from the earnest discussions of male philosophers in ancient Greece, yet for Nava this case study of modernist consumerism constitutes an affective rather than cognitive or explicitly ethical dimension of cosmopolitanism. They qualify as part of the cosmopolitan constellation, in her view, inasmuch as modernist white women's desires and world views became associated with culturally repudiated social groups outside the dominant rational Western political and cultural mainstream. Women in this example become active makers of cosmopolitan culture from below, as a counter-culture of modernity.

The second example deals in a different way with cities as supportive milieux for cosmopolitan rights for asylum seekers, emphasizing the need to take up the historic legacy of cosmopolitanism from the ancient world, Christianity and the Enlightenment. It draws on a speech made by the French post-structuralist writer Derrida in 1996 to the International Parliament of Writers (IPW) in Strasbourg. This called for cities to take up the role as protectors and promoters of rights of refuge for asylum seekers, a number of whom are writers and artists whom repressive regimes have tried to silence (Derrida, 2001). The immediate context for this was the tightening of French immigration restrictions in the mid-1990s, through the Debret Laws directed at border-crossers without official papers, which asylum seekers typically lack. Derrida was speaking on behalf of a worldwide IPW campaign which by 2001 had seen a number of writers and political activists facing censorship and imprisonment resettled through IPW networks. They included Svetlana Alexievitch from Ukraine, condemned as a literary traitor for critical commentary on the post-Chernobyl world, re-settled in Tuscany; Alia Mamdouth from Iraq, censored for discussing women's rights and sexuality, re-settled in Paris via Beirut and Rabat; and Bashkin Shehu from Albania, previously imprisoned for criticism of the Hoxha regime, re-settled in Spain (Banks, 2001: 2–3). This example reminds us that while the classical Occidental political legacy of cosmopolitanism no longer holds a privileged position, it cannot be discounted as irrelevant.

The third example is drawn from Rustom Barucha's (2006) study of Rabindranath Tagore, Nobel prize-winning Indian poet, educational reformer and political activist, and Okakura Tenshin, Japanese art curator and cultural commentator. Living and working in the late 19th and early to mid-20th centuries, Tagore and Okakura were indefatigable world travellers and centres of extensive global networks of 'rich donors, dealers, agents, diplomats, connoisseurs, disciples and friends' (*ibid*: 112–13), and of political activists and writers (Holton, 2008). In an epoch of Empire and global political instability, they both supported the national resurgence of India and Japan, and the regional resurgence of Asia as a cultural and civilizational force. While neither claimed the identity of a cosmopolitan – regarded by Tagore as 'colourless vagueness' (Barucha, 114) – each travelled extensively in Asia and the West and engaged in cross-cultural conversation, conflict and sometimes polemic. While not self-styled cosmopolitans, Barucha presents them not as bearers of the Western traditions of philosophical and political universalism, but as examples of a militant kind of 'subaltern cosmopolitanism' (119–23).

These three examples cover a wide range of themes in time and space. Thematically they suggest the multiple origins and types of cosmopolitanism, which is very far from being an exclusively Western gift to the world. They not only indicate the uncoupling of cosmopolitanism from any sense of universalism derived from a particular social source, but also, taken together, reveal some of the ways in which a universalistic 'one size fits all' approach to cosmopolitan has been eroded in favour of a multiplicity of approaches.

A further important point concerns explicit and implicit senses of cosmopolitanism. Whether or not individuals and movements associate themselves with cosmopolitanism, as such, is of less centrality than the characteristics of what is thought and done, and how far what are effectively cosmopolitan practices (such as the Cities of Refuge), become part of sustained relationships and institutions. The three cases, the first provided by a sociologist based in the UK, the second by a French philosopher, and the third by an independent writer and theatre director living in Calcutta, are also symptomatic of the range of academic disciplines and writers that are currently contributing to the proliferation of commentary on cosmopolitanism. And they are but a small sample of a far greater diversity of theme and interest, a diversity which will be explored in terms of a systematic typology of cosmopolitanism in Chapter 2.

Meanwhile, having seen that cosmopolitanism is, in a metaphorical sense, a coat of many colours, it remains to be established what different kinds of threads are evident, how much strength the coat manifests, and how easily the coat may be unravelled by internal weaknesses, tensions, or faults in the fabric. Can a single coat really be made out of all this diversity? And what differences are evident among observers and wearers of the coat? Do all observers see it in the same light, or are we talking of a range of cosmopolitan apparel whose attractiveness is influenced by differences of cultural perception and inequalities of class?

Two initial cautions are certainly necessary as we move from metaphor to empirical analysis. One is to ensure that the numbers of unsung cosmopolitans are not exaggerated through absence of clear definition. It is as important to indicate the limits as much as the scope of cosmopolitanism. The second caution, however, is to be even-handed in recognizing complexities involved in assessing the extent of any worldview, whether conservative or socialist, nationalist or cosmopolitan. Such calculations are sometimes messy because the attitudes and practices of individuals and groups are often internally contradictory when judged by pristine evaluative criteria. Distinct and apparently obverse positions may sometimes be combined, as with nationalist cosmopolitans or cosmopolitan nationalists identified in recent research. Sorting out these complexities is important, and will be an extended feature of later chapters. Until this is done we should avoid the assumption that because there is so much nationalism around, there really is very little cosmopolitanism to speak of. Equally, we should avoid the converse assumption that because many instances of cosmopolitanism (explicit and implicit) can be identified, this represents, to switch metaphors, the tip of some gigantic cosmopolitan iceberg floating around out there whose wondrous dimensions are yet to be determined. Possibly so, but a good deal more analysis is required to be sure.

One strong and recurring political thread in the evolution of cosmopolitanism across time and space, is the dimension recently termed cosmopolitics (Cheah and Robbins, 1998; Archibugi, 2003). This alerts us both to the connection of cosmopolitanism with visions of the good society (of which world government is one), with policies designed to enlarge and enhance citizenship (such as global human rights) and ways of generating increased social participation and social cohesion (such as global civil society). The call for a league of nations to curtail war by the philosopher Kant at the end of the 18th century and the 20th century emergence of cosmopolitan law within and around the expanding array of global institutions are testimony to the robustness of this political thread. Theorists with an interest in post-colonialism have also emphasized this thread in ways which direct attention to non-Western or post-Western contributions (Cheah and Robbins, *ibid*). A final example of the resilience of political cosmopolitanism is the idea that cosmopolitan democracy might be a way of creating political institutions able to meet the current absence of effective and legitimate modes of global politics – that is, to meet the much-debated global democracy deficit.

Such ambitions, in turn, raise questions both about the political feasibility of cosmopolitics and its relationship with power structures.

Is cosmopolitanism simply a way of managing cross-border processes and inter-dependencies from above dominated by empires, powerful nation-states, global regulatory institutions like the World Trade Organization, business corporations and dominant Western cultural assumptions about the desirability of secular reason, democratic politics, and individualism? Or can it equally be seen in terms of cross-border forms of cultural life and politics that operate from below? Settings where cosmopolitanism has been identified as operating from below involve globally oriented social movements and networks of political activists, professionals and workers, intellectuals, migrants and artists linking cities and communities. So where does this diversity lead us? Is there, for example, a necessary and unbridgeable conflict between cosmopolitanism from above and from below?

It is clear that cosmopolitanism is, in a number of respects, a world-view and way of life suited to the more powerful and wealthy. In this vein critical comments have seen it as the class consciousness of frequent flyers (Calhoun, 2007), detached from the social realities of inequality and suffering. While cross-border mobility is not a monopoly of the privileged, it is far easier for those with wealth and power, who can both afford to travel, and who may have assets and interests in more than one territory or nation. Elite cosmopolitanism may also be connected with luxury consumption and a life divided between multiple residences in a number of cities and resorts. What matters here is not loyalty to and dependence upon a single national community, but the capacity to do without a national domicile, whether for reasons of cultural preference or tax avoidance. To this combination of global access and global interest, many critics would add a third feature of cosmopolitanism, namely a disdain for the national, local and parochial, as a less desirable and exciting way of life, with narrow horizons and small-minded prejudices.

In spite of the reality of elite cosmopolitanism, the argument developed in this book sees cosmopolitanism from below as an equally robust phenomenon. The connection between cosmopolitanism and domination is contingent rather than necessary. As will be expanded on in Chapter 3, there are many reasons why the less powerful and affluent may identify and connect with aspects of the world beyond their immediate origins. This may be as a way of escaping or resisting forms of local power in the name of the more universal claims of religious or political commitments, whether aimed at religious salvation or social revolution. Equally direct experience of geographic mobility and the creation of wide-ranging networks of cultural reference that span nations and territories, are to be found amongst migrants and kinship groups, as well as refugees and asylum seekers.

The anthropologist James Clifford (1992: 106–8) was one of the first to emphasize that cosmopolitanism was not an exclusively elite phenomenon, drawing attention to unprivileged as well as privileged travellers. These included companion servants and guides of the more prominent well-to-do travellers as well as large numbers of migrant labourers. This point has been well documented by others (Gilroy, 1993; Werbner, 1999, 2006; Waxer, 2001), leading to the development of notions of working class, vernacular or plebian cosmopolitanism. In the latter case, Gidwani and Sivaramakrishnan (2004: 339–41), writing of the Indian city of Chennai and northern rural districts of Tamil Nadu, identify class inequalities between higher income 'patrician cosmopolitans' working as skilled professionals in information technology and mobile 'plebian cosmopolitans' who migrate from villages to perform domestic labour for them, straddling in the process two 'cultural worlds' (341).

It is mistaken therefore to assume that it is only elites and dominant classes who inhabit what Castells (1996) calls 'the space of flows', while the less powerful live largely immobile lives in 'the space of place'. Inequalities of power are very important but they do not map so neatly onto the social geography of the globe. Meanwhile burgeoning innovations in communications technology render interconnections across space more feasible and affordable, linking those who remain physically immobile, though far from immobile in their thoughts, hopes and fears.

Whether all global inter-connections, whether from above or below, constitute cosmopolitanism, is perhaps a more relevant but certainly a far more difficult question to resolve. Global connections may after all be trans-local, as amongst migrant diaspora or criminal fraternities, rather than potentially open to or somehow inclusive of the interests of all. This is an example of a third area of caution, in addition to two raised earlier, in this case, relating to the misleading equation of cross-border with cosmopolitan.

Cosmopolitanism: History, Conflict and Opposition

Cosmopolitanism as we have indicated has a long and diverse history. At some points in the ancient, medieval, and contemporary worlds it has been prominent, at other points its feasibility and dynamic has been seen to be over-ridden by contrary trends, while in all periods its incidence and impact is controversial. For some the cosmopolitanism of the 18th century European Enlightenment, marked by an outward-looking study of the world beyond Europe, represented a world of greater fluidity and openness to strangers than the 19th century consolidation of European nation-states and competitive Imperial rivalry (Hopkins, 2002). Whereas the former gave birth to a sense of universal rights that transcended particular feudal jurisdictions as well as to the anti-slavery movement, the latter saw an increasingly tight Imperial and racial dichotomy between human social groups, reserving civilization for the West, justifying colonial annexation and missionary conversion harnessed to nationalist rivalries between European powers. Cosmopolitanism, in the more open-hearted 18th-century sense, was on the wane, only to revive in the period before 1914 in the form of liberal and socialist internationalism (Lyons, 1963), wane again between the two World Wars, and revive yet again in the period after 1945. These long waves of expansion and contraction will be examined in more depth in the historical sociology of cosmopolitanism attempted in Chapter 3.

In this long history, cosmopolitanism has clearly been confronted by scepticism, opposition, hostility and sometimes active repression. In many settings the terms 'cosmopolitanism' and 'cosmopolitan' have been terms of abuse rather than forms of self-identification. In this sense it is important to be alive to the significance of discursive power in the way that cosmopolitanism is conceived, ranging from its emancipatory claims as the way to global solidarity and democracy at one extreme, to its abject debasement as an unnatural and divisive form of treachery to nation and people.

Outright opposition is evident, for example, within Nazi Germany and Stalinist Russia, social settings in which the worldwide allegiances of cosmopolitanism were seen to challenge primary official allegiances to particular states and political cultures. Cross-border mobilities and connections were seen as generating 'rootless' and thus irresponsible individuals and groups, unable and unwilling to participate in national life and thus dangerous to social solidarity. Groups such as the Jewish financial and trading diaspora, or internationalists within socialist movements were singled out for severe criticism and repression.

Other far more considered criticisms have come from nationalists or nationally minded democrats and socialists, who in different ways wish to challenge the presumption that worldwide rather than national loyalties are capable of sustaining effective democracy and citizenship rights. A good deal of this considered debate is encapsulated in an edited collection of essays published under the title of *For Love of Country* by Nussbaum and Cohen in 1996.

Amongst the points made are the following. Why should one engage with others with whom one feels little in common, with different traditions, ways of life, and values, some of which may be anti-democratic or seemingly incompatible with core values shared in particular nations and communities? And even if such connections are seen as potentially desirable, it remains possible to argue that they are rarely able to prosper, since most people's loyalties and affections remain on a smaller more localized and intimate scale.

The fortunes of cosmopolitanism have expanded and contracted, but have never been far from controversy and disagreement. The episodic character of cosmopolitan expansion, decline and renewal, however, requires close attention to processes of social change over the long term, as much as to arguments in debate. The most promising way of analysing such patterns is in terms of an historical appreciation of the long-run dynamics of globalization, an account which also requires appreciation of its discontents. Since globalization is an often ill-defined and poorly conceptualized process (Hirst and Thompson, 1996; Holton, 2005), some initial clarification is needed before its relationship with cosmopolitanism can be fully appreciated.

Globalization is often equated with contemporary economic processes that cross borders such as free trade, foreign direct investment, technology transfer and economic deregulation. These not only create profound inter-dependencies and power differentials between capital and labour, and between rich and poor nations, but also, so many think, profoundly undermine national sovereignty and political autonomy. Many more recent theorists of globalization (Held *et al.*, 1999; Scholte, 2005; Holton, 1998, 2005), while not discounting these processes and their impacts, treat globalization as a more complex multi-dimensional set of processes with autonomous origins involving culture, religion and politics as much as economic life. The world religions, movements for human rights or environmental sustainability, for example, cannot be regarded as simple effects of free trade or corporate power, in part because conflicts between the economic, political and cultural globalization are important, and in part because many aspects of globalization in areas such as religion or language and technology transfer pre-date today's global capitalism.

Within this multi-dimensional long-run historical approach, cosmopolitanism may be regarded as one aspect of globalization. Above all, its inter-cultural globally oriented political and cultural focus exhibits all the general characteristics associated with globalization, namely (a) cross-border activity, (b) inter-connection and inter-dependence, and (c) consciousness of the world as a single space (for further discussion see Holton, 2005). Periods in which cosmopolitanism has advanced have been those in which cross-border activities of one kind or another have expanded, whether through trade, migration, imperial conquest, war, religious proselytization for converts, or some combination of these. They have also been ones where inter-connections and inter-dependencies, forced or chosen, deliberately engineered or the product of unforeseen circumstances, loomed large in the lives of those affected. Meanwhile, different world-views have also been in play, whether religious or Imperial, diasporic or politically focussed.

While Kwame Anthony Appiah (2006: xii), in his influential recent study, rejects any close nexus between cosmopolitanism and globalization, he does so because he sees this term either in narrowly economic terms, or alternatively as a vague over-generalization. This rather summary one-line dismissal is somewhat arbitrary and superficial. It is certainly incompatible with the work of many recent theorists of globalization who have felt well able to avoid both these potential traps (Robertson, 1992, 1995; Held *et al.*, 1999; Holton, 2005). If, however, we examine the West African context from which a good deal of Appiah's personal interest in and views about cosmopolitanism derives, it is hard not to see the effects of globalizing processes at work in the creation of the cultural and political milieux that Appiah draws on to elaborate his discussion of cross-cultural engagement among strangers.

The context is the Ghanaian trading town of Kumasi in the 1950s in the midst of impending colonial independence and its immediate aftermath. Appiah, raised in Kumasi by an Asante father and English mother, remembers it in the 1950s as a place of cosmopolitan conversation between traders, migrants, and colonial personnel. Here Indian, Lebanese and Syrian traders existed alongside Africans and a smattering of English and other European officials and professionals. While Appiah admits that 'conversations across boundaries can be fraught', he is equally of the view that 'they can also be a pleasure' (Appiah, 2006: xx). Such conversations might be about politics in the home country, but often simply about getting things done drawing on a range of sources including patronage. The point about all this is not that Kumasi is presented as a model of intimate inter-cultural harmony, but rather, through the juxtaposition of difference, a milieu in which conversations across boundaries was possible.

But where does globalization fit in? 'If by globalization you have in mind something new and recent', says Appiah, 'the ethnic eclecticism of Kumasi is not the result of it (102). This is because cultural mixture has been going on for centuries' including a long-run linkage with the world of Islam to the North and East. But if we do NOT regard globalization as necessarily new and recent – even if more intensely felt today – then the connection between cosmopolitanism and globalization is restored. It is moreover restored from a wider perspective than is found in Euro-centric conceptions of its genesis in the outward expansion of Europe and the West. For what comes into focus, if we start from Kumasi, is Islamic cross-border globalization and the long history of migration and re-settlement, as much as Western imperialism and colonization. In this sense, it is preferable to analyse cosmopolitanism as a range of practices and institutions that very often transcend the divides between West and East (Delanty, 2006c).

Has globalization created such a profound new inter-dependence of peoples across political and cultural boundaries, that the human condition has now become cosmopolitan (Beck, 2006)? To the extent that it has, is this now a foundation for a new cosmopolitan politics and ethics that might create enduring cosmopolitan law and governance (Held, 1995)? Or is cosmopolitanism rather more sharply circumscribed limited to some social groups rather than others? Does cosmopolitanism take different forms in different locations? To the extent that it does, is there one basic template for cosmopolitanism or is it multiformed and varied? And if so, what common features lie behind the variety?

Cosmopolitanism is therefore a live issue in a number of inter-related senses. In a practical sense it is concerned with how we live our daily life in the face of the many human challenges created by the cross-border mobilities and inter-dependencies brought about by globalization, while in a more philosophical or theoretical sense it has re-emerged as a major preoccupation amongst scholars and thinkers engaged with questions as to the direction of social change and the possibility of creating a global political community of citizens able to engage with social inequalities, cultural conflicts and political instabilities of the early 21st century. The possibility and desirability of cosmopolitanism have provoked major debates not only among philosophers and historians, but sociologists, anthropologists, geographers, political scientists and academic lawyers.

This book provides a critical guide to this debate, the questions that have been raised and the answers offered. Given the proliferation of debate and discussion across many disciplines and traditions of thought, a good deal of intellectual mapping is required to make sense of the many cross-currents of argumentation involved and the complexity generated.

Any author engaging with wide inter-disciplinary topics and questions, inevitably brings their own disciplinary approaches to bear. In my case these derive from a background in *sociology* and *history*. This book has however been written with the aim of speaking across disciplines, and is intended to be accessible to readers with other intellectual backgrounds. From sociology I derive an interest in general patterns of social change, power, inequality and opportunity, focussing both on structures of social life and institutions, and simultaneously on social actors' worlds and the way these are expressed within and shaped by institutions. Meanwhile from history I derive an interest in continuity and change across time, and in the ways that social actors use arguments about past, present and future to inform and inspire the search for a better and more satisfying life.

Beyond this, the building of wider inter-disciplinary links is reflected in several features of this study. First, bridges to *moral philosophy and ethics* are evident in the focus on the normative aspects of cosmopolitanism and its claims to create a better world. These are identified, not simply as moral positions in their own right, but also scrutinized in terms of the social locations that generate cosmopolitanism and the relationship of cosmopolitanism to other norms such as equality and justice. Second, bridges to the study of *politics* and *law* are evident in the focus on political institutions and concerns to identify whether and how far cosmopolitanism is capable of generating new types of governance and democracy grounded, in part, on new legal norms.

Third, there are bridges to the study of culture, which is itself widely distributed across disciplines like *cultural studies* and *anthropology*, as well as inter-disciplinary studies of post-coloniality, migration, diasporic communities, identity and language. Work in these genres often proceeds from a sense of the importance of recognizing 'new voices' and a diversity of forms of knowledge and experience that enter into cosmopolitan ways of life. The sociological and historical approaches from which I start out, overlap in part with this body of work, but may also derive much from it in terms of aesthetic and performative aspects of cosmopolitanism. The emphasis on cosmopolitanism as performance, for example, encourages an approach that is not simply tied to the texts that cosmopolitan philosophers or political leaders write down, but extends to the ways that cosmopolitan life is performed through conversation, song and consumption of goods, sexual preference and inter-personal relationships. This in turn breaks down any supposition that cosmopolitanism is of the mind, rather than the body.

The intellectual mapping of cosmopolitanism must then deal with both complexity and with a further characteristic of debates over globalization, namely an excess of conjecture and speculation over empirical analysis and the careful sifting of evidence. Theory and the empirical analysis of evidence, whether in relation to cosmopolitanism or anything else, should clearly not be read as separate and self-contained domains. This is because understandings of evidence are framed in terms of theoretical assumptions (whether explicit or implicit), and because there is constant feedback between evidence and theory.

These considerations raise general questions of epistemology in social analysis to do with the status and reliability of knowledge. General debates at this point usually rehearse the strengths and weaknesses of a positivist epistemology, in which it is claimed that facts and values can be easily separated, allowing rival interpretations of evidence to be tested with factual evidence. In addition to general criticisms and re-appraisals of positivism within the philosophy of science and social theory, Appiah (2006: 13–31) in his recent work on cosmopolitanism has indicated some of the problems in using a narrowly positivist approach in this particular area of enquiry. In what amounts to a post-positivist stance (for this approach see Alexander, 1982), Appiah seeks to balance two considerations. One is the importance of a realist perspective on the world, in which we cannot indefinitely hold on to erroneous factual beliefs without constantly confronting their inadequacies. Another is the irreducibility of values and value-laden interpretations of the world to questions of fact and techniques of analytical reason.

Discourses, debates and practical conflicts connected with cosmopolitanism cannot therefore be settled simply by the positivistic application of empirical analysis to conjecture, insofar as conjecture is based on values. What can be done is to review empirical evidence and collect or generate additional evidence with which to confront conjectures that rely on beliefs about fact. And in so doing it is important to emphasize with philosophers of science like Lakatos (1978) and Feyerabend (1993), that the problems posed in any research agenda cannot be settled simply by falsifying single propositions about the world. Rather research agenda, in this case around cosmopolitanism, comprise sets of testable propositions, nested within other kinds of intellectual devices such as organizing concepts and underlying philosophical assumptions. These nests of thought require unravelling, and cannot easily be dismissed through simple-minded testing of particular elements alone. Furthermore, their plausibility depends on their relative robustness as compared with rival interpretations, rather than their plausibility taken in isolation.

These epistemological considerations are intended to clarify the status of empirical analysis that forms a crucial part of this book. Research into cosmopolitanism has in recent years begun to take seriously the previous excess of theoretical speculation that characterized this area of enquiry. Work by writers such as Werbner (1999), Szerszynski and Urry (2002, 2006), Nava (2002, 2007), Nowicka (2006) and the empirical research agenda developed by Beck and Sznaider (2006a) is indicative of a turning-point in research into cosmopolitanism. This turning-point replaces theoretical speculation with theoretically informed empirical analysis. The present book takes this turning-point as given and seeks to push forward beyond it, elaborating a more systematic intellectual map of what we currently know about cosmopolitanism, and what areas of analytical difficulty and confusion persist.

Defining Cosmopolitanism as a Subject for Research

In the first sections of this book, discussion jumped straight into a variety of currents of thought, ways of life, and institutions associated with cosmopolitanism. The key task of defining cosmopolitanism was deliberately delayed in order to emphasize the proliferation of ways in which the term has been used, and the problems of delineating the scope *and* limits to cosmopolitanism. We have, so to speak, collected along the way a series of ideas and prompts that are useful in constructing a definition, including ideas such as cross-cultural engagement, hospitality, world citizenship and cosmopolitics. How then may a clearer definition of cosmopolitanism be established, and how to discriminate between what is and what is not cosmopolitanism?

One way of proceeding would be to live with the diversity, and avoid definition altogether. Pollock *et al.* (2000), have argued that 'Cosmopolitanism may be a project whose conceptual content and pragmatic character are not only as yet unspecified but also must always escape positive and definitive specification, precisely because specifying cosmopolitanism positively and definitively is an uncosmopolitan thing to do'. They write from a post-modern perspective that seeks to challenge the coherence of unitary concepts in the name of diversity and complexity. Post-modern playfulness or irony towards excessively formalized definitions of emergent and rapidly changing social trends may be a salutary corrective to over-structured and mechanistically defined research problems. The alarming evasion of any definition at all seems nonetheless to be a classic instance of the self-defeating character of sceptical argument. If we apply scepticism to this example of post-modern scepticism, the argument is self-defeating because it cannot specify any substantive content to cosmopolitanism, leaving the term as a 'free-floating' discursive *geist* in search of material manifestation and embodiment. This is vulnerable, as Skrbis *et al.* (2004) point out, to serious problems of indeterminacy.

A more constructive way of proceeding here would be to resume the search for a generic definition, but to move beyond philosophical to a more sociological definition. A shift of this kind is a key part of the recent turning point in approaches to cosmopolitanism discussed above. The pioneering work of Ulf Hannerz (1990, 1996, 2004b) is of particular importance in this endeavour. Hannerz draws a key distinction between 'cosmopolitans' and 'locals', developed in part from older work by Robert Merton applied to towns and communities, rather than cross-border processes. Merton (1968) picked up on Carl C. Zimmerman's translation of Toennies' well-known distinction between *Gemeinschaft* and *Gesellschaft* (*ibid*: 447n7). Locals represented a commitment to *Gemeinschaft* or community, having parochial concerns and conducting ways of life based on maximization of useful contacts within their locality. Cosmopolitans, by contrast, represented *Gesellschaft* in the sense of a world of voluntary organizations, having ecumenical concerns beyond the locality, and life projects connected with the acquisition of skills and knowledge. Cosmopolitanism focusses here on cognitive capacities based around trans-contextual knowledge rather than immediate inter-personal worlds.

Hannerz applied aspects of Merton's formulation to the global arena, focussing on social actors who could be distinguished as cosmopolitans who moved across borders, as distinct from locals who didn't. This social action framework perspective is distinct from approaches centred on systems of philosophical ideas or institutions. The key quality of the cosmopolitan is openness to others, akin to bridge-building rather than the erection of walls. The cosmopolitan 'needs to be in a state of readiness a personal ability to make one's way into other cultures through listening, looking, intuiting, and reflecting' (1990: 239). Cosmopolitanism, on this basis, is seen as 'a perspective, a state of mind, or...a mode of managing meaning' (*ibid*: 238). This gives social action a highly rationalized meaning, that contrasts markedly with conceptions of cosmopolitanism as a set of feelings and desires (Nava, 2002, 2007; Walkowitz, 2006).

In Hannerz's definition, cosmopolitanism requires inter-cultural openness and knowledge. The mere fact of cross-border movement is insufficient, since this need not involve cognitive skills and sympathies. Accordingly, Hannerz in this earlier work was sceptical as to whether migrants, tourists, or refugees would qualify as cosmopolitans. Cosmopolitans, he felt, could be distinguished not simply from 'locals' seen as 'representatives of more circumscribed territorial cultures'. They also differed from 'frequent travellers', whether tourists or migrants whose world of meaning was, so to speak, carried internally within social networks that travelled with the groups, thereby inhibiting inter-cultural contact with others. Those who were seen as qualifying were trans-national professionals like foreign correspondents or oil engineers whose professional life demanded inter-cultural skill and competence.

Bruce Robbins has called for greater 'intellectual order and accountability' in debates over cosmopolitanism, which he sees as characterized by 'gushingly unrestrained sentiments, pieties, and urgencies' and lack of a discriminating lexicon (1999:9). Hannerz's overall approach has been influential as a key reference point in this definitional confusion, in spite of the criticisms levelled at it. His influence is clear enough in recent empirical analysis by Szerszynski and Urry (2002) where cosmopolitanism is taken to be '...a cultural disposition involving an intellectual and aesthetic stance of "openness" towards peoples, places, and experiences from different cultures, especially those from different nations' (*ibid*: 469). This definition is interesting in adding aesthetic to intellectual openness, thereby including senses other than intellectual reason into cosmopolitanism. Visuality is one of these (Szerszynski and Urry, 2006), linking cosmopolitanism with the impact of visual representations of the world as a single place. This in turn directs our attention to imaginary or virtual travel as part of the cosmopolitan experience, whether through utopian projections or communications media, rather than actual physical travel.

The two most damaging criticisms of Hannerz's definition, are first that it privileges elite cosmopolitanism, thereby discounting cosmopolitanism from below (Tomlinson, 1999, *passim*; Werbner, 2006), and second that it ignores the ethical side of cosmopolitanism (Tomlinson, *op. cit.*). On the first point, it seems arbitrary to include some mobile groups such as professionals well able to give an account of their cross-cultural engagements, but exclude others such as migrants or tourists, whose engagements may in some contexts be similar, but which may be harder to discern. The qualities of openness involved may not in fact be necessarily connected with any particular social or occupational group, an issue to be explored later in this study. On the second point it seems problematic to exclude ethical issues, such as cosmopolitan values and commitments to the cosmos or world as a whole, or at least to principles and institutions that operate on this level.

In a more recent systematic review of problems of definition (Hannerz, 2004a), much of the thrust of these criticisms is accepted. Following Clifford and others, he now believes that more subtlety is required in analysing the relationship between cosmopolitanism and different mobile groups – whether elite or working class. Hannerz also re-emphasizes that his earlier stress was on professionals (and their cognitive orientations), rather than managers and elites *per se*. Meanwhile, he has taken up the missing ethical dimension to earlier work, suggesting that definitions of cosmopolitanism must now come to terms with the dual character of this wide-ranging phenomenon. Cosmopolitanism, he argues, has two faces (*ibid*: 71). One is the cultural face, with which his research started out. The other is the political face, an aspect of cosmopolitanism which seems to subsume issues of ethics.

The former face is a 'happy' one, and has both intellectual and aesthetic aspects. It includes both knowledge of cultural repertoires and practices other than one's own, as well as what he sees as consumer cosmopolitanism, involving the enjoyment of new cuisines, music, and literatures. Happiness in this sense comprises both intellectual and cognitive satisfaction, as well as the satisfaction of desires through consumption of other cultural products and ways of life. There is no necessary relationship between any of this and cosmopolitan concern for global social inequality, the democratic deficit, and political change. These features belong to what he sees as political cosmopolitanism, which wears a 'worried' face. This is concerned, by contrast, with community, society and citizenship, focussing on rights and obligations rather than knowledge and desire. There is no necessary concern here with cultural enjoyment or engagement with others, indeed it would be possible to be a political cosmopolitanism acting from philosophical principles alone.

The evolution of Hannerz's definition of cosmopolitanism has been dealt with at some length, in part because of his long experience of research in the field, but mainly because it consolidates a central presumption of this book. The presumption is that cosmopolitanism can no longer be treated as a unitary phenomenon. This position has been advanced first by taking account of the enormous proliferation of themes and aspects taken to be examples of cosmopolitanism, drawing on literature which itself comments on issues of proliferation. The second line of argument here is evident in the evolution of Hannerz's thinking. His distinction between the cultural and political offers a relatively straightforward way of grasping a fundamental distinction between two modalities of cosmopolitanism, the relationship between which is contingent rather than necessary.

Two important issues remain. The first is the question of what common element is found in the two types of cosmopolitanism. The beginnings of an answer focus on the common property of 'openness' to the world, whether in an inter-personal or political and ethical sense. Skrbis and Woodward (2007), rightly point to the diffuseness and ambivalence of cosmopolitan openness, which is rarely absolute as well as taking multiple forms. This serves as a cautionary note, but does not foreclose on openness as a central category. Following Tomlinson (1999: 185), openness may still be used as a basis for the definition of cosmo-politanism in terms of a

> disposition which is not limited to the concerns of the immediate locality, but which recognises global belonging, involvement, and responsibility, and can integrate these broader concerns into everyday life practices.

Here 'belonging, involvement, and responsibility' can take a diversity of forms. These may of course be incompatible with each other, as in involvement in personal consumption activity while remaining indifferent to what is consumed or how it has been produced, by-passing ethical and political concerns.

A second issue, following on from the first, concerns the relationship between culture and politics in this approach. The two may be distin-guished for analytical purposes, as a basis for identifying different kinds of disposition to the world. They are also usually seen as distinct in ideologies of liberal free trade, where consumer choice is not required to display political or moral responsibility for the organization of production of goods and services. Empirically though the two are inter-twined in many senses. This is primarily because culture is not a politics-free zone. Politics, in the sense of power over the allocation of resources and the distribution of cultural goods, is intrinsic to culture, whether that is defined as the way of life of a social group, or in terms of particular symbolic resources and practical techniques of living that are created by and available for adoption by individuals, institutions, and communities.

The case of fair trade coffee makes this point well. We may drink coffee to be able to face the day, smooth over the exigencies of paid and unpaid labour, or as the completion of a meal. The use of coffee in this way is more culturally widespread in some contexts than in others, where tea may be the drink of choice. Most coffee marketing has hitherto been controlled by corporations who buy in markets supplied by small farmers, either for re-sale in retail shops and supermarkets, or, in the case of Starbucks, through direct sales. In either case coffee is powerfully marketed as part of modern culture. The power of cor-porations is far greater than that of farmers who receive prices that do not reflect the profitability that big business can extract from the market, though coffee consumers are freer to buy coffee or not, and with the best information to choose which coffee they buy. The fair trade movement (Holton, 2005) has grown up as a critical response to the poor prices many producers in low-income regions get for their produce. It is an attempt to re-distribute income from corporations and consumers to farmers.

So what does all this have to do with culture and politics, and with cosmopolitanism? Firstly, behind the cultural taste for and uses of coffee, lies a political dimension, represented, in the first instance, through the market power of corporations, and then in the counter-politics of fair trade. Secondly, a cosmopolitan disposition may be practised through consumer behaviour in the area of coffee-drinking. Most coffee drinkers may not care where their coffee comes from or how it is produced. However cosmopolitan coffee drinkers might do so, but in two different ways. For the consumer cosmopolitan coffee drinker, a gourmet interest in different types and ways of roasting beans, may also be linked with an awareness of different areas of production, and the characteristic tastes of coffee from such areas around the world through websites like *The Global Gastronomer* (2008). The political background is not of interest, even though it affects price and availability.

For the political cosmopolitan coffee drinker, by contrast, a similar interest in types and quality may be combined with concern for whether exploitative child labour is used in growing coffee, whether coffee is marketed through fair trade principles, as well as concern for the reliance of many poorer countries on coffee production. These concerns represent an explicit linkage of culture and politics and invest consumer purchase with some kind of political or ethical dimension in terms of choice of fair trade and country of origin. For others such concerns have taken the form of boycotts of Starbucks over its stance on the intellectual property rights of Ethiopian coffee farmers in a particular variety of bean.

Plan of Book

The remainder of the book is divided into two parts, followed by a conclusion.

In Part I attention is given to theoretical, conceptual and historical issues in the understanding of cosmopolitanism. Chapter 2 presents an in-depth review of attempts to conceptualize cosmopolitanism, expanding on and deepening the focus in the present chapter on both multiple modalities and multiple types of cosmopolitanism. The aim is to provide a systematic mapping of this expanding and proliferating field starting out from the six-fold conceptualization of different modalities of cosmopolitanism recently offered by Vertovec and Cohen (2002). This spans a range of disciplinary fields, and offers a useful way of charting the dozens of types of cosmopolitanism that have emerged in the last twenty years of scholarship.

Chapter 3 deals with a major theme in the book, namely the elaboration of a new historical sociology of cosmopolitanism. One prominent feature of my argument centres on problems with the influential theory of cosmopolitanism as the second age of modernity, developed by Ulrich Beck (2002a, 2006). His argument is noteworthy for the greater emphasis given to change rather than continuity in the recent historical evolution of modernity. The historical basis of Beck's argument on the relationship between new forms of modernity and cosmopolitanism is subjected to systematic assessment and critique and found wanting. The chapter goes on to develop an alternative historical sociology to that of Beck. This focusses both on the long-term connections and discontinuities between cosmopolitanism in ancient, medieval and modern worlds, and on different spatial contexts and modalities of cosmopolitanism both within and outside what is often referred to as the West. This chapter serves both as a contribution to the history of cosmopolitanism, as well as an understanding of modernity.

In Chapter 4 the coherence of cosmopolitanism is discussed in relation to the development of social theory. What do cosmopolitan perspectives add to theories of society? Consideration will be given to a number of the theoretical currents that have exposed cosmopolitanism to critical scrutiny, including theorists of capitalism and modernity, feminism, post-modernism and post-colonialism. In the second part of the chapter, attention is given to recent arguments that methodological cosmopolitanism should replace both methodological nationalism and methodological globalism, as proposed by Beck (2006). Does this represent a much-needed re-direction of thinking, or is it to vastly over-extend the scope and impact of one social trend into an axial principle of social life? However the balance is struck here, it remains interesting that the language of cosmopolitanism has recently been resurgent in a number of different discourses, from ethics and education to political activism and marketing.

In Part II concern shifts to empirical analysis, bringing together and making sense of a mass of detailed multi-disciplinary research. This part of the book is intended as the first state-of-the-art review of evidence relating to cosmopolitanism. It moves beyond the speculative theoretical mode of much existing writing, while also adding substance to current programmatic calls to research cosmopolitanism more thoroughly.

This section of the book starts out in Chapter 5 from a general discussion of the 13 research questions proposed by Ulrich Beck, to which several missing areas of enquiry, such as cosmopolitan law, are added. A number of methodological difficulties that complicate resolution of these questions are identified. These include the problem that much available data is collected at a national level rather than in a form that engages with the incidence of cosmopolitanism, and the problem that a good deal of research that is explicitly concerned with cosmopolitanism fails to discuss limits. Attention is also given to the challenge of establishing the impact and incidence of cosmopolitanism as a popular and practical, as distinct from an elite and philosophical, disposition.

In the second part of the chapter attention turns to research findings on the socio-cultural rather than legal and political aspects of cosmopolitanism. Accordingly the focus is on analyses that link cosmopolitanism with consumption, employment, migration and settlement, travel and tourism, and mass media. These are treated separately and in terms of their relationship with each other. There are a number of important debates involved here, including the significance of travel or mobility to cosmopolitanism, and whether it is possible to be a physically immobile virtual cosmopolitan through new communication technology.

Chapter 6 examines political and legal aspects of cosmopolitanism. This theme deserves a chapter of its own because it has been underplayed within many of the cultural discourses on cosmopolitanism, and because relevant literature is spread across a wide range of disciplines, not only political science but philosophy, law and policy studies, that have not always been well integrated into sociology and social theory. The focus here is very much on cosmopolitan principles such as human rights and cosmopolitan institution-building, including cosmopolitan law and much that has been labelled as multiculturalism.

A much neglected question in many theoretical analyses of cosmopolitanism is the question of popular attitudes to cosmopolitan institutions and policies. This issue is discussed in terms of recent research, providing a sense of the extent to which nationalist or cosmopolitan attitudes prevail, and whether it is possible to combine the two.

In the final section of the chapter particular emphasis is also given to work which claims that Europe is the major source of contemporary progress towards cosmopolitanism. This begins with discussion of the comparative importance of human rights principles in Europe, Asia and Africa, investigating the sense in which non-European cultural practices may either obstruct or provide openings for engagement with cosmopolitanism.

Chapter 7 provides a case study of cosmopolitanism in Ireland, including both historical and contemporary material and commentary. This case study has been chosen because it dramatizes the paradox that countries with strong forms of national identity have simultaneously been homes to cosmopolitan thought and practice. This brings together themes of religious cosmopolitanism connected with Catholicism, literary cosmopolitanism associated with the work of writers like Joyce, the contribution of Irish performers to popular culture, the global marketing of 'Irish' products, such as Guinness, together with migration and the Irish diaspora. Attention is given here both to the social construction of cultural cosmopolitanism, as much as cosmopolitanism as a form of social practice from below. The Irish case also raises questions about the limits to cosmopolitanism, limits that arise where certain trans-national processes are closed rather than open.

In the concluding chapter, the main features of the recent re-casting of cosmopolitanism are summarized, showing how the subject has been transformed from a philosophical enquiry into the nature of political rights and obligations to a far broader plurality of social and cultural as well as political and legal questions. Attention then turns to the broad findings of research arranged under the 13 elements of Beck's cosmopolitan research agenda, plus the additional theme of cosmopolitan law. Discussion then returns to the question with which the book began, namely whether cosmopolitanism represents a fruitful way of addressing many of the most pressing problems of the age, including war, global poverty and cultural conflict. Here ten theses on cosmopolitanism are presented, indicating bridges between analytical and evidence-based research and the normative plausibility and feasibility of cosmopolitanism. The argument is sceptical but still optimistic.

Part I

Theoretical, Conceptual and Historical Issues

2

Conceptualizing Cosmopolitanism: A Re-appraisal

In this chapter a systematic attempt is made to chart the proliferation of modalities and types of social activity that have been associated with cosmopolitanism. This extends and deepens the analysis of proliferation in Chapter 1. Cosmopolitanism, as described there, is a coat of many colours, composed of a variety of threads, new and old, cultural and political, pertaining both to what is and what ought to be. There are twin dangers here.

One is to simply go with the flow, adding new types of cosmopolitanism to the dozens that already exist, identifying new ways in which social processes, institutions, ways of life and ways of thinking about the world may be seen as cosmopolitan. This adds to the existing proliferation and appears to offer exciting new insights. Once we abandon the presumption that cosmopolitanism is singular, Western and universalistic in form, many alternative sources and types are opened up for analysis, arising from particular origins within and beyond the West, post-colonial as well as colonial, understanding outreach to others in a variety of ways (Robbins, 1998a, 1998b).

Nonetheless this proliferation equally runs the risk of intellectual or analytical chaos. If cosmopolitanism, like globalization before it, is a term that is everywhere affecting everything, then severe doubts are in order as to whether it displays much constancy of meaning. Conversely, if we stay close to the philosophical traditions and elite activities that cosmopolitanism has often been associated with, then order has been bought at the price of dismissing the complex social and moral challenges of the contemporary world.

In an attempt to avoid these dangers, attention is directed first at modalities of cosmopolitanism, and second at questions of typology.

29

Modalities of Cosmopolitanism

Modalities represent the different kinds of social structure and social action within which cosmopolitanism is articulated and institutionalized. Vertovec and Cohen (2002), in their editor's introduction to a seminal collection of essays entitled *Conceiving Cosmopolitanism*, have produced a check-list of six distinct modalities. These form the basis of Table 2.1. All six fall within the generic definition of cosmopolitanism developed in Chapter 1, which emphasized the centrality of an open disposition to 'the world', a term which serves as a broad symbol for 'others' or 'strangers' beyond one's own group or world. This generic definition may be developed individually or collectively, and within culture and politics. What then do Vertovec and Cohen add to this?

Table 2.1   Six Modalities of Cosmopolitanism

1. As a socio-cultural condition
2. As a philosophical world-view
3. As a political project to build trans-national institutions
4. As a project for recognizing multiple identities
5. As a mode of orientation to the world
6. As a set of competencies which enable us to make our way in different cultures and countries

Source: derived from S. Vertovec and R. Cohen, 2002: 9–14.

What is immediately striking about their check-list from a sociological perspective is that it embraces the structure/agency distinction. Cosmopolitanism appears in this respect both as a condition or structure within which social actors operate, as well as within various modalities of action. As we go through the six modalities, both the contemplative and the practical sides of cosmopolitan action are stressed, embracing both world-views and competencies. Similarly both individual and institutional projects are also indicated. In this sense cosmopolitanism is far more than a virtuoso ethic of personal cross-cultural competence, being equally involved with the construction of institutions of governance and law, echoed in the last 60 years in the development of human rights and cosmopolitan law.

Social action, as analysed by Max Weber (1978 vol. 1: 22–6), involves the relationship between the ends of action and the means by which they were achieved. Such links comprise different rationalities for action, by which is meant logical connections that link ends and means, whether or not these are consciously present in the social psychologies of actors themselves. Hannerz (2004a: 77), in his recent discussion of the definition of cosmopolitanism, notes the distinction

Table 2.2 Types of Social Action and Cosmopolitan Modalities

Weber's types	Means-ends connections	Cosmopolitan modalities
1. Instrumental	Means are instruments to achieve given ends	Cross-border co-operation in institution-building Cross-cultural skills
2. Value-relevant	Means are embedded within value ends.	Open world-views that valued human rights and cultural diversity The world as an imagined community, whether of citizens or co-religionists
3. Expressive	Means are expressive and affectual	Feelings and emotions that engender cross-cultural solidarities in personal or community life
4. Habitual	Action is minimally rationalised	Habitual openness as a taken-for-granted feature of everyday life

Source: columns 1 and 2 derive from M. Weber (1978), vol. 1, 22; column 3 developed in the present book.

between a cosmopolitanism of means and a cosmopolitanism of ends. These approximate to two of Weber's four types of social action, as outlined in Table 2.2. This set of types, it must be emphasized, provides an abstract typology depicting different logics behind action, which in reality may be combined in a variety of ways.

Here Type 1, instrumental action, approximates to the cosmopolitanism of means. This is to be found in a range of modalities such as institution-building (as organizational means to regulate social relations according to cosmopolitan principles), and cross-cultural competence that allow goals to be met. Type 2 value-relevant action, meanwhile, approximates to the cosmopolitanism of ends, typically found in world-views which value openness and commitment to other world citizens or co-religionists or strangers, as fundamental human goals that are valued in their own right.

This still leaves two types of action unaccounted for, within the least developed expressive and habitual aspects of Weber's typology. Can these perhaps be linked with further specific modalities of cosmopolitanism that are not included in the schema presented by Vertovec and Cohen (2002)? In the case of expressive rationality, it is certainly arguable that cosmopolitanism may sometimes be a feeling, linked with emotions and desires that are neither rationally calculated nor necessarily disciplined according to particular values. Beck, for example, speaks of cosmopolitan empathy based on 'the globalization of the emotions' (2006: 5–6). Another version of this kind of connection has also been made by Mica Nava (2002, 2007) in her work on consumption and what she calls 'visceral cosmopolitanism'. This is influenced by feminist theories of desire, as discussed in Chapter 1. Another converging argument developed by Bruce Robbins seeks to displace nationalism as the sole paradigmatic form of political feelings (1999: 69–72). The implication is that a seventh modality of cosmopolitanism should be added, namely as a set of feelings and emotions.

This addition goes against the conventional argument in which cosmopolitanism is seen as the preserve of manipulative elites who, if anything, lack emotion. This is evident, for example, in Balibar's (1994), argument about cosmopolitan philosophers of the 18th-century Enlightenment. While claiming to be acting universalistically in the name of humanity, he sees their cosmopolitanism as flawed by the divide between such elites and the masses (*ibid*: 74). Here, as Robbins points out, authentic feelings are curiously regarded as a monopoly of popular attitudes, rather than available to anyone. This assumption is arbitrary and untenable.

Finally, there remains habitual action, taken up and re-formulated by Bourdieu, in terms of the notion of habitus. This represents dispositions to actions that are reproduced over time, without recourse to constant reflexive monitoring. Can this also be added to the check-list of modalities? This prospect is certainly possible, in a context where philosophical approaches have been displaced from a central role, and where in consequence greater attention has been given to non-elite vernacular types of cosmopolitan endeavour. Although Appiah's (2006) account of Kumasi, discussed above, occurs within a philosophical study, it is clear that he sees cosmopolitanism has something that grows out of ways of life which bring strangers together and which offer the possibility of cosmopolitan conversation. A strong sense of habitus is present. This is based firstly on the co-mingling of people from different places, which, as a child, Appiah 'never thought to wonder' (xix) about, in order to determine why 'people travelled so far to live and work in my hometown' (xx), movements which brought together his English mother with his Asante father. Secondly it is based on the movement of his own people, including children who previously lived across the road from him, to other global cities in different countries. Eventually of course habitus is overcome by conscious thought about this kind of world, but for a period it remains part of the natural horizon.

Recognizing the cosmopolitan habitus may be difficult inasmuch as observers are wedded to an excessively mechanistic developmental approach to socialization that starts from the immediate and intimate world of the family and works outward. At the level of the individual person, this emphasis on primary socialization makes sense. Secondary socialization outside the immediate familial or kinship circle comes later. Even so there is a danger that this process of transition may be conceived in a rather mechanistic way, as if we start from family, then surrounding geographic community, then nation, regions, and finally the wider world. This steady sense of progression outwards may be particularly misleading where the habitus that surrounds the immediate circle of family is already opened up to global or trans-contextual influences as in Appiah's discussion of Kumasi. This opening up may occur through a mixture of trade and migration, or alternatively where war, social disruption, and the creation of refugee populations mean that an immediate intimate circle may not exist.

On the basis of this Weberian commentary on the modalities of cosmopolitanism, a revised eight-point check-list is now proposed, including affective and habitual modalities in addition to the six-point check-list developed by Vertovec and Cohen.

Table 2.3   Revised Check-List of Cosmopolitan Modalities

1. As a socio-cultural condition
2. As a philosophical world-view
3. As a political project to build trans-national institutions
4. As a project for recognizing multiple identities
5. As a mode of orientation to the world
6. As a set of competencies which enable us to make our way in different cultures and countries
7. As feelings and emotions
8. As a habitus

Cosmopolitanism as a Socio-cultural Condition: Towards a Typology

Amongst these eight modalities, further discussion of the first, cosmopolitanism as a socio-cultural condition, is warranted for a number of reasons. The primary reason for this is to provide a way of linking social structure with social action, directing research to the kinds of ways in which cosmopolitanism may be linked with certain specific social structures or conditions. The second reason is that 'condition' may be interpreted less structurally, and more ontologically, as a term which refers to the nature or essence of being (i.e. living). Put less technically, cosmopolitanism may be, or have become, intrinsic to the human condition, a position recently advanced by Beck (2006). These possibilities will be looked at in turn, drawing on literature dealing with different types of cosmopolitanism.

Typologies are sometimes seen as little more than descriptive detail of rather minor interest to social theory. This kind of response can, under certain circumstances, be superficial, especially when the intellectual coherence of a key concept or field of study has generated a proliferation of complex and ambiguous meanings or empirical examples. It is because this problem of proliferation has become endemic to the study of cosmopolitanism that detailed attention now turns to a typology of cosmopolitanisms. This is intended as a preliminary intellectual mapping of the immense scope and diversity of rapidly expanding discourses of cosmopolitanism. The full listing of typologies is contained within the Appendix to this book. Selections from this listing are discussed within the next section of this chapter, under thematic headings, starting with positions in the social structure that may generate or encourage a number of different types of cosmopolitanism.

Cosmopolitanism has been linked with a variety of structural positions within society. The most prominent of these have emphasized power structures (including business and Empire), migration and movement, cities and urban living, migration and movement, and institutions of knowledge and belief. These may be separated for analytical purposes provided it is realized that they intersect and are often connected with each other in reality. After all empires radiate power through expansive movement, creating or re-structuring cities and discourses about social processes, though they have no monopoly over movement, nor are they in any way the sole animator of cities or forms of knowledge.

(a) Power Structures

The emphasis on power structures is used here in a broad-ranging sense to incorporate dominant classes, status groups, institutions of governance and discourses. The operation of such structures is reflected in the labels chosen for a number of types of cosmopolitanism:

Bourgeois: Levenson, 1971: 19–55
Colonial: van der Veer, 2002
Corporate: Connelly, 2000: 602
Despotic: Beck, 2006: 44–5, 151–2
Forced: Malcolmson, 1998: 240
From Above: Kaldor, 1996
Hegemonic: Nwankwo, 2005

Laissez-faire: Reich, 1991: 315
Managed: Mignolo, 2000
Market: Kleingeld, 1999: 518–21
Merchant: Malcolmson, 1998: 239
Military: Connelly, 2000: 602
Of Dependency: Abbas, 2000: 778
Upper Class: Dehija, 2006: 113

and the identification of cosmopolitan qualities in the following phenomena:

Capitalism: Beck, 2005: 59
Capitalists: Hamilton, 1999, *passim*
State: Beck, 2005: 8
World Order: Beck, 2002a: 65

There is a strong emphasis here on economic power and social processes and locations within which it is concentrated such as mercantile and corporate activity, as well as capitalism driven by capitalists. This has been extended to forms of state activity and Empire that may be linked with capitalism, as well as to a range of spatial settings especially in the West and Asia. The argument here is not that capitalism and capitalists are necessarily cosmopolitan in orientation, since the nation-state has been a major institutional pre-condition for the consolidation and protection of capitalist property rights. The point is rather that capitalism, with its expansive movement across borders in search of markets, labour, raw materials and sources of or outlets for capital, has thereby created structural conditions that encourage cosmopolitanism in its other modalities. These included *laissez-faire* cosmopolitan worldviews associated with free trade, and bourgeois cosmopolitanism, seen by Levenson (1971) as an alternative to communist cosmopolitanism.

As with theories of globalization, however (see Holton, 2005), there is a large analytical problem of reductionism in assuming that because capitalism is a major feature in cosmopolitanism, it is therefore the leading and necessary feature, to which all else pertains. Michael Mann (1986) has argued for the existence of four rather than one type of social power across history, as well as for the autonomy of each of the four types, namely ideological, economic, political and military. From this perspective an account of cosmopolitanism from the top down need not rely simply on a theory connecting cosmopolitanism with capitalism. Rather it may draw upon other sources of power and dominance, including proselytizing religions and forms of imperial power-seeking, which may be linked with each other and with economic power. These may equally operate outside the dominance of capital, as occurred historically before the rise of modern capitalism, or culturally in processes driven by religious or imperial world-views connected with the expansion of the realm of gods and emperors on earth (Hopkins, 2002). Such processes are discussed more fully in the following chapter.

In addition to the point that there may be top-down forms of cosmopolitanism other than those dominated by capitalism, is a further major point, namely the existence of cosmopolitan conditions that involve and mobilize beyond the most powerful and dominant social groups and discourses. Their importance is reflected in the following labels given to types of cosmopolitanism:

Aboriginal: Connelly, 2000: 602
Anti-Colonial: van der Veer, 2002
Anti-Imperial: Malcolmson, 1998: 238
Anti-Proprietary: Posnock, 2000: 809
Emancipatory: Beck, 2006: 45ff
Feminist: Connelly, 2000: 602
From Below: Kaldor, 1996; Kurasawa, 2004; Nwankwo, 2005: 14
Marginal: Bhabha, 1996: 195
Migrant: Beck, 2006: 106
Minority: Beck, 2006: 106
NGO: Beck, 2006: 107
Non-Elite: Robbins, 1999: 100
Oppositional: Schein, 1998
Popular Non-Western: Robbins, 1999: 100
Vernacular: Bhabha, 1996; Diouf, 1999; Werbner, 2006
Working Class: Werbner, 1999: 23; Waxer, 2001: 223ff

and to the following kinds of 'cosmopolitans':

Minoritarian: Pollock *et al.*, 2000: 582–3
Subaltern: Barucha, 2006: 119–23
Working Class: Werbner, 1999

In many such cases, cosmopolitanism from below is very much a response to cross-border processes and interdependencies which threaten the interests of those who either lie outside dominant social groups (classes and elites), evident within aboriginal, anti-colonial, anti-imperial, and working-class cosmopolitanism, *and/or* a response to dominant discourses, evident in anti-proprietary, emancipatory or minority cosmopolitanism.

Not all types of cosmopolitanism can however be neatly divided into the categories 'from above' and 'from below'. Some, as will be shown below, are more ambivalent in relation to structures of power. In large measure this reflects theoretical difficulties in treating society in terms of some kind of basic binary divide. Leading examples of this kind of thinking include Marxist-inspired two-class models of society divided between capital and labour, the powerful distinction made by critical theorists between system and life-world, and finally discursive post-structuralist binaries between dominant social forces and their Others.

Some of the examples already cited, have elements of ambivalence within them. An interesting example arises within van der Veer's (2002) discussion of colonial and anti-colonial cosmopolitanism in the 19th century. On the one hand, processes of colonization at this time were often carried through by means of top-down forms of control linking capitalist, diplomatic, missionary and educational activity, carried forward through elites. On the other hand, there grew up during the late 19th and early 20th centuries, movements critical of the forceful and racist ways in which Empire and colonization operated.

Other examples of ambivalence may be drawn from studies of migration. Migrant cosmopolitanism, for example, is often rightly taken as a typical case of cosmopolitanism from below involving working class and often marginalized groups seeking a foothold for survival in a new context, drawing on the cross-border linkage and resources of diasporic populations. Yet migrant diasporas are themselves internally stratified and often generate dominant groups and centres of power. The Jewish diasporic community in Amsterdam as it had developed by 1900, was, for example, stratified between *Sephardic* Jews of Iberian origin and concentrated in trade and business (Swetschinski, 2000), distinct in economic status from *Ashkenazy* Jewish migrants and refugees from Central and Eastern Europe, confined in the main to wage labour and small business.

In other cases working-class migrants may gain cultural strength if not formal power through cosmopolitan intersections between economic and cultural life. Pnina Werbner (1999) demonstrates this through the example of Hajji Sulieman, a Pakistani migrant to the Gulf region, son of a watchmaker, but also a devout Muslim and member of a transnational Sufi sect. The Gulf highway, she argues, is one 'along which many different nations travel, meet, and interact, getting to know one another while working side by side' (23). Whereas some 'trans-national' migrants remain embedded within their existing cultural groups, Werbner argues that others realize the cosmopolitan possibilities inherent in their conditions of employment, through an openness to others.

Sulieman learned Japanese, the language of his employers, but also English and Arabic. He also observed the customs and ways of life of other groups, including Hindus, Arabs, and Bangladeshis, and developed cross-cultural friendships.

All this speaks to cosmopolitan 'openness' towards and competence in dealing with others. But added to this, Werbner also demonstrates the interaction between the world of employment and the religious world of Sufism. Sulieman, acting against his employers' wishes, went on the *haj* pilgrimage to Mecca, and maintained strong connections with his Sufi Shaikh and mentor. Confronting his manager on his return he drew strength from the image of his religious leader, escaping dismissal and negotiating a new position within the company in Baghdad. Sulieman, it seems, drew on the importance of his faith as a source of respect among co-workers, and mentioned in interview the interest of Japanese in Sufism. Werbner uses this detailed example to demonstrate how social conditions engender the possibility of working-class cosmopolitanism as distinct from migrant trans-nationalism. But Sulieman's story may equally be taken as an instance of cosmopolitan bargaining power from below, since his cross-cultural competence appears to have been recognized as an asset by his employers. Sulieman himself continued to combine work and religion in his new posting in Baghdad, and the case study ends with his contemplation of moving to the Netherlands with its significant Islamic population but where the sect currently has little presence. For Werbner, this world of travel is closer to 'triumphant mastery' of conditions rather than the alienation that many other working-class migrants, including many women domestic workers in the Gulf, experience.

Drawing from these examples, it is clear that the relationships between cosmopolitanism and power are complex, rather than being set in a singular 'top down' mode. One way of putting this is to speak of ambivalence, with both top-down and bottom-up relationships evident, requiring constant attention to the interaction of those in different class positions, mediated through forms of cultural power.

Cosmopolitanism 'from below' is evident in a number of cases from the general listing in Appendix 1 including:

Anti-colonial: van der Veer, 2002
Black: Posnock, 2000: 804; Nwankwo, 2005
Democratic: Honig, 1998: 13
Migrant: Beck, 2006: 106
Emancipatory: Beck, 2006: 45ff
Feminist: Connelly, 2000: 602
Oppositional: Schein, 1998

but perhaps with more ambivalence in relation to combinations of 'top down' and 'bottom up' in the following further types:

Christian: Kristeva, 1993: 26–7; Sennett, 1994; Connelly, 2000: 602
Ethical: Giri, 2006
Fraternal: Harland-Jacobs, 2007, *passim*
Islamic: Connelly, 2000: 602; Euben, 2006: 174–97
Left: Beck, 2005: 270–6

The issue of ambivalence here is partly about cross-class involvement in political forms of cosmopolitanism that span classes and social groups, as in supporters of cosmopolitan democracy, anti-colonial cosmopolitanism, left and feminist cosmopolitanism or those who seek an emancipatory cosmopolitanism able to resolve leading world problems. In such settings, radical mobilization from below can create institutional change affecting the structure of politics and law. This is evident in recent NGO struggles for human rights as a central feature of cosmopolitan world order. Ambivalence here surrounds the interaction and inter-penetration of civil society and state, rather than their separation into sharply distinct modes of political cosmopolitanism.

Ambivalence is also equally evident in cultural forms of cosmopolitanism, in areas like religion or consumption, which are hard to link exclusively with top-down or bottom-up types of activity. Euben (2006), for example, in her discussion of cosmopolitanisms in the Islamic and Western worlds, notes that neither is culturally homogenous, each has certainly developed varieties of cosmopolitanism, but these vary culturally and in their relationship with dominant institutions.

The opposition between the sacred abode or world of Islam (*dar al-Islam*), and the profane abode or world of war beyond (*dar al-Harb*), represents an important distinction, but it should not be read as excluding cosmopolitan currents within Islam. For Euben, these include the cosmopolitan imaginary or world-view built upon the idea of the *umma* (religious community), as well as sacred texts including the Qu'ran, which a number of Islamic scholars read as giving encouragement to seeking out the 'presence of and moral and religious diversity of human beings' (Hashmi, 2003: 81). In the context of theories which see Islam as composed of a multiple set of networks (Lapidus, 1975), Robinson (1997) has pointed to cosmopolitan circuits of the Sunni world constituted by scholars, families and individual travellers across political and cultural borders and boundaries. Euben sees these as enacting the Islamic cosmopolitan imagery.

All this is of course only part of the picture. Juridical rigidity in the *shari'a* law and the political authority of Islamic political empires – Safavid, Ottoman, and Mughal – also meant that power structures mattered. While networked linkages across space and time might in one sense have a life of their own (see Robinson, 1997: 173 on scholarly networks), it is equally true that patterns of cosmopolitan or ecumenical knowledge are significantly affected by shifts in political power. When political regimes were strongest they were more likely to tolerate more open contacts with non-Muslims, a situation reversed in periods of weakness and difficulty.

Further commentary on Islam and cosmopolitanism will be provided in Chapter 3 below. For the moment, it is a more general point that is emphasized, namely the lack of any necessary relationship between structures of power – material or discursive – and cosmopolitan outreach. The relationship is more complex and ambivalent. Attention now turns to the second possible connection between social conditions and cosmopolitanism linked with movement of some kind.

(b) Migration and Movement

Movement across all manner of frontiers and boundaries – cultural as well as political – has also been seen as a major structural condition conducive to cosmopolitanism. This structural condition is interconnected with relations of power, as we have already seen, yet the issue of movement is so analytically important that it needs attention in its own right.

In a very simple sense the contemporary age of mass migration is widely seen as an age of cosmopolitanism. The theme of migration and movement is however both broader than simple movement across borders, and in a paradoxical sense not quite so indiscriminately spread across time and space. It is broader in two major ways:

(a) because some kinds of movement, notably travel and tourism, are not usually related to migration in search of employment or directly connected with re-settlement outside the country of origin

(b) because non-physical movement is possible through the imagination, aided in many cases by particular communications media and technology, including letters, books, and film, as well as television, and computer-mediated internet communication. Travel in this sense need not involve physical movement.

Focussing at the outset on physical bodily migration, this is, as already indicated, a deeply ambivalent process *vis-à-vis* distinctions between cosmopolitanism from above and from below. Put very simply, it is equally possible that movement across borders may encourage or discourage positive cosmopolitan relations with others encountered within the context of migration. Positive relations may emerge where migrants work with others, encounter them as neighbours or citizens with common interests, as well as where closer inter-personal relations are established through friendship or more intimately within marriage. Cross-cultural ties may ensue which involve a sense of common feeling, solidarity, or obligation to others. Negative relations may emerge, by contrast, where movement creates adverse reactions in new places of settlement, such that common ties and solidarities are obstructed, sometimes violently so, or simply because of exclusionary practices towards migrants denying them jobs, social recognition and political rights. Here migrants may look to and stay within their own group for resources and sociability. This may also occur where coercion is absent, but where preferences for one's own group are more powerful than any cosmopolitan tie.

Whether positive or negative, the relations arising from physical mobility create no necessary connection with outward looking forms of cosmopolitanism. This is a major theme in Werbner's (1999), study of working-class labour migration and trans-national ethnic worlds. The story of Sulieman Hajji, discussed above, provides a striking instance of how migration may create conditions suited to cross-cultural openness. Equally, however, migration may remain enveloped in ethnic worlds, no matter how many boundaries are crossed. Werbner notes in this respect the ways in which it is not simply migrants who travel along global pathways. Pakistani goods, brides and tourists also do, alongside and often closely connected with Pakistani labour migrants. Men who have gone ahead to work subsequently marry and brides travel to them, as do tourists visiting relatives abroad. Gifts, commodities, and ritual objects connected with marriage also do. None of this necessarily leads to cosmopolitan openness, because culture and place of origin travel alongside people. This does not mean that culture remains the same, rooted in an unchanging tradition. Even tradition adapts to new circumstances, such as the broadening of the spatial context from which marriage partners may be drawn, extending from villlage-level kinship and personal affinity groups to a wider global arena.

Migration is nonetheless not the sole form of physical movement that may be linked with cosmopolitanism. Travel and (non-kin-based) tourism have also been seen as providing many of the conditions under which cosmopolitanism has emerged, though rather more on the cultural than political sides. The association of travel and cosmopolitanism has also been controversial, especially where global travel is regarded as a form of cultural imperialism. Instead of the much vaunted cross-cultural openness, many post-colonial theorists, from Said (1978) onwards, have taken travel and travel commentary by Westerners to involve colonizing and orientalizing discourses and practices which render non-western populations as inferior to others. This line of critique is important for underlining the conditions of gross social inequality that often surround travel. To challenge the old adage, it may be said that travel does not necessarily broaden the mind. It may rather be associated with projects of colonial rule, racial domination and sex tourism.

Such criticisms have not however prevented further productive elaboration of connections between cosmopolitanism and travel. Euben (2006), in particular, has noted that travel is not the sole pre-rogative of powerful Westerners, being endemic in the Islamic world over many centuries. A number of writers argue that over-emphasis on cultural imperialism renders the Western gaze on those Others it encounters through travel as far too monolithic (Sen, 2005). This often obscures the cultural agency of the colonized and neglects the poss-ibility for cross-cultural communication, solidarity and co-operation (Holton, 2008). Such considerations leave considerable space for the possibility of cosmopolitanism, though this is typically re-conceived as multiple rather than singular in origin, and something that emerges from the active engagement of social actors drawn from a range of particular socio-cultural contexts, rather than the gift of the West to the rest.

The significance of travel as a socio-cultural condition underlying cosmopolitanism has been traced in historical depth by Binney (2006), and elaborated sociologically by Szerszynski and Urry (2006). For Binney, travel, by confronting travellers with the unfamiliar, encour-aged not simply commentary on difference, but also a re-assessment of classical cosmopolitan presumptions of the universality of human-kind. Whereas the cosmopolitan world-view (in our terms modality 2 – see Table 2.3) grounded this universality in our common nature, Binney argues that greater emphasis on socio-cultural differences arising across the centuries through travel required a greater attention to the challenge of how those from different social backgrounds might come together. This, he feels, had become pressing by the second half of the 18th century with the rise of cultural particularism, the product of increased travel, trade, and interaction with other nations.

In the face of emerging nationalist argument that such commonalities are weak, rendering cosmopolitanism impossible or unnatural, cosmopolitans had henceforth to ground cosmopolitanism in some kind of unity within difference. Binney cites Kant's commentary on what is morally sublime and beautiful to identify this new approach. 'Thus the different groups unite into a picture of splendid expressions', says Kant, 'where amidst great multiplicity unity shines forth, and the whole moral nature exhibits beauty and discipline' (Kant, 1960: 75 [1764]). Published in 1764 at a time of heightened world trade and travel, these comments represent a re-formulation of cosmopolitan ideals that draw on an extensive background of corporeal and imaginative mobility.

Much of the argument linking cosmopolitanism with travel has drawn on elite experience. This either features the personal travel of explorers, writers, and aristocrats engaged on the Grand Tour, or the imaginative travel of educated writers who wish to compare and contrast what are perceived as different cultures, civilizations, and institutions. This association with elites should not however exclude others. Corporeal travel is now a mass phenomenon, while imaginative travel is even more accessible, whether involving a sense of religious or political community, or the mass communications media including books, film and television. The internet, meanwhile, introduces notions of virtual travel.

For Szerszynski and Urry (2006), cosmopolitanism can be conceptualized very largely in terms of travel in its widest sense, curiosity about the world, and consumption. In their own typology (Table 2.4), there are six pertinent dimensions, reflecting their view that accounts of the cosmopolitan condition should include 'intellectual and aesthetic

Table 2.4 Cosmopolitan Predispositions and Practices

1. 'Extensive mobility, in which people have the right to "travel" corporeally, imaginatively and virtually...'
2. 'The capacity to consume' other 'places and environments' through travel
3. Willingness to take the risks involved in dealing with others
4. Ability to map one's culture and make aesthetic judgements about different places and societies
5. Semiotic skills that enable the interpretation of images of others, 'what they are meant to represent', and 'when they are ironic'.
6. An openness to other peoples and cultures, including a willingness to appreciate aspects of 'the Other'

Source: Szerszynski and Urry (2006): 114–15.

orientations toward cultural and geographical difference and distinctive types of competence' (114). The notion of conditions here is extended well beyond structural conditions to the cultural and ideational prerequisites of cosmopolitanism. In particular, the emphasis here on willingness, capacities, abilities, and skills, signifies an action frame of reference, rather than dependence on structural conditions independent of will and consciousness. This harks back to Hannerz's conception of cosmopolitanism as a cognitive accomplishment, but adds to it aesthetic elements, which are closer to ideals of connoisseurship. It is also cosmopolitanism with a happy rather than worried face.

Movement in the imagination rather than of the body represents an important aspect of cosmopolitanism that may be linked with forms of thought and technologies of communication. This emphasis is clearly not unique to Szerszynski and Urry, but their work is of particular interest in teasing out some of the critical aspects of non-corporeal travel, notably through the concept of visuality.

The argument here is that the 'conditions of existence' of cosmopolitanism depend not simply on an array of communications forms and technologies, from letters and postcards to telephones and emails, but also, more specifically, on visual means of communication, such as television. This enables the world to be seen 'from afar'. A striking example of this is the visual depiction of Planet Earth, whether from space on the US moon-landing missions, or within environmentalist depictions of the planet as a space which we share with each other. Televisual depictions of the globe, they go on to suggest, have become a given, almost taken-for-granted feature of contemporary life, a kind of banal cosmopolitan visual back-drop.

A related way of looking at 'the blue planet', suggested by Franklin, Lury and Stacey (2000: 27–32), is that of panhumanism. This combines a sense of technological mastery of nature that makes possible the transmission of images from outer space, with a sense of human vulnerability in the face of the extra-terrestrial cosmos.

Could this banal everyday visual cosmopolitanism or panhumanism have any stronger resonances than this, and could it perhaps be linked with a kind of visual image of potential global cosmopolitan citizenship, bringing together culture and politics? Szerszynski and Urry are somewhat sceptical of this, one problem being the rather abstract God-like perspective from which Planet Earth is visually represented. Cartographies of global power have typically utilized such images, and seem therefore incongruent with notions of cosmopolitan democracy. In popular consciousness too there is often a contrast between the lived experience of particular places that seems to contrast markedly with generalized cosmopolitan projections of a single world, somehow united in difference. The link with cosmopolitan citizenship therefore remains hard to make within this particular line of argument.

What is nonetheless clear is that ways of experiencing corporeal and imaginative mobility are not solely abstract or somehow sealed off from the practical exigencies of employment, personal relationships, friendship, consumption and religious life. Cosmopolitanism in a cultural sense need not be seen as abstract and de-contextualized. The story of Sulieman Hajji makes this point very well. It is precisely a story about the exercise of trans-contextual capacities and abilities across several specific cross-cultural settings, yet a story that is not simply enmeshed in cultural particularity or localism. The cosmopolitan and the local are not as distant as in the evidence assembled in Szerszynski and Urry's discussion of visuality, place and cosmopolitan citizenship.

Mobility in its various senses remains therefore an important condition for the emergence of cosmopolitanism, though connections between the two are far from necessary or invariant. Such connections may be stronger rather than weaker, where additional conditions conducive to cosmopolitanism are also present. Cities and urban ways of life have been seen as offering a third connection of this type, which often intersect closely with movement. We have seen this already in Sulieman's story which is not simply a story about movement, but a story in which global cities such as Dubai, Baghdad, and Amsterdam play a key role as intensified settings of cross-cultural encounter and possibility.

(c) Cities and Urban Living

Cities have widely been seen as conducive to the emergence of cosmopolitanism in both its cultural and political senses. This kind of argument is both historical and contemporary. Historically it is present at the outset of cosmopolitanism as a world-view in the expanding city-states and imperial adventures of ancient Greece and Rome. The urban focus is subsequently reproduced in a number of cities of the Christian and Islamic worlds, and in the Western cities of the 18th-century Enlightenment. Trading cities too, play a significant part in this connection, whether the port cities, through which cross-cultural encounters were a necessary part of business transactions, or the Imperial cities which, through force or attraction, pulled in wide-ranging social groups, living in close proximity with each other. Cosmopolitan is an adjective applied to many urban spaces today. It occurs not merely in real estate brochures encouraging cultural diversity, but to cities as intense cultural settings which encourage diverse forms of social experimentation in the construction of the built environment and through alternative diverse and syncretic ways of living.

The idea of civilization itself is intrinsically connected with cities not simply as centres of power and authority, but also of cultural life and learning, and enhanced freedom from tradition and conservatism. The old adage 'urban air makes free' encapsulates this connection with freedom, opportunity, and political virtue. Here the cultural and political sides to cosmopolitanism come together. And while such qualities have often been seen as primarily Occidental in character, and hence lacking in cities outside Europe, this distinction is almost certainly overdrawn. Contrasts between Western urban freedom and Eastern urban despotism are prominent in Marx and Weber, but they should not become invariant stereotypes, so as to obscure elements of urban freedom and openness outside the West nor elements of non-cosmopolitan exclusion and closure within it (Holton, 1986). Jewish ghettoes were after all very much a historic product of Western exclusionary anti-Semitism. Meanwhile Mediterranean port cities of North Africa (see Larguèche, Clancy-Smith, and Audet (2001) on the open city of Tunis) and the Middle East (see Watenpaugh (2005) on Aleppo in Anatolia) , together with similar Asian maritime cities (Harper, 2002), were the product of multiple economic, political and cultural influences.

Meanwhile under conditions of globalization over the last 200 years, it becomes very unclear how far cosmopolitan cities such as Shanghai, Bombay, or Cairo depended for their cosmopolitanism solely on the impact of Western socio-cultural institutions and how far autonomous sources of openness were drawn upon. Ackbar Abbas (2000), for example, argues that cosmopolitan cities during the epoch of colonization and Western power should not be read as the simple effects of cultural imperialism, and still less as following a unitary model of dependency. Shanghai during the 1920s, often described as the Paris of the East, was a treaty port where multiple Western interests had a privileged political and legal status. A range of architectural styles and cultural institutions such as the department store and race course were taken from the West, yet Shanghai was also a site where multiple jurisdictions permitted space for Chinese autonomy to be negotiated and Chinese versions of cosmopolitanism to be developed. Cosmopolitanism in Shanghai, he argues, differed in this respect from the more direct dependency on Britain evident in Hong Kong.

How then is the cosmopolitanism of cities best characterized? One strategy, following Simmel, is to connect the cosmopolitanism of cities with the restless dynamic spirit of modernist cultural innovation creating 'a highly diversified plurality of achievements' (Simmel, 1903: 336, cited in Keane, 2006: 7). Drawing very much on his native city of Berlin, Simmel saw city life as complex, restless and diverse, involving individuals in multiple though often fragmentary sets of relationships and multiple kinds of civil organizations that transcend the simple dominance of capitalism or markets. For Vertovec (2006), writing of the 20th century, Berlin's cosmopolitanism is linked both with its reputation during the 1920s as a home of foreign intellectuals and artists, and in the late 20th century as a demographically multicultural recipient of mass Turkish migration. Such characteristics are seen as indicators of world-openness (*Weltoffenheit* in German). This no longer simply means a sense of welcome to the world, since the world is now very much constitutive of Berlin as an economic and cultural centre with a high proportion of non-native migrants (288).

Another way of understanding the city as cosmopolitan institution is through the characteristics and development of the built environment. New York, for example, has been presented as a cosmopolitan city through its modernist architecture, as much as its migrant melting pot. Robinson (2006) argues that its skyline has become a potent symbol of modernity symbolizing world power and boundless confidence in the dynamism and vitality of the New World. Its modernist architecture is not however cosmopolitan by virtue of its export to other places as a model of what modern cities should look like, but more through its borrowing and re-invention of styles from elsewhere. Mumford (1966), for example, as Robinson indicates, notes the importance of clean Japanese lines in the work of American architect Frank Lloyd Wright, together with incorporation of the Indian verandah, the widespread global origins of the industrial machines that influenced architecture, and European *beaux-arts* influences (Robinson, 68). For Benton *et al.* (2003: 71) the ornamentation of the New York skyscraper included Moorish, pre-Columbian and German expressionist elements, as well as elements derived from classical and gothic traditions. It is in such diverse borrowings and their recombination, that New York's claims to a cosmopolitan built environment are, in Robinson's view, to be seen.

Taken overall the material and moral milieux of cities provides a further condition for cosmopolitan development that adds further to the inter-connected influences of power and movement. Cities also bring together, as we have seen, both the political-normative and cultural strands of cosmopolitanism. Further elaboration of these points will be provided on a historical canvas in Chapter 3, and with reference to more contemporary evidence in Chapter 5.

(d) Institutions of Knowledge and Belief

A final set of conditions often linked with cosmopolitanism concerns knowledge and belief. This is clearly present, as we have seen, at the historical outset of cosmopolitanism as a primarily philosophical doctrine developed by the Stoics. Science and the professions may also be connected with cosmopolitanism in the sense that such forms of knowledge claim a universal logic and applicability. It is also closely linked with certain religious sources of knowledge and belief, embracing currents within Christianity, Islam (Euben, 2006) and ecumenism, as well as more spiritual beliefs such as theosophy (van der Veer, 2002). In such cases, it is not necessary to presume that some prior social structure determines the forms of knowledge and belief in question, since forms of knowledge may vary independent of structural conditions (Weber, 1978; Collins, 1998).

The existence of connections between science or religion and cosmopolitanism may stretch the credulity of those who see only intolerance and bigotry in such forms of knowledge, or at the very least, knowledge claims that exclude alternative forms of understanding, even where they claim universality. Such objections may point to religious persecution, inquisitions, and genocide, as well as the service to which science has often been put in the name of nation or fatherland, as in the Nazi holocaust. However powerful such objections may be, they do not, in and of themselves, undermine the possibility of connections between forms of knowledge or belief and cosmopolitanism. What they rule out is the possibility of any necessary connection between the two.

What may be left after this is conceded, is not a merely random connection between particular ideas and their consequences in how people act, but rather one of 'elective affinity' between certain ideas and certain consequences, as proposed in Weber's sociology (Weber, 1949: 56, 61 [1904] see also Howe, 1978 for alternative translations to those of Shils and Finch in Weber (1949)). By this is meant the possibility of a logical connection between the substance of a belief and particular patterns of action that follow from it – whether intended or not. In the case of Weber's argument about the Protestant ethic (Weber, 1961 [1904]), the elective affinity between religious asceticism and the spirit of modern capitalism was not based on conscious intention. It arose rather through a logical affinity between ascetic practices in the religious sphere involving disciplined action to the glory of God, and disciplined asceticism in business leading to economic innovation.

Are there then elective affinities between science or religion and cosmopolitanism? One strong possibility here is a connection between the singular all-embracing scope of science, or the monotheistic religions that posit a single order of God's will, on the one side and a singular all-embracing cosmopolitan order, on the other. In such cases the epistemological or theological claims to singularity rest on a claim to the universality of the beliefs or knowledge asserted, whose truth is secured either through universal reason or universal faith. Since such characteristics of science or religion have not led inexorably to global cosmopolitanism, it is worthwhile identifying why they may not have done as well as why they may do. The connection may for example be broken when universalistic claims to knowledge or religious revelation are arbitrarily associated with a particular people or set of knowledge holders, who are closed against knowledge and belief that arises from other sources. This may involve exclusions based on status or caste, class, ethnicity, gender and age, or a mix of all of these. Claims to universalism may in other words be socially monopolized, whether from custom, prejudice or the will to power.

Elective affinities between forms of knowledge and belief and cosmopolitanism may be more plausible, where claims to monopoly are rejected for any particular social group. Ideals of religious ecumenism among Christians have been around for centuries yet have taken centuries to achieve, to the extent that they have been achieved. Yet to do so required relaxation of the denominational monopolization of truth and wisdom among Protestants, Orthodox, and more recently Catholics (Gheorghiu, 2007). The elective affinity here then is between monotheistic ecumenism and cosmopolitanism, but the connection, like that of Weber's Protestant ethic theory, is not a strong invariant one.

Among scientists, meanwhile, a degree of cosmopolitan openness may certainly be associated with the rise of the international scientific conference and international refereed publications. The scientist may appear here as the epitome of trans-contextual cosmopolitanism. The norm of truth-seeking would appear to require attention to strange and unfamiliar results and sources of insight rather than the mere following of convention. Yet this heroic picture is a complacent one, since positivist research methods have not spontaneously liberated scientists from particular intellectual and political allegiances. These have not necessarily stood in the way of good science, but they have equally introduced extra-epistemological considerations into the problems that science has recognized and taken up for research, as well as introducing arbitrary rhetorical and political elements into what forms of argument are deemed acceptable scientific reasoning. There remains some kind of elective affinity between a universalistic scientific worldview and cosmopolitanism, but in the real world the heroic ideal is very far from being universal.

Having examined four specific ways of linking the cosmopolitan condition with particular social practices and institutions, we now turn to a more comprehensive and far-reaching claim that the human condition is now a cosmopolitan one.

Cosmopolitanism as an Emergent Feature of the Human Condition

The claim that cosmopolitanism is a key ingredient of the human condition has recently been advanced by Ulrich Beck (2006). The argument here is that cosmopolitanism penetrates all of life, rather than selected institutions and processes, such as movement or cities. This cosmopolitan condition is closely connected, in his view, with the multiple processes of globalization, conceived as a set of cross-border relationships that create increased inter-connection and inter-dependency. Beck offers a number of examples (*ibid*: 2–3). They include global terrorism which impacts on small local ways of life as much as global politics. They also include both economic globalization through capital mobility and markets, together with reactions against it, whereby economic globalization has engendered movements of political globalization that seek to reform or transcend markets in the name of alternative principles of democracy and law. Nothing now escapes such processes, since there are now no borders or boundaries which are able to remain impervious to global impacts.

Cosmopolitanism for Beck represents the contemporary human condition, whether or not it has been willed or chosen. He consolidates this argument in two ways: the first takes up the cosmopolitanization of reality, while the second talks of banal cosmopolitanism. Cosmopolitanization arises, in large measure, from what Beck sees as modern social changes, whereby the self-contained national societies that emerged with industrialization have been overrun by the interpenetration of global, national and local processes. This, in a sense, means the cosmopolitanization of everything, leading him to coin dozens of further types of cosmopolitanism, the effect of which is to make any sense of the limits of cosmopolitanization very hard, if not impossible, to draw.

This indiscriminate approach not only makes sociological analysis of the scope and limits of cosmopolitanization difficult, but also smuggles in the normative assumption that cosmopolitanism is now such a natural part of everyday life that it is an inevitable given. This is all very well, if one is a supporter, but not if one is an opponent. A premise of the remainder of this book is that scholarship can do better than presume the cosmopolitanization of everything, leaving normative questions open for endlessly proliferating debate.

Continuing with Beck, attention now turns to the connections he makes between cosmopolitanization, banal cosmopolitanism and the cosmopolitan outlook.

Because cosmopolitanization is unwilled, Beck also sees it both as 'involuntary cosmopolitanism' (107), and 'banal cosmopolitanism' (10: 40–4) – a term also picked up by Szerszynski and Urry (2006). Banality here, drawing on Billig's earlier (1995) concept of banal nationalism, refers to aspects of the human condition or everyday experience that are taken for granted aspects of life. In the nationalist versions they include national flags on official buildings or national symbols on coinage. In Beck's cosmopolitan version they are to be seen in the ways in which social distinctions 'between us and them are becoming confused, both at the national and international level. The modest, familiar, local, and circumscribed and stable, our protective shell is becoming the playground of universal experiences'. This idea can be made more concrete through examples such as eating national dishes whose ingredients derive from other parts of the globe, or driving cars whose branding includes a national element but whose components are made and assembled at a number of places in the globe. We are, as it were, caught up in cosmopolitanization without knowing it. This in turn leads to further typological ideas such as the 'cosmopolitanism of side effects' (124), that exists without deliberate intention, or 'deformed cosmopolitanism' (161) achieved without struggle.

This emphasis on unintended consequences means that explicit conscious agency is not required to create cosmopolitanization. This enables Beck to avoid top-down conspiracy theories whereby cosmopolitanism is driven by 'global capitalists', or 'an American play for global domination' (48). Nor, on the other hand, is cosmopolitanization driven by the altruistic well-meaning values of cosmopolitans seeking a better or more just world. Social agency enters in subsequently as a response to cosmopolitanization and the creation of a cosmopolitan human condition. For Beck, agency is embodied in the idea of a cosmopolitan outlook.

Before this is outlined, it is important to note that this general argument reproduces the quasi-Marxist presumption that social conditions somehow determine social consciousness. Unlike Marx and many Marxist schools of social history (Thompson, 1963; Brenner, 2003), however, Beck's model seems to avoid any close attention to the history of agency and struggles over cosmopolitanism, prior to the point where cosmopolitanization takes place. This is because his argument depends on what he sees as a unique 20th century social transformation in the human condition. Before the present cosmopolitan age, the human condition was not, as it were, ripe for cosmopolitan values and politics. Now we have entered this age he believes it is, and that it will be Europe that leads it, because it is somehow better represented within the recent consolidation of the cosmopolitan outlook.

In Chapter 3, this approach is challenged as profoundly mis-conceived as to the historical dynamics of globalization and their rele-vance to the present. Both cosmopolitanization and cosmopolitan outlook are evident through time and space, though episodically with advances and declines. A number of historical and non-European examples have already been mentioned in passing in the present con-ceptual chapter. It did not take a great transformation to engender them, nor is contemporary Europe necessarily best placed to imple-ment cosmopolitanism, which, if the foregoing analysis is valid, cannot be regarded simply as a unitary world-view or one-dimensional modality.

These general problems with Beck's argument are important. Yet his concept of the cosmopolitan outlook remains of interest, for the way in which it seeks to bring together a number of strands of argument. This outlook is formally defined as:

> Global sense, a sense of boundarylessness. An everyday, historically alert, reflexive awareness of ambivalence in a blurring of differentiations and cultural contradictions. It reveals not just the anguish [of being aware of war and crisis worldwide] but also the possibility of shaping one's life and social relations under conditions of cultural mixture. It is simultaneously a sceptical, disillusioned, self-critical outlook. (3) [my parentheses and paraphrasing]

The cosmopolitan outlook, as depicted here is, is closely linked with *conditions of globalization*, what Beck calls cosmopolitanization, as in the reference to boundarylessness and cultural mixture, with the *blur-ring of sharp distinctions* between the global and the local, drawing on Roland Robertson's concept of glocalization (Robertson, 1992), with anguish as a *cosmopolitan feeling*, and with conceptions of *reflexive modernity as a critical life project* (Beck *et al.*, 1994). The theoretical underpinnings of this concept are discussed further in Chapter 4. For the moment the idea of the cosmopolitan outlook is filled out in more substance.

The outlook is constituted for Beck through the intersection of five major elements. These commence with what he sees as a common

Table 2.5 Beck and the Cosmopolitan Outlook

1. Experience of the crisis in world society
2. Recognition of cosmopolitan differences and the resulting cosmopolitan conflict character
3. Cosmopolitan empathy and perspective-taking
4. Impossibility of living in a world society without borders
5. Melange principle

Source: Beck, 2006: 7.

sense of 'crisis in world society' born of our common sense of inter-dependence which generates a 'civilizational community of fate'. The second feature refers to a recognition that social differences are real and will generate conflict, but need not undermine a common cosmo-politan project. Thirdly, as foreshadowed, reference is made to cosmo-politan empathy, which means we can empathize with others because we are in virtually interchangeable positions. The fourth and fifth aspects, like the second, accept social differences. The fourth point, on borders, accepts that an entirely open world is impossible, in part because the longing for borders seems a basic feature of social psychology. Fifth and finally is a re-assertion, through what he calls the melange principle, of the idea of the inter-relations of local, national, and cosmopolitan cultures and traditions. This is evident in his adage that 'cosmopolitanism without provincialism is empty, provincialism without cosmopolitanism is blind'.

Some very interesting currents of thinking are well represented in this concept. Of foremost importance is the way that Beck has pro-vided a defence of cosmopolitan views, by detaching them from any sense of aloofness from particular local or national sentiments. While cosmopolitanism as a universal principle has been criticized precisely for being remote from everyday life, Beck has taken up sociological and anthropological writing on its ordinary, rooted, and vernacular characteristics. These, as we have seen above, displace cosmopolitan-ism from its unitary philosophical modality in which the general and universal is seen as a primary and superior obligation in relation to the local and parochial. For Beck, by contrast, the cosmopolitan outlook emerges from a situation in which the global and the local inter-relate and inter-penetrate. He describes this as a 'both-and' rather than 'either-or' principle. Our lives partake both of the global and the local, even if the two are in conflict, rather than there being a global life for some and a local one for others. This melange principle contrasts markedly with Castells' (1996) argument in which global social stra-tification means the privileged inhabit a mobile 'space of flows', while the dis-privileged are consigned to a 'space of place'.

Beck: A Preliminary Verdict

Beck's arguments about cosmopolitanism range far wider than issues of cosmopolitanization and the cosmopolitan outlook discussed so far. They deal not only with changes in the human condition and social life, but also with the ways in which scholars study the world. Cosmopolitanism, in addition to its other modalities, is also, in his view, a new methodological principle for the study of social life. And all these endeavours are bound up with a normative commitment to cosmopolitanism as a fruitful form of contemporary political engagement.

The immense breadth of this work requires further discussion in later chapters. In Chapter 3, we consider the historical plausibility of Beck's view of the cosmopolitan age of modernity, in the context of an alternative historical sociology of cosmopolitanism. In Chapter 4, attention turns to the theoretical and methodological issues concerning the place of cosmopolitanism in social theory, including a critique of Beck's concepts of methodological cosmopolitanism. For the remainder of the present chapter we return to issues concerning ideas of a cosmopolitan condition.

In one sense this idea is simply a re-conceptualization of the idea of a global condition in other terms. Just as globalization theorists argue that inter-connections and inter-dependencies across boundaries now profoundly influence social processes and ways of life within bounded nations and regions, so Beck essentially says the same but in the language of cosmopolitanization. So what advantages, if any, does this bring?

One possible advantage derives from the normative connotations that are associated with some strands of cosmopolitanism. These, as we have seen, point to ideals of a different more just global order, where rights and obligations cross institutional boundaries. To speak of cosmopolitanization, therefore, carries normative as well as analytical and historical resonances. This draws attention to a powerful, though not necessarily the most influential, world-view evident within global politics, where inter-state relations are still seen by most observers to be grounded in national self-interest more than cosmopolitan politics. It remains nations rather than trans-national interests that in this view dominate international organizations.

The relationships between cosmopolitanism and global politics will be explored in more depth in Chapter 7. For the moment attention is limited to Beck's general approach to global realpolitics. This approach rejects the view that contemporary power politics is simply dominated by national self-interest. The normative meaning of cosmopolitanism is rather stretched to include contemporary developments, such as the role of the US and its allies in military interventions across the globe. These are seen less in terms of national strategic and economic interests, and more in terms of a cosmopolitan sense of military humanism. Here the national rights of countries such as Kosovo or Iraq are violated in the name of human rights and democracy. In this sense he believes we are seeing the cosmopolitanization of international relations (*ibid*: 119–29).

Leaving aside the substantive plausibility of this rather controversial view of military intervention and imposition of externally-legitimated institutions on the unwilling, concern here is primarily about Beck's preference for cosmopolitanization and cosmopolitanism rather than globalization and globalism, as the key organizing concepts to understand the contemporary world.

Here doubts remain as to whether Beck has established the need for any set of key concepts beyond globalization. This term has rightly been criticized for its vagueness, for lack of precision in distinguishing trans-national from international processes, and for what many see as its normative association with free trade, economic liberalism and corporate power. Beck tends to discount it for such normative limitations. Yet there are already far richer and multi-dimensional accounts of globalization available that are neither restricted to economic processes or liberal world views. A rich vein of work, including Robertson (1992, 1995); Held *et al.* (1999); Tomlinson (1999); and Holton (1998, 2005, 2008) identifies cultural and political as well as economic and technological aspects of globalization. In the process a number of normative developments and challenges have been identified and discussed. These, following Robertson's pioneering work in the 1990s on understandings of the world as a single space, already occupy the ground that Beck has now claimed for cosmopolitanization. In this sense it is unclear how much is really added.

Beck himself seems to regard his emphasis on cosmopolitanization as the linkage of global with local (and national) elements, as an advance on previous approaches. This may be so in relation to older theories of cosmopolitanism, that saw it as a de-contextualized universalistic philosophy. But it is by no means novel in relation to theories of globalization. Here earlier first-wave theories of hyper-globalism seen as sweeping nations and localities way into oblivion, have been rejected as misconceived through lack of attention to global/national interconnections rather than conflicts (for a systematic review see Holton, 2005). Beyond this, Robertson has developed the notion of glocalization, precisely an inter-penetration of global and local, in which inter-dependencies between the two scales define the global condition. While the term glocalization may seem clumsy, it is directed at just the same processes that Beck is trying to get at, and does so without introducing the positive normative aura that surrounds terms like cosmopolitanism. Of the two it is arguable that glocalization is a more fruitful and less confusing term.

Such questions are pursued more theoretically in Chapter 4. Attention turns meanwhile to a more systematic historical assessment of cosmopolitanism across time. This is designed in part as a critique of Beck's attempt to link cosmopolitanization and the cosmopolitan outlook with contemporary social trends. But it is also intended, in a more general sense, as a contribution to a long overdue historical sociology of cosmopolitanism grounded in evidence more than rhetoric.

Conclusion

This chapter covers a good deal of ground. Its aim has been to provide a systematic intellectual mapping of the complex ways in which cosmopolitanism has been understood and analysed. Attention has been given to the wide variety of modalities within which cosmopolitanism has been expressed, and to the proliferating typology of cosmopolitanisms that have been identified. This exercise is fundamental if the extraordinary complexities and profound ambiguities of the topic are to be appreciated. They raise the very real analytical problem that debates over cosmopolitanism are in danger of intellectual chaos and incoherence.

Complexity has its problems, but so too does over-simplification. One important conclusion that may be drawn from this chapter is the serious inadequacy of those approaches which take one modality or type of cosmopolitanism as a necessary feature of cosmopolitanism in general. Cosmopolitanism may be found in the West, among elites, and within cities. Yet important as these connections may be, they are neither necessary or exclusive features of cosmopolitanism in general. Non-Western, non-elite and non-urban cosmopolitanisms have been identified, challenging the simplistic recourse to familiar unitary stereotypes.

Another associated problem, located in the important body of work on cosmopolitanism by Ulrich Beck, is the tendency to see cosmopolitanism everywhere, such that it becomes almost limitless, and thus close to the defining spirit of the age. This too is a problematic consequence of the proliferation of cosmopolitanism, as well as the outcome of a simplistic cosmopolitan philosophy of history. In Chapter 3 an alternative contribution to a historical sociology of cosmopolitanisms is presented.

3

A Historical Sociology of Cosmopolitanism

Is cosmopolitanism primarily a modern phenomenon, and if so, can it be regarded in Beck's terms as the defining feature of the contemporary modernity of the 20th and 21st centuries? Or does it have a much longer and more complex history? This chapter is designed as a historical sociology of cosmopolitanism. The aim is to scrutinize Beck's argument in comparative historical depth. The broad argument here is that Beck's position is mechanistic, ahistorical and largely misconceived. Such problems have been noted by other critics of Beck, such as Fine (2007), but no alternative historical sociology of cosmopolitanism has yet been formulated. The chapter goes on to sketch one possible alternative, bringing history back into the sociology of cosmopolitanism. The first part of this book concludes in the following chapter, where some theoretical and methodological implications of this critique of Beck are elaborated.

The Two Ages of Modernity Argument

Ulrich Beck's contributions to the understanding of cosmopolitanism (notably Beck, 2002, 2006; Beck and Sznaider, 2006a) represent a major advance in scholarship. They have done more to re-connect the study of cosmopolitanism with sociological theory than any other writer, provide an important array of new concepts such as cosmopolitanization to the analysis of social processes, and re-invigorated connections between social analysis and normative arguments in favour of cosmopolitanism. This latter theme will be explored in the concluding chapter of this study. For the moment, attention will focus on the historical plausibility of Beck's arguments about cosmopolitanism and modernity, which connect discussion with the rise of the nation-state and globalization.

Theories of modernity abound in sociology, but often within rather different historical frames. Modernity may in this respect be regarded as commencing with the 18th-century Enlightenment, Industrial Revolution or French Revolution, or be projected backward in time to 16th- and 17th-century Protestantism, or processes of colonization and agrarian change at roughly the same time. The backward moving historical escalator, may equally return us to the 15th- and 16th-century Renaissance, to late medieval processes in the 12th and 13th centuries, all of this focussed primarily on European initiatives. Or perhaps we should return even further to the classical world of ancient Greece and Rome, an older argument recently revived and extended by Inglis and Robertson (2004, 2005). Bundled into this welter of origins and key turning points are issues relating to the modernity as institutional change, linked with capitalism and rationalization, and modernity of the self, evident in the intellect and in aesthetic taste.

No systematic attempt is made here to dis-aggregate all the various issues at stake in such arguments. What is important is to note that Beck belongs to those who see modernity primarily as a very recent development. This somehow starts around the 18th century, and draws on 'Great Transformation' (Polanyi, 1957) assumptions about processes of social change. These typically distinguish tradition from modernity and link tradition with an older world. Here key modern characteristics such as rationality, the invention of the self, and the (apparent) achievement of social dominance over nature through technology and work organization remain subdued by religious faith, arbitrary power and economic traditionalism.

Like Polanyi (1957), Marx and Engels (1962) [1848], and Hegel (1956) [1837] before him, Beck sees modernity very much as a revolutionary or radical qualitative change, pregnant with new opportunities, but also fraught with challenges and problems. The normative presupposition underlying this is that modernity, or some preferred version of it, is better able to meet human wants or express the dynamic of human strivings for freedom and justice, than what went before. Like all good things, however, one needs to struggle to achieve and consolidate its progressive features in the face of associated problems. For Beck, one of the biggest challenges is the increase in socially generated risk associated with industrial modernity. This contrasts with what he sees as a naturally generated risk of traditional societies and thereby reinforces binary divides between past and present, tradition and modernity. In such schema, cosmopolitanism becomes aligned with universal progress and against the particularisms of tradition, with its historical genealogy very much associated with the euphoria and hubris of modernity.

The 'Great Transformation' assumption, leads those who use it to reject the idea that social change is often less dramatic and more gradual or faltering in its impact, in favour of grand philosophies of history that are believed to divide historical epochs and ages. 'Traditional society' is somehow either written off or caricatured as the passive obverse to the more dynamic modernity, the task then switching away from history to an elaboration (and often celebration) of the modernity in which we live, and of which cosmopolitanism is seen by many as a part.

This switch away from history is however unfortunate, because it leaves intact presumptions such as those of the Great Transformation argument, and rather naïve grand-narratives tied to epochal events such as the Renaissance or Enlightenment. Its neglect matters even more in Beck's argument because in addition to such presumptions is the theory of two modernities, the first of which is believed to take a national form, the second a cosmopolitan one. Rather than treat such matters of history as either settled within philosophically loaded grand-narratives, or somehow epistemologically incoherent because one can only really know the present and its construction of the past, this book takes an alternative approach. Drawing on traditions of historical sociology in work by Weber, the Annales school, and Michael Mann, (for elaboration of these traditions see Holton, 2003) it is proposed that the past is neither epistemologically unavailable to the present, nor best understood through grand-narratives bearing normative assumptions about progress. In the alternative approach advanced in this chapter, the past can be known, not as it was directly experienced by those living in the past, but through logical and empirical analysis of evidence, directed by theoretical questions, and alive to epistemological problems of translation between past and present, and across cultural difference. This represents a post-positivist research strategy which retains notions of truth and reliability of interpretation, without falling into the traps of positivist objectivity, on the one side, or subjective relativism on the other.

Beck's theory of two modernities is encapsulated in Table 3.1. This identifies the changing institutional forms associated with the two modernities, parallel changes in social risk profiles, and further parallel changes in methodologies of social science scholarship required to comprehend such changes. Just as a 'great transformation' was seen as separating as separating tradition and modernity, so another very profound change or 'epochal distinction' (Beck, 2002: 62) separates the two modernities. Once again though, change is seen as far more crucial than any kind of continuity. Accordingly the shift to cosmopolitan modernity is associated with 'a new kind of capitalism, a new

Table 3.1   Beck and the Two Modernities

Type of modernity	Institutional forms	Risk profile	Scholarly methodology
1. National	Nation-state, in which economy, polity and culture are subsumed International law	Socially derived risks linked with industrial revolution	Methodological nationalism based on analysis of nation-states
2. Cosmopolitan	Interconnected global processes involving cosmopolitan nations	Trans-national risk communities	Methodological cosmopolitanism based on the analysis of world society
	Human rights law		

Source: constructed from Beck (2002), (2006).

kind of economy, a new kind of global order, a new kind of politics and law, and a new kind of society and personal life…[that are] clearly distinct from earlier phases' (*ibid*: 63).

Beck is not alone in detecting the emergence of a 'post-national' epoch in the evolution of modernity. Habermas, for example, speaks of a 'post-national constellation' associated with globalization (2001). For Köhler, this transition is represented as a shift from a 'national' to a 'post-national' public sphere, 'thanks to the social activity and the deliberate will of a population sharing common values and interests, such as human rights, democratic participation, the rule of law and the preservation of the world's ecological heritage' (1998: 231). While for Beck, the institutional changes associated with this epochal shift from national to global configurations of organization are paralleled by transitions in both the risk profile and the scholarly framework involved in the two kinds of modernity.

The national societies that Beck sees being consolidated in 19th-century Europe involve both high levels of system and social integration. At a systemic level this mean that each national society has its distinctive complex of national economy, national polity, and national culture. These three are, so to speak, isomorphic, with national culture expressed through national identity, being associated with class struggles over distribution of the fruits of the national economy being conducted through increasingly democratic national polities. In this way system integration is associated with social or cultural integration into national forms of politics. These kinds of national social integration – referred to by Beck as 'patriotic-national' modes of production' (2006: 107) – are not however the same thing as national social consensus, given high levels of class conflict over the risks associated with market economies driven by social deregulation.

A final component of this first modernity concerns relationships between nations. International relations within this framework are seen as organized on a state-to-state basis, very much according to what has come to be known as the Westphalian system that emerged from the debilitating Thirty Years' War. This is taken to have cemented the idea of the territorial integrity of states as a basis for international law. Under this system it is nations rather than individuals or groups that are party to international legal processes. We shall return to debates over the realities of this system and doubts as to its historical characterization, later in this study.

In cosmopolitan modernity by contrast, as indicated in Table 3.1, radical changes are evident. These are associated very closely with global inter-connections and inter-dependencies. Yet for Beck, it is cosmopolitanism rather than globalization that becomes the over-riding master process and concept here. This is not because Beck disputes the increasing intensity and cultural salience of cross-border processes of capital mobility, migration, governance, and law to the cosmopolitan age of modernity. The preference for cosmopolitanism as the leading concept in Beck and a number of others seems rather more to do with perceived problems with the scope of the term global-ization. As Mignolo (2000) puts it, globalization seems more to do with managerial designs for world domination, whereas cosmopolitanism is a more open term, containing within it critical and emancipatory possibilities.

Another reason for Beck's avoidance of globalization and preference for cosmopolitanism as an organizing concept is that globalization has often been seen as the binary opposite of the local or national. While sharp distinctions between the global and the national and local are very far from being necessary connotations of globalization (Robertson, 1992; Holton, 2005), they were crucial in early theories of hyper-globalization (e.g. Ohmae, 1990, 1995), and linked very largely with economic and technological processes. The assumption here was the global would erode the national and local. More recent work has accepted that global processes do not necessarily have this effect, that they may consciously or unwittingly rely on or re-inforce sub-global scales of activity, and above all, that national institutions and identities remain strong, what-ever the relationship between them and globalization.

Beck's work, too, takes up this line of argument. Here, as again seen in Chapter 6, it is not that the institutions of cosmopolitan modernity are singularly or unambiguously trans-national. He speaks rather of 'cosmopolitan nations', whose conditions of existence have been profoundly shaped by their inter-connections and inter-dependencies with others, but whose national distinctiveness has not disappeared.

As argued in Chapter 2, this reflects the re-casting of cosmopolitanism away from general universal institutions such as world government and de-contextualized world identities, and toward relations between groups and institutions that recognize each other as different, but who somehow value the inter-play of difference. Here particulars engage with each other while providing points of stabilization (Beck, 2006: 62) amidst the risks and uncertainties of everyday life.

All this clearly accepts much of the criticism levelled at cosmopolitanism for being too remote, abstract, and over-generalized as an identity, and implausible as a form of governance, without abandoning cosmopolitanism itself. When we come to empirical analysis in Part II of this study it does however render identification of what is and what is not cosmopolitanism more difficult to determine, insofar as national scales of activity do not in and of themselves rule out Beck's re-formulated versions of cosmopolitan modalities.

In addition to cosmopolitan nations, Beck focusses on cosmopolitan law as another key institutional change. Whereas in national modes of modernity, legal relations between nations are conducted (if at all) through international law, under cosmopolitan modernity, their legal form, in his view, is expressed through the cosmopolitan notion of human rights (*ibid*: 120–2). Unlike the previous age of relations between territorially bounded sovereign states using international law as a route to peace, the new age grounds law within the global arena in transnational rights of a higher order. Such 'human rights' apply to all, and are extendable to individuals and groups as much as nation-states. One indicator of this is the emergence of norms of humanitarian conduct as a necessary feature of international relations. Overall human rights represent '…the dream of a new, more humane global order: all peoples, states, religions, ethnic groups living united under human rights raised to the status of law'. And this dream, he acknowledges, represents 'an age-old principle which can be traced back to the philosophy of the Stoics and which had already become policy, or at least a political ideology during the Roman Empire' (141).

Objections to the Two Modernities Argument?

What then are the objections to the 'two modernities' argument? Beck's discussion does not deny that longer-term historical legacies influence the present. The 19th century and early 20th century, meanwhile, might well be thought of as a more nation-centred epoch than the present, in which states and peoples sought national unification or national independence. And the argument that 'international law' preceded the development of human rights might also seem very plausible. Why in short does history matter?

It may not matter so much if the discussion is primarily about the credentials of cosmopolitanism as moral philosophy, and as an inspiration to address and re-make the modern world. If cosmopolitanism is simply seen as more desirable than nationalism then this would apply irrespective of its historical emergence or connections with theories of modernity. Of course there may be added rhetorical force to arguments in favour of cosmopolitanism if it could be shown that it is somehow a position specially suited to the challenges of our times. It is possible, on this basis, to interpret Beck's 'two modernities' argument as adding rhetorical force to the moral case for cosmopolitanism. Yet this leaves the analytical basis to his argument unexamined. If his sociology of cosmopolitanism turns out to be historically inadequate or misleading, then this is a highly important analytical issue in its own right. In addition, it also has implications for the moral claims of cosmopolitanism. If this has no special claims to be uniquely suited to contemporary challenges, then this might weaken the rhetorical force of the normative case in favour. Conversely, if cosmopolitanism in some shape or form has been present in a range of contexts across time and space, then this might provide an alternative route to a more positive normative evaluation of its claims.

For the remainder of this chapter, the focus is primarily analytical. What is at stake here is firstly whether Beck's two modernities argument makes historical sense, and secondly whether there is an alternative way of constructing a historical sociology of cosmopolitanism.

There are two major objections to the two modernities argument. One is the gross neglect of cosmopolitanism and processes of cosmopolitanization across time and space. The other is a specific misunderstanding enshrined in Beck's notion of the first modernity, of the historical emergence of nation-states, national institutions, national identity and nationalism in relation to cosmopolitanism. Let us look at these in turn.

Overcoming Blinkered Historical Perspectives on Cosmopolitanism

Cosmopolitanism, like globalization, have often been seen as cross-border phenomena that are new and qualitatively different from what went before. Relevant instances of contemporary novelty cannot be denied, whether in the form of virtually instantaneous communications technology or high levels of economic interdependence. But it is equally important to acknowledge historical continuities in cross-border phenomena, such as high levels of cross-border trade and migration, warfare, religious imaginings of a single global community, and the periodic presence of cosmopolitanism itself. How then do we recognize both change and continuity?

To achieve this requires serious attention to the evidence for continuity, rather than accepting the case for novelty at face value. As soon as this question is asked it becomes very clear that historians, anthropologists, and sociologists have brought forward many instances of cosmopolitan thought and activity in the past, involving most if not all modalities of cosmopolitanism discussed in Chapter 2.

A useful starting-point is provided in Euben's (2006) study of Western and Islamic travellers since the latter part of the first millennium, which she uses as the basis for a key chapter 'Cosmopolitanisms Past and Present: Islamic and Western' (174–97). Globalization and cosmopolitanism have long histories, but they are not well remembered and often only invoked in passing, if at all (*ibid:* 174–5). Echoing parallel arguments in the collection of essays entitled *Globalization and History* (Hopkins, 2002) and in *Making Globalization* (Holton, 2005), history is claimed to matter not for some kind of antiquarian interest, but because of a tendency for analysts of cosmopolitanism to retreat into the present. This tendency obscures the way in which the past, as perceived and analysed 'is as important a comparison for the present as contemporary cultural constellations are for each other' (175). This in turn invites attention to complex processes of historical change and interaction, to earlier cosmopolitan moments, and the mobilities, cultural inter-connections, antagonisms and melanges of the past. Relationships between the global and local have existed throughout history, implicating power and values, institutions and culture. They are not a sudden novelty.

Such a historically informed focus is of course ruled out if we accept Beck's presentist and empirically ungrounded analysis of cosmopolitanization and cosmopolitanism as uniquely central features of contemporary life. Euben and others seek to identify other cosmopolitan moments in time and space and to explore linkages between them. Beck in the main does not, relying for the most on episodic historical references to thinkers like the Stoics or Kant. The uniqueness of the present is, in other words, asserted rather than sustained through historical analysis.

There are, however, as Euben goes on to argue, further spatial and cultural dimensions to approaches to the history of cosmopolitanism. If Beck foreshortens this history to the last two centuries of what he sees as modernity, others tend to link cosmopolitanism with the expansive character of the European world and its colonized Others. This focus allows a greater historical dimension evident, for example, in Mignolo's (2000) work tracing such processes from colonizations of the 16th and 17th centuries to the contemporary post-colonial period. But it is a focus that can narrow attention to a primarily European and European-induced genealogy, as well as limiting attention to philosophical rather than action-oriented cosmopolitan modalities.

How then might these blinkered historical perspectives be overcome? And what substantive insights would a richer historical sociology of cosmopolitanism yield?

The main lines of an alternative approach can be illuminated through attention to long-run processes of intellectual thought, religious development, Empire, mobility and trade and the intersections between them.

We start with intellectual thought, and the important recent work by Inglis and Robertson (2004, 2005). This identifies the development of an ancient Greek 'ecumenical sensibility' (2005: 104) in the period from the time of Alexander the Great in the later fourth century BC to the eventual demise of independent Greek ascendancy with the rise of Rome. This is linked not so much with Stoicism as Alexander's conquest of the east as far as India, and the Hellenization of populations in the Eastern Mediterranean and beyond. This in turn encouraged changes in the ways that Greek intellectuals understood the world, moving away from narrow horizons of 'Greek chauvinism' to a 'general Hellenic universe'. These intersected with more familiar philosophical doctrines of the Cynics and Stoics in the spread of cosmopolitan ideals and practices, and were further elaborated in Greek historiographies of 'world history', which according to Inglis and Robertson were invented over two millennia ago, rather than over the last two or three hundred years. History writing was, they go on to claim, revolutionized away from particular polities to the whole ecumene (*oikoumene*), and away from localized empirical contexts, to those of trans-local interactions. Such approaches were further extended in Roman historical writing against the background of new phases of Empire.

Such developments speak not only to far earlier 'pre-histories' of globalization than many 21st-century writers acknowledge, but also consolidate existing awareness of the significance of ancient cosmopolitanism in philosophy and beyond. They also serve to de-mythologize some of the leading conceits of modern Western thought, including the suppositions that reflexivity and sociological theory are somehow recent products of the Enlightenment. For Inglis and Robertson (2004), sociology has an 'ancient inheritance', and this includes a kind of methodological ecumenism, supposed by Beck and many others to have emerged comparatively recently.

In the case of religion, and in particular the world religions such as Christianity and Islam, Roland Robertson (1992) regards these as further early forms of globalization. Each treats the world as a single place, re-inforced by mono-theistic faith in a single divinity. For Muslims the *dar al Islam* is the sacred world of God inhabited by the *umma* or community of the faithful, distinct from the profane *dar al-Harb*. This community is not necessarily static and certainly not uniform. It contains within it multiple, though not always mutually exclusive bodies of thought and practice. In addition, there is considerable mobility, inter-connection and cross-fertilization through the mobility of pilgrims to holy places, and of those seeking knowledge wherever it may be found. It may then be regarded, following Bamyeh (2004: 223), as founded on an 'imagined unity' within a rather heterodox global civil society (Euben, 2006: 88).

Christian notions such as St Augustine's *civitas dei*, or city of God, also represent similar all-embracing conceptions of religious community. Again there is a binary divide separating the sacred from the profane (Edwards, 2001: 35–6), where the cities are allegorical representations of living with God (Jerusalem) and living with the Devil (Babylon). The city of God is also represented as mobile, as a kind of 'wandering in the world' (*ibid:* 36). In this sense, as Edwards points out, the Roman political taxonomies are reversed, for it is no longer the enfranchised citizen of a particular place that is valued, and the foreigner or alien seen as marginal. The heavenly city transcends such bounded entities, valourizing *peregrinus* (mobility) over *civis* (static citizenship).

Such world-views are what would now be called global imaginaries. They may be regarded as encouragements to religious cosmopolitanism, in the sense that all, regardless of ethnicity, gender or skin colour, are equal before God. As St Ambrose put it, the world is a *patria* (or homeland) for all humankind (*ibid:* 37). This recognizes the possibility of what Edwards calls the 'virtuous pagan', living outside knowledge of the God and the Church. Here spiritual virtue is cosmopolitan rather than local or particular in form.

In practice, of course, religious community is very clearly connected with particular places, cultural traditions, and ethnicities. Such particularities do not, in and of themselves, rule out cosmopolitanism, since, as we have argued in Chapters 1 and 2, it is a mistake to regard cosmopolitan impulses as free-floating forms of universalism unconnected with time and space. The limits of religious cosmopolitanism are set rather by intolerance to others including other co-religionists.

Intolerance has often been prevalent in inter-religious terms, including Christian-Muslim conflicts such as (what Westerners call) the Crusades, as well as in intra-religious partisanship and conflict in the application of religious power and justice in relations between branches of Christianity such as Catholics and Protestants, or within Sunni, Sh'ia and Sufi currents in Islam. These characteristics do not however rule out religious sources of cosmopolitanism altogether, as secular critics often imply. Religious ecumenism and inter-faith dialogue, for example, represents a different side to religion. What they do suggest is that connections between religion and cosmopolitanism are not necessary, but are potential features that arise in certain circumstances rather than invariably.

One way of identifying such circumstances is to look at the intersections between religion, mobility, and political organization. In the case of Islam, Euben (2006), using Islamic travel narratives as evidence, has identified 'the Islamic ethos of travel in search of knowledge' (*ibid*: 178) as a rich strand in the genealogy of Islamic cosmopolitanism. In contrast with contemporary portrayals of Islam as 'anticosmopolitanism par excellence', Euben notes the Qur'anic emphasis on the moral significance of human diversity, as reflections of the plurality of God's design, together with injunctions to seek knowledge wherever it may be found.

These themes encouraged enormous personal mobility within the *umma* over more than a millennium, sometimes attached to the *hajj*, or pilgrimage to Mecca. They created, as it were, a cosmopolitanization of Islamic experience. This is evident in the Islamic travel writing discussed by Euben. It is also evident from data on the biography of 50 leading Islamic thinkers (Jackson, 2006) from the 7th-century circles around the prophet Muhammad, to 20th-century figures such as the Iranian Ali Shariati and the Tunisian Rachid Ghannoushi. Here currents of thought and pathways of action circulated across political and cultural boundaries within the network-like structure of the Islamic world (Lapidus, 1975). This typically involved study in more than one centre of knowledge. The 11th-century theologian, philosopher, jurist, and mystic al Ghazzali, born in Iran, studied there, then moving to study in Baghdad, and moved subsequently through Syria and Palestine, as well as making pilgrimages to Mecca and Medina (Jackson, 2006: 86–9). For Ibn Khaldun, the 14th-century historian, cosmopolitanization was built into his family's experience of movement from Arabia into North Africa and Moorish Spain.

Cosmopolitanization of this kind was present before Western colonization, and before the contemporary phase of modernity that Beck labels as cosmopolitan. Emphasis on cosmopolitanization in this historical, cultural and spatial context renders Beck's approach both Euro-centric and historically foreshortened. But what of the cosmopolitan outlook, a more explicit commitment to outward-looking engagement with others?

Within Islam, there are both cosmopolitan and anti-cosmopolitan moments, both outward-looking and inward-looking processes and elements. Inward-looking processes may be a reaction against external pressures, or may reflect the predominance of local worlds. They may be used as a basis for the perceived purifying of Islam, and sometimes for its aggressive outward reassertion, as in Al Qu'aida's recent campaigns. These are anti-cosmopolitan in their divisive thrust against Western materialism, though they speak to the continuing cosmopolitanization of the Islamic experience of Christendom and Europe over the last millennium.

Euben (2006: 179) provides a number of historical examples of what she calls 'a counter-genealogy of cosmopolitanism' emphasizing Islamic rather than Western 'practices, moments and ideas' and which also appear and persist in cultural memory. These range from the Abbasid dynasty of Damascus , where Islamic law is understood 'as a response to a fluid syncretic milieu', through the more widely known cities of Andalusia (*al Andalus*) under Cordoban Umayyad rule from the 9th to the 11th centuries, where Muslims, Christians and Jews lived together in relatively tolerant conditions (Menocal, 2002), and through long-distance interchanges between the multi-ethnic Ottoman, Safavid and Mughal empires in the 17th and 18th centuries (Robinson, 1997), coming finally to the contemporary 'virtual umma... enacted and reconfigured electronically by Muslims across the world' (Karim, 2002; Mandaville, 2002). This last example, it should be emphasized, is positioned within a long history of cosmopolitan engagements, rather than being a recent manifestation of some supposedly emergent Islamic cosmopolitan modernity. It speaks to the need to re-think the concepts within which any history of cosmopolitanism is framed, both in terms of the supposed centrality of the second modernity and in terms of narratives centred on Europe.

The example of cosmopolitan engagement in Andalusia is worthy of attention, in indicating the enormous possibilities of tolerance and harmony within Islamic and Arabized settings. For Menocal (2002), the caliphate of Andalusia, centred on Cordoba, established in the second half of the 8th century AD by the exiled Umayyad Islamic figure Abd al-Rahman, has enormous significance for the history of inter-cultural openness. These represent the impact, in the culturally diverse context of Iberian Europe, of ideas, institutions and cultural practices of the world beyond Europe. This diverse context is consistent with Beck's concepts of cosmopolitanization, in terms of successive waves of migrants from Phoenicea, Carthage and Greece, invasions by Visigoths and the more recent passage of Islamic Syrian Arabs and converted Berbers from North Africa, creating a multi-religious population including Muslims, Christians and Jews. Underlying such movements was an expanding Mediterranean trading economy.

Rahman was the last remaining member of the Umayyad Caliphate based in the cosmopolitan city of Damascus, whose family was slaughtered and replaced by the Abbasid rulers, soon to move the caliphate eastward to Baghdad. Rahman, seeking to follow the relatively open governing practices of the Umayyads, ushered in a period of over 200 years of significant cross-cultural harmony. This, according to Menocal, had both an Islamic and Arab dimension. The Islamic dimension involved recognition of other monotheistic Abrahamic religions – or *dhimmi* – meaning Peoples of the Book. These received religious protection and private if not public rights of worship. Such rights were probably more significant to Jews, who had the lowest status for previous Visigoth rulers, than Christians, for whom rights to public religious disputation were denied. Many Christians of course converted by choice. Both Jews and Christians could also hold public office. This represents significant though not unlimited evidence of cosmopolitan openness and tolerance, providing a milieu that is not mere cosmopolitanization but also has elements of a cosmopolitan outlook. This argument may be further sustained by reference to a second element in the Andalucian mix.

The Arab influence, according to Menocal, was more cultural in form, involving language, (pre-Islamic traditions of) poetry, literature, scholarship and architecture. Christians and Jews became culturally Arabized, even if they chose not to convert to Islam, and the built environment fused together a range of culturally distinct architectural styles. Meanwhile Latin use declined among Christians. It was through the medium of Arabic too that the outward-looking orientation of the Baghdad caliphate who set about translating classical authors of ancient Greece was transmitted to Cordoba and its environs. The pursuit of intellectual truth was a marked feature of Cordoba, evident in its many libraries containing work in many languages, as well as through the presence of leading scholars. For Menocal it is the influence of Arabic poetry that is a crucial feature of cultural openness, insofar as this contained commentaries of discordant features of life rather than settled orthodoxies. Poetry was thereby a way of speaking of desire and the erotic, as much as obligation and duty.

The Umayyad caliphate of Andalusia did not survive beyond the early 11th century when an epoch of disorder and conflict ensued between Muslims as well between Islam and Christianity. Intolerance became more marked including book-burning and oppression of minorities. Nonetheless some of the earlier traditions survived or were amplified, many around the new intellectual capital of Toledo, which whether under Muslim or Christian rule became by the end of the 11th century 'the intellectual capital of Europe', yet at the same time 'a Christian city where Arabic remained a language of culture and learning... It was by way of Toledo that the rest of Europe – Latin Christendom – finally had access to the vast body of philosophical and scientific materials translated from Greek' (144–5) on a journey from Baghdad to Cordoba and thence Toledo. In these ways the pathways to European cosmopolitan worlds of letters, science and tolerance had non-European origins.

Aside from the example of Andalusia, a good deal of the other examples in Euben's argument feature Muslims talking and engaging with each other across political, ethnic and sectarian divides. Is this to be regarded unambiguously as cosmopolitanism? The answer depends on the yardsticks used. If by cosmopolitanism we mean a philosophical and practical openness to *all* others then maybe not. However by this yardstick many other examples of cosmopolitanism, including Christian or liberal-democratic types would also need to be excluded. The religious ecumenism that emerged within movements culminating in the bodies like World Council of Churches was, for example, derived from linkages between sections of Christianity – Protestant, Orthodox, and Catholic (Gheorghiu, 2007) – rather than all world religions.

Practical modalities of cosmopolitanism extended to all others may be difficult to achieve, either because not all the diverse others of the world are present in any given context, and in part because the terms of openness may vary across different settings, with some 'others' being more acceptable than other 'others'. We will return to problems of variability in what constitutes openness later in this study. For the moment we emphasize that complete unambiguous cosmopolitanism is far easier to assert, as it were theoretically or philosophically, than practically. This might lead sceptics to the conclusion that cosmopolitanism in being restricted to vague over-generalized commitments to universalism is not feasible as a practical orientation to the world. This is clearly unsatisfactory for those who see cosmopolitanism as practical and this-worldly, rather than as 'a product of induction from some sedentary hiding place' (Bamyeh, 2000: 103). His riposte is to see cosmopolitanism emerging from practical exigencies of life, though still somewhat enigmatically, as 'an outcome of conducting one's life on a route to a number of destinations'. How might this clue be elaborated?

One way of building such an alternative practice-centred approach, recognized by many recent sociological and anthropological writers, accepts that open orientations to the world are typically incomplete and circumscribed by social context. Yet they remain relevant to socio-logical if not philosophical assessments of cosmopolitanism as this affects ways of life and social relationships. Another way of putting this is that cosmopolitanism is always in some kind of dialogue with the local, and this applies not merely to practical, but also to philo-sophical categories, which are equally grounded in time and space, whatever their universalistic aspirations. It is upon this basis that most current literature as well as this study proceeds.

This approach is nonetheless vulnerable to the problem of where to draw the line between cosmopolitanism as re-conceptualized here, and its obverse. If openness is regarded in a conditional manner, then this logically also applies to closure. How closed does one have to be to finally qualify for allocation to the category of non- or anti-cosmopolitan? This problem arose, as we saw in Chapter 2, in Hannerz's pioneering work seeking to distinguish 'cosmopolitans', 'trans-nationals', and 'locals'. This wrestles with issues of relative openness in its discussion of migrants who may be trans-national in moving from one location to another, but not in the sense in being open to engagement outside their diaspora group. This problem re-appears in a more religious setting, in Diouf's (1999) discussion of a Senegalese trading diaspora. Based on the Murid sect, this diaspora has been active in trade in North America, Europe, and Asia, but nonethe-less very much turned inward, without any cultural as distinct from business engagement with others.

Standing alongside religion as a profound influence on the develop-ment of cosmopolitanism, is the institution and circulating practices of Empire. These, to repeat the argument, are not necessarily connected with cosmopolitanization or the cosmopolitan outlook, and may well be vehicles of closed particularistic forms of dominance and outlook. Each nonetheless has the potential for openness of one kind or another, including the generation of connections and solidarities across cultural differences. This may be a product of outward-looking proselytizing religious zeal, of Imperial strategies of rule across diverse vernacular cultural domains by means such as multicultural recruitment into officialdom or internal policies of toleration.

Sheldon Pollock (2000) develops a further dimension to questions of cosmopolitanism and Empire, via language, and in particular the rela-tionship between trans-local politico-religious and local vernacular languages. This is centred on South Asia and the growth of vernacular languages between 1000 and 1500 where previously trans-regional

Sanskrit had become the dominant language of political will in public literary expression (*ibid*: 11). Rather than take this process as an indicator of the decline of an official cosmopolitan language in favour of localism or proto-nationalism, Pollock takes a more subtle approach.

Sanskrit, while a dominant political language linked with South Asian empires, was never the medium of everyday conversation. In this respect it was similar to other Imperial languages such as Latin in Europe or Persian in West Asia. In the case of Sanskrit its function became very much a means of imagining supra-local Imperial space through epic literature. The rise of vernacular languages was not however in opposition to this but a way of translating Sanskrit epics into local spaces, whether in the Indian sub-continent or Java. Pollock rejects the idea that sectarian religious choices mandated vernacular language, in favour of vernacularization of the Sanskrit literary ecumene in order to reach the masses. This pre-modern example indicates not only the centrality of Empire for many instances of cosmopolitanism in this epoch, but also the significance of global-local interactions and inter-penetrations within multi-lingual and multi-ethnic Empires.

For the Mughal Emperor Akbar, emperor of India through the last half of the 16th century, reason and dialogue between different viewpoints rather than formulaic tradition was an important feature of the good ruler. Descended from the Mongol military rulers Tamerlane and Genghis Khan, Akbar at first consolidated his rule through successful military campaigns. Having secured this, he set about promoting dialogue between religions (Hindu, Muslim, Christian, Jew, Parsees) in the context of Imperial neutrality, reflected in the abolition of discriminatory taxation against non-Muslims. Akbar even attempted, in the end unsuccessfully, a generic synthesis of religious currents. Amartya Sen (2005: 288–9) sees this as an example of the importance of inter-cultural engagement through public debate. While not explicitly referring to this epoch as cosmopolitan, it clearly counts as an ecumenical form of inter-cultural engagement.

This discussion of Empire suggests that stability and a sense of security may be important in encouraging outward cosmopolitan outlooks and practices, while conversely that insecurity may create a more inward-looking orientation. This would apply both to Imperial rulers, especially where they rule culturally mixed populations, as well as democratic publics in more modern contexts. Religious groups may be more outward-looking, for example where surrounding political arrangements are more stable, allowing significant levels of religious autonomy. Euben (*ibid*: 83), cites Francis Robinson's (1997) work on Islamic religious ecumenism as a case in point. Religious and scholarly traditions are not tightly determined by political power (see Collins,

1998 for a similar argument about the autonomy of philosophical debates). Nonetheless, Robinson argues that where Muslims felt confidently in power in periods of Imperial consolidation they were more likely to discern divinity even amongst non-Muslims, and to take up 'rational subjects, which at times served a bulwarks against congealing orthodoxy'. Periods when Muslim power was in jeopardy served by contrast to curtail outward linkages and suppress ecumenical knowledge in favour of moral reconstruction (*ibid*: 172–3). This political insecurity factor may help explain why contemporary radical Islamists adopt the inward reconstruction rather than outward ecumenical option.

In addition to religion and Empire, a third analytical distinct element in any historical sociology of cosmopolitanism is mobility itself, sometimes forced and sometimes voluntary. While religion and Empire, along with changes in transport technology, encourage mobility, it may also be connected with long-distance trade, with what James Clifford refers to as 'travelling cultures' (1992). Mobility may in short be seen as a feature of the human condition.

The significance of long-distance trade for cosmopolitanism involves social practices, institutions and ways of life that cross political and cultural boundaries. Across the last two, in some cases three millennia, trade of this kind was linked with high-value luxury goods like silk, spices, and precious metals. Their level and volume also fluctuated across historical periods, with reversions and interruptions due to political instability, border closure and epidemic disease. By the late medieval period, there had nonetheless grown up a number of interconnected circuits of trade linking Asia in the East with Northern and Western Europe through maritime and land-based trade routes (Abu-Lughod, 1989). The significance of such circuits, together with the challenges in associating them with cosmopolitanism, may be grasped by reference to the Silk Road.

First coined by the explorer von Richtofen in 1877, the 'silk road' or *Seidenstrasse* linked China, with central and West Asia, with further extensions into the Near East and Mediterranean Europe (Wood, 2002). Products like silk, satin, jade and precious stones, spices, carpets and furniture were traded along what was more a network of interconnected trading routes rather than a single pathway. It was the route along which members of the Venetian family of Marco Polo travelled east in the 13th century, as well as the route along which diplomatic emissaries and religious figures travelled to and fro. Buddhism, for example, was brought into China by this route around 2000 years ago, while Chinese Buddhists in subsequent centuries travelled back to India in search of texts to be translated into Chinese. Cities developed along the way included Samarkand (formerly Marakanda), Bokhara and Dunhuang. These developed a range of functions over time, within changing economic, political and military conditions. Such functions included trade, politics and religion.

In what sense then may this mobile world be regarded as cosmopolitan? Some care is needed in answering this question, in part because of sparse evidence. Wood (2002) also points out that the Marco Polo story, taken out of context, suggests a rather false impression that all movements along the silk road were long-distance. While commodities often moved a considerable distance, people may rarely have done so, in part because goods were passed between many intermediaries. The presence of traders from different backgrounds may also have meant periodic co-presence in markets rather than more intensive forms of inter-cultural connection. It may be that religious mobility along routes carved out by traders and warriors was more central to any cosmo-politanism that arose within the world of the silk road. Certainly the remarkable archaeological findings in the western Chinese desert oasis of Dunhuang – location of the Caves of a Thousand Buddhas – suggest a world of interaction connected with mobile Buddhist scholars and travellers. Texts and paintings discovered in Dunhuang, dating from around 400 to 1000 AD, represent what may be 'the world's first paper archive' (*ibid*: 90). Most texts were in Chinese, but Sanskrit, Tibetan, Hebrew and Sogdian (language of a people based in Samarkand) are also represented, as are religious texts from Confucian and Taoist to Jewish, Manichean and Nestorian sources.

Other more recent kinds of mobility have been discussed by Clifford, through the notion of 'travelling cultures' (1992). Travel across borders is seen not merely as a feature of trade or migration, but as a discursive cultural practice in scholarship, literature, and politics. In this context, the ethnographic encounters which anthropologists used to study in local settings have been displaced by a 'global world of interconnected import-export' (*ibid*: 100). 'Natives', as the discursive objects of enquiry, cannot under these circumstances simply be treated as localized unsullied by wider contact (Appadurai, 1996: 39), any more than the more familiar Western populations of 19th-century Europe. For Clifford, this line of thinking should not lead to the replacement of the figure of the authentic local 'native', with the inter-cultural, hybrid (and we might add cosmopolitan) traveller, but 'concrete mediations of the two'…including the 'dynamics of dwelling/travelling' analysed comparatively (101).

Gilroy's (1993) account of the Black Atlantic provides a graphic example of the complex cross-border mobilities among African, African-American and populations of Caribbean origin during the 19th and 20th centuries. Slaves and the children of slaves made this world, which linked many countries and which appears in a range of cultural settings. Rather than see such connections as links between distinct and separate and self-contained 'cultures', Gilroy takes the entire Black Atlantic as a 'transcultural international formation' (4). This arose in the context of Empire, slavery, colonization, trade and racial domination, but it represented far more than this. The mobilities of slaves, former slaves and later migrants were linked sometimes with ships and autonomous maritime communities, but also with the circulation of musical genres, books and long-playing records. These display the active agency of Black Atlantic populations. It is a world of cross-fertilization and hybridity (see also Berlin's (1998: 17) idea of an Atlantic Creole) and one, it might be added, where cosmopolitanization in Beck's sense is built into the conditions of existence of such mobile groups.

Gilroy's study also pursues what might be called (though he doesn't use these terms himself) the cosmopolitan outlook of the Black Atlantic as an example of a counter-culture of modernity. Rather than thinking of communities of former Africans scattered through North American and European nations trying to preserve traditional ways of life in an authentic manner, he emphasizes a modern transcultural and outward-looking stance. This is based in large measure on an opposition to slavery of any kind in the name of a more universalistic sense of humanity, traced through Black Atlantic writers such as Martin Delany, William du Bois and Frederick Douglass. Gilroy does not dispute the presence of nationalist elements within their thinking (*ibid*: 35). This reflected a view that successful nation-building would create strength and security. At the same time this did not displace broader aspirations and identities to Africa and sometimes to Christianity, what Gilroy calls an 'open Blackness', alongside more inward-looking practices, such as Black Power. In this sense we might say that as with Islam, there are cosmopolitan as well as non- or anti-cosmopolitan moments in the Black Atlantic.

Some sense of what cosmopolitan openness might mean in this context is provided in Featherstone's recent (2007) work on transnational political networks in the later 18th and early 19th century around the radical London Corresponding Society. This body of 'tradesmen, shopkeepers and mechanics' has previously been identified by E.P. Thompson as a significant aspect of *English* struggles for political reform and for the making of an *English* working class (my italics). Featherstone, by contrast, identifies broader linkages with the ex-slave, free black activist Olaudah Equiano (who then went under the name of Gustavus Vassa). For Thomas Hardy, leader of the LCS, 'our views of the Rights of Man are not confined solely to this small island, but are extended to the whole Human Race, Black or White, high or low, rich or poor' (*ibid*: 431). Esquiano, for his part, defined himself very clearly as a 'citizen of the world'. He represents one of a number of mobile former slaves who established links with radical political movements in London at around the turn of the 19th century (Gilroy, *op. cit*: 12).

Featherstone cites other examples of linkages between mobile Afro-Caribbeans and British radicals in the first half of the 20th century including C.L.R. James, author of the celebrated book on the black Haitian revolution of the early 19th century against French colonial rule (James, 1988 [1938]). Evidence of this kind does not of course dispose of the significance of nation and various kinds of nationalism to a range of radical and conservative social and political movements throughout this period. These do not however displace Empire and colonization as central and continuing themes in processes of cosmopolitanization.

Mobility in different forms and settings exerts some kind of continuity across history, as much as settlement and a sense of rootedness in particular places. In this sense, as Appiah (2006: 192) points out, humankind is a travelling species, rather than one locked into territorial stability. This applies both through epochs regarded as traditional, and within and beyond Beck's purported first age of modernity. Settlement and senses of place are clearly important to processes of agriculture, state-building and identity. They do not however exert a monopoly upon human experience, which is better thought of in terms of a dialectic between movement and settlement.

Insofar as movement and settlement are conditions entered into voluntarily, then both sides of the dialectic hold opportunities as well as constraints. Cross-border movement may bring access to new land, food, economic opportunity, solidarity and security that comes from being part of a larger group, but it may equally bring greater risk, rejection by those encountered in new settings, and new uncertainties not faced or imagined before. Continued settlement in one place may bring greater comforts and securities by being part of communities one knows, a surer grasp of identity, and less uncertainty than movement. But it may equally create limits to knowledge affecting what can be achieved, leading to frustration and conflict, may stifle innovation and reduce long term-flexibility by refusal to countenance what lies beyond familiar practices and horizons.

Once we bring coercion and constraint into this hitherto rather unrealistic model, the dialectic is further complicated. Coercive pressures in one setting may force movement to another, as occurred in many contexts with enslavement and transportation. The resultant mobilities may bring tragedy, abuse, and even genocide, yet on the other hand, new unintended opportunities for freedom, with resistance creating the possibility of new kinds of cross-border life. Similarly escape from unacceptable repression and abuse in the case of refugees may lead to multiple outcomes from being stuck indefinitely in the limbo of camps, or where re-settled being subjected to abuse and exploitation in new settings. Such settings may, by contrast, offer up new opportunities, not least those available to those with cross-border experiences and knowledge, including cross-border linguistic, cultural, religious and business linkages and capacities.

This dialectic is important in understanding the social rootedness of cosmopolitanism. As elaborated in Chapter 2, the task is not to seek out cases of outward-looking orientation that are somehow divorced from any particular context, and thus appear as 'pure' philosophical universalism. Even philosophy, as Collins (1998) points out, must be set, however subtly, within its social context, which in turn influences the problems tackled and the concepts and arguments developed, though not mechanically or deterministically. The rootedness of cosmopolitanism means that contextual origins matter, rather than being discordant and embarrassing lapses from ideal cosmopolitan virtue. This applies to Western cosmopolitanisms, which often picked up the legacy of Enlightenment reason or Christianity, without taking account of violence and racism on which many Western structures of global power rested. The general influence of context in a variety of forms also applies to the rootedness of cosmopolitan elements in Islam and in the Black Atlantic.

In this section we have demonstrated that a rich historical sociology of cosmopolitanism can be constructed across time and space. Neither cosmopolitanization nor the cosmopolitan outlook can be understood, as Beck has attempted, in terms of the present and its recent past, with the odd reference back to ancient Greek philosophers. Rather the historical sociology of cosmopolitanism is connected with long-term trends in religion, Empire, trade, and mobility. Such trends are, moreover, world-wide rather than centred only upon Europe or the West.

We now turn to the second major issue concerning nation-states, and Beck's conception of the first modernity. Was there really a nation-focussed modernity that has now been transformed by cosmopolitanization?

Nations, Cosmopolitanism and the First Modernity

Beck's conception of a first modernity, as we have seen, stands in marked contrast to the second more contemporary phase. Whereas the second modernity is seen as cosmopolitan in its conditions of life and cultural outlook, the first is constructed as founded on nation-states and national modes of thinking about identity, culture and relations with others. These are constituted through international relations, by which is meant relations between bounded sovereign entities, resting on national capitalisms and political communities.

The argument here takes a strong form, that contrasts with what might seem to be a quite reasonable emphasis on the 19th and early to mid-20th centuries as periods of nation-state construction, unification and nationalist conflict, compared with what went before. The weaker version of this argument is that nations and national scales of activity mattered a great deal at this stage, but do not exclude either international or trans-national developments. The late 19th and early 20th centuries were after all a period of colonial expansion, increased free trade, mass cross-border migration, new global technologies such as the telegraph, telephone and radio, as well as new moves towards human rights in the shape of the Geneva Conventions on rules of warfare and imprisonment. In the weaker argument such developments can be seen emerging from within or at the very least alongside nationally focussed activities.

Beck's stronger 'national' account of the first modernity is of a rather different order. Here we find 'separate nationally organized societies' dominated by a 'social image of frozen, separate words and identities' (Beck, 2006: 5). Prevailing nationally centred views of the world are referred to elsewhere as a 'territorial prison theory of identity, politics, and society' (*ibid*: 7). 'During the national phase of modernity', he continues, 'cosmopolitanism could only be grasped intellectually, in the head, but could not be felt as a living experience' (*ibid*: 19). This is because 'nationalism…took possession of people's hearts'. The rhetoric here is eloquent, but unflinching, both unconditional and without complexity. This strong argument may be bold, but this is not sufficient to offset its ahistorical limitations.

An incident from the 19th-century European world of the arts may be an appropriate starting-point for a critique of Beck's approach to the first modernity. The date is 1835 and the evidence entries in the guest register of the Hotel d'Union in Geneva where the composer Franz Lizst and a number of his friends were staying (Taylor, 1986: 46). Lizst himself signed in as follows:

Place of birth: Parnassus
Occupation: Musician-Philosopher
Arriving from: Doubt
En route for: Truth

The writer Georges Sand for her part wrote:

Place of birth:	Europe
Residence:	Nature
Arriving from:	God
En route for:	Heaven
Date of passport:	Infinity
Issued by:	Public opinion

How would one characterize this moment? The answer can scarcely be in terms of some 'territorial prison theory of identity, politics, and society' organized around bounded national notions of sovereignty and cultural identity. While Lizst as a composer was posthumously claimed by the new state of Germany in 1881, he was born in an Austrian region of the Austro-Hungarian Empire, in a village with a primarily Magyar population. While German was the language of the household his family name was spelt in the Hungarian (Lizst) rather than German (List) manner. And in the midst of struggles for German unification, he himself thought and acted more in terms of a cosmopolitan Romanticism, for which Europe was home and within which truth and doubt rather than national destiny were in his heart and the classical site of Parnassus, mythical home of the muses of poetry, art and music, his symbolic birthplace.

In such cases Romantic cosmopolitanism clearly involved something more than experience 'in the head'. Romantics after all sought to live as they thought. Such aesthetic versions of cosmopolitanism are clearly to do with modernity, but have little or nothing to do with nationally bounded territorial sovereignties.

Of course it may be objected that this kind of orientation is not of mass significance, being the province of a privileged elite, detached from broader cultural sympathies. There are further difficulties, nonetheless, in assuming that when we look to popular culture, here at least will be found nationalism in the hearts of the people, who may thenceforth be represented as denizens of the territorial prison view of the nation.

One cannot of course deny mass nationalist sentiment, evident in struggles over national unification, and symbolic representations of the nation – *la patrie* – as bearers of values that in the language of the day undergird national character and national achievement. From national wars conducted by sovereign states in pursuit of national interests, the increasing control of border-crossing through passports, to more banal everyday symbols of nation, in flags, monumental buildings and currency, the evidence seems both widespread and compelling. And yet this is far from the case for several reasons.

The first is that region and locality rather than nation may have been the primary frame of reference for many less privileged peasants and workers. Very telling evidence of this comes from migrants from Europe obliged to declare their previous place of residence to immigration officers in the US. Much of this was regional rather than national in focus. This suggests that national sentiment was not as yet lodged in many people's hearts whether in places like France which had well-established nation-states, or like Germany and Italy, which only achieved national unification during the second half of the 19th century. Nationalist mass populations may then be products of the 20th century, and may in the contemporary epoch be, at least in part, responses to globalization, rather than products of a previous epoch of modernity.

Accordingly for mid- to late 19th-century state-builders, the challenge often remained of creating national sentiment, rather than relying on its spontaneous location in people's hearts. For Massimo d'Azeglio, first Prime Minister of the newly created Italian nation-state in 1861, the partial unification of geographical territories into the Kingdom of Italy had one major limitation. This is summed up in the slightly misquoted comment, 'We have made Italy. Now we must make Italians' (see Doyle, 2002: 39–40). This highlighted the persistence of highly significant regional affiliations separating North and South, as well as particular Northern and Southern regions from each other, economically, politically and culturally. Similarly Eugen Weber (1977), writing of late 19th-century France, commented that one prevailing issue was how the centralized French state could turn peasants with regional and local loyalties into Frenchmen.

The second objection involves the continuing salience of multi-ethnic Empire right through most of Beck's first modernity – and certainly up to the end of World War One (Calhoun, 2007). Britain and France, Austro-Hungary and the Ottomans were not single bounded nations in which economy, polity, and culture were unitary and thoroughly congruent, even though nationalist currents were a significant element in their internal politics. Each Empire contained multiple nations, ethnicities, and internal boundaries, and each was characterized by significant levels of internal mobility of people, ideas, cultural repertoires and ways of life, as well as influences from outside.

Such kinds of imperial melange are obscured, as Calhoun also points out, by the presumption that the ideal of the Westphalian system of distinct bounded nation-states approximated to reality. This is doubtful in that it exaggerates the extent to which nation-states were 'effective and discrete power-containers' (*ibid*: 14). This image marginalizes Empire, and neglects the de-stabilizing effects of attempts to create a world of nation-states by force. Empires were in any case the major players in global politics between 1648 and 1914.

Distinctions between nation and Empire were certainly available during the supposed national age, providing instances of a cosmopolitan outlook. This is made clear by British Prime Minister Disraeli in a speech at the Crystal Palace, London, in 1872 (cited in Robbins, 1999: 110–11). England, declared Disraeli, would have to 'decide between cosmopolitan and national principles... The issue is no mean one. It is whether you will be content to be a comfortable England.... Or whether you will be a great country – an Imperial country – a country where your sons, when they rise, rise to paramount positions and obtain not merely the esteem of their countrymen, but command the respect of the world'.

What significance does this have for Beck's depiction of the first modernity? Firstly, Empire amounts to cosmopolitanization in Beck's sense, because Imperial inter-connections and inter-dependencies define the conditions of existence for those within it. Empires, in the second place, are also capable of generating forms of cosmopolitan outlook that find expression outside the head, in both imperial and anti-colonial forms of cosmopolitanism. While Beck's framework remains intact they can neither be recognized as such, nor be compared and contrasted with earlier and later forms of cosmopolitanism. This in turn profoundly unsettles Beck's purported two modernities theory, by undermining its historical credibility.

Conclusion

In this chapter an alternative historical sociology of globalization is presented to that offered by Beck. This has three main features. First, it rejects his assumption that both cosmopolitanization and the cosmopolitan outlook are essentially very recent phenomena. For Beck this was pre-figured by what went before, but only philosphically, 'in the head', rather than within broader social processes and institutions. The alternative view presented here is that cosmopolitanization and the cosmopolitan outlook are evident across time and space. More specifically, the potential for cosmopolitanism is present wherever religion, Empire, trade and mobility are present, but as one rather than the only possible orientation possible under such conditions.

This does not mean that each cosmopolitan moment is exactly similar to those that precede it. But it does mean that continuity must be given more emphasis than Beck supposes in analysing the relationship between cosmopolitanism and social change. This leads on to the

second feature of our account. This disputes the theory of two modernities. The idea of a first nationally contained modernity, giving way
through some great transformation to a second cosmopolitan age, is
simply not sustained by the historical evidence. This problem is not a
secondary matter to do with a more complex appreciation of forebears
or anticipations of contemporary cosmopolitanism. It is rather a major
attempt to provide cosmopolitanism, and theories of social change
associated with it, with a more plausible historical sociology.

From the analysis presented here, it is clear that cosmopolitanism
has arisen in a range of contexts – traditional and modern – Western
and non-Western. There is therefore no necessary or strikingly new
relationship between cosmopolitanism and modernity in general, or
second 'late' modernity in principle.

A third feature of this historical approach is that the contemporary
conjuncture is not the point at which cosmopolitanism has come of age.
This proposition, reflected in the two modernities argument, derives
more from normative than analytical concerns. The argument of this
book is that cosmopolitanism is not necessarily a product of recent
modernity, and that its contemporary revival cannot be seen as the
product of some profound structural shift that ushers in a new cosmopolitan age. This proposition reads very much like rhetorical special
pleading. Cosmopolitanism has been around for a long time in a
variety of modalities and special settings.

While many contemporary concerns, such as global warming or
global inequalities, may be seen as requiring global solutions, so too did
earlier concerns for religious salvation and the transformation of
earthly arrangements to better express God's will and the vanquishing
of evil. Empires, meanwhile, tended to have the same internal problems
of how to achieve and maintain unity in the midst of cultural diversity,
as is evident in today's challenges posed by multicultural populations
created by mass migration. The analytical point here about continuities
does not disturb any kind of normative case for cosmopolitanism, only
those cases which claim that the moment for cosmopolitanism has
now come.

This chapter pursues a historical sociology of cosmopolitanism, but
has not fully dealt with some interesting questions of social theory that
have arisen here and in earlier chapters. In the next chapter, a number
of these are taken up. They include questions of social change including the relationship between cosmopolitanism and modernity, and
problems of social order arising from relationships between global
and local, universal and particular features of social life.

4

Cosmopolitanism and Social Theory

Debates over cosmopolitanism are of major significance for social theory and moral philosophy (Fine, 2007). They raise questions about the nature of human society, processes of social change, conflict and order, globalization, prevailing forms of political and cultural identity, and the evolution of law and legal institutions. An important aspect of such debates are questions about the direction in which society is moving, and indeed whether there is any clear sense of direction.

These questions about what is happening are closely connected, as we have seen, with concerns about what social relationships should be like and where society should be moving. A major normative feature of cosmopolitanism is the hope that war, racism and global injustice can be effectively countered through some kind of over-arching human solidarity grounded in sustainable institutions. This close relationship between sociological analysis and philosophical or moral concerns is not in any way unique to debates over cosmopolitanism, or indeed globalization. For many, such concerns are what makes the fruits of knowledge in the analysis of cosmopolitanism worthwhile. Social theory cannot however be reduced simply to moral and political commitments, whether these favour, oppose or are indifferent to cosmopolitanism. What it can do for social actors, as Max Weber argued, is to help us understand what we can do and clarify what it is we wish to do.

In understanding what we can do, sociology, anthropology and geography, in particular, have played an important role in claiming knowledge of the conditions under which certain ways of life, normative ideas and value orientations can prosper, and what kinds of challenges arise for those who are involved in them. In debates over cosmopolitanism, this body of scholarship provides insights into the conditions under which cosmopolitanism of various kinds is possible. This provides understandings relevant to the search for a stable and just world community, as well as insights into the possibility of open engagement between individuals and groups under conditions of cultural difference and cross-border mobility.

Many theoretical currents have fed into contemporary debates around cosmopolitanism, as noted in Chapters 1 and 2. Older traditions of Stoic and Enlightenment moral and political philosophy, based very largely on doctrines of natural law (Fine, 2007), have been joined by sociological theorists of modernity, and most recently of all by post-modern, post-structuralist, post-colonial and feminist approaches. These recent currents have broadened and enhanced earlier challenges directed at the idea that cosmopolitanism is to be regarded simply as a kind of ethical universalism grounded in common values. As Binney (2006: 1–10), points out, the 18th-century encounter of Europeans with the world beyond had already revealed weaknesses in earlier assumptions that cosmopolitan virtue takes a universal form that somehow exists on a higher moral plane than any particular cultural constellation. Cosmopolitanism, in his view, shifted at this time from what he calls representative (i.e. universalistic) to complex forms that take account of particularism. Cosmopolitanism as an explicit outlook was no longer unitary but could take a variety of forms not restricted to Christian or classical philosophical forms.

What recent scholars have done is to vastly expand and elaborate this point with Islamic as well as Christian, working class as well as elite, and imaginative and emotional as well as instrumental varieties and modalities, identified and explored. More importantly, perhaps, recent debates have gone some way towards de-throning cosmopolitan virtue from its previous ethical pinnacle, identifying how sovereign and discursive power and inequality may be built into ostensibly cosmopolitan orientations and activities (Mignolo, 2000). This critical re-appraisal of the normative status of cosmopolitanism is important, but it remains the case that the continuing use of this concept presumes some kind of common core, the most important characteristic of which is cross-cultural openness towards others.

Jeffrey Alexander (1982), in pursuing the challenges facing social theory, argued against its reduction, whether to political partisanship, to methodological preferences (e.g. positivist or hermeneutic), or to rival models of society (e.g. Marxist or functionalist). He argued rather for its importance in tackling fundamental generic problems arising from any kind of theory. This required giving attention to presuppositions made in conducting theoretical analysis, as well as to the fruitfulness of specific concepts, and to engagements between theory and empirical analysis.

In this chapter, an attempt is made to apply the spirit and substance of this general approach to social theory to questions of cosmopolitanism. This focusses on the two generic problems that Alexander identified – namely *the problem of action*, and the *problem of order*. This approach, working outward from social theory to cosmopolitanism, contrasts with Fine's (2007) valuable critical exegesis and evaluation of what he identifies as 'cosmopolitan social theory'. Nor is discussion here restricted to very general abstract theoretical questions. Rather a bridge is provided between general theory and more substantive issues about cosmopolitanism, issues which general theory may help to illuminate.

Cosmopolitanism and the Problem of Action

The problem of action, as discussed by Alexander, is one of two generic problems inherited from classical social theory and the work of Talcott Parsons (1937). The focus here is on the structure of social action, and in particular the generic elements that go to constitute action. These have conventionally been defined in terms of the relationships that pertain between the ends of action and the means used to achieve such ends. The concern here is not so much with explicit intention or social psychology, but with the logic of action whether explicit or implied. The foremost issue in debate is between two kinds of theoretical argument. The first of these is rational actor or rational choice theory, while the second involves theories that focus on norms and values.

Action in the first of these arguments is the outcome of rational choice over the best means to achieve an end or objective that is given. No attention is given to the values or norms which enter into the determination of objectives, which many rational choice theorists believe are questions beyond scientific or theoretical reach. In the second argument about action, by contrast, attention must be given to both means and ends, and to how these are connected. In this option it is both possible and desirable to ask about the normative or value-based component in action, whether these are deemed rational or not. Amongst other things, this approach considers questions as to where values and norms come from and how they affect how we act.

Alexander's general approach to the problem of action may usefully be translated into a more substantive context by considering how the two arguments rehearsed above enter into cosmopolitan action. One way of doing this is by considering the world of actors engaging with each other across cultural and political divisions, represented in Appiah's telling phrase as the challenge of 'living with strangers'. Within this existential context, it is possible to link cosmopolitanism both with certain versions of rational choice theory as much as with norm- or value-based approaches to action.

Within rational actor theory, self-interest remains the key orientation to action. This might appear to be the obverse of cosmopolitanism, in that there are no obligations to anyone other than oneself or one's country. Such a position might be termed unenlightened self-interest, in which individuals or states seek to maximize their welfare whatever the cost to others. Taken literally this encourages evasion of community responsibilities, whether to near neighbours like oneself, to strangers, and to countries other than one's own. In more practical terms this can mean indifference to the sufferings or injustices faced by others, as well as a more active and controlling relationship with others, furthered through war, colonization or unequal modes of exchange.

Such a world, unregulated by any other normative concern, would consist of short-run self-interested transactions in which no longer-term common interests emerge and within which opportunistic pursuit of individual advantage is paramount. Such an atomized and anarchic world is certainly recognizable as a feature of the world in which we currently live, and as such sets limits to moral and political forms of cosmopolitanism. Its anarchic character is also hard to link with cultures of cosmopolitanism, based on some kind of way of living that crosses political and cultural boundaries rather than being limited to self-interested individuals and states. It is nonetheless capable of institutionalization through states and the international system of states, as well as through discourses that elevate the particular interests of individuals, states, and peoples over cosmopolitan outreach and co-operation.

Realist theorists of international relations of various kinds (Morgenthau, 1992; Waltz, 1979) see states as pursuing self-interested strategies in international relations, complying with trans-national or cosmopolitan norms only insofar as they promote national self-interest. National sovereignty, from the viewpoint of rational choice theory, is a sufficient basis for action requiring no reference to broader norms. This standpoint clearly downplays norms as central features of social action. It has been challenged on two main fronts. First it downplays the growth of trans-national institutions of governance at global or regional levels alongside national ones, institutions which limit sovereignty in practice if not in theory (Held, 1995; Rosenau, 1990). Second, and more germane to the present discussion, it downplays the development of trans-national norms in areas such as human rights, which challenge the exclusive focus on nation-states and national sovereignty. There are currently many social actors, in both non-government and government organizations who are concerned with emergent global or cosmopolitan norms, and whose influence if not power has transformed the agenda of global politics.

For Berman (2004–5), the major problem with realist constructions of self-interested states is a focus on the means of implementing law, rather than with the substantive normative content of law itself. The obsessive focus on national sovereignty and whether it is being undermined by globalization bypasses a more subtle question, namely the ways in which sovereignty is becoming more diffuse 'in order to accommodate various international, transnational, or non-territorial norms' (*ibid*: 527). To assert that states simply avail themselves of norms that suit them, fails to appreciate how emerging norms influence how states conceive of their interests. Legal jurisdiction, an issue that becomes more complicated under conditions of intensified cross-border processes, is not only a question of who possesses coercive power, but equally a matter of 'norm articulation and persuasion' (*ibid*: 533). Law in this sense is not simply a matter of the coercive power of sovereigns, but 'a language for imagining alternative future worlds' (*ibid*: 534). Examples cited in support of this argument include cases where national courts were influenced by the deliberations of international courts and tribunals that held no direct power or jurisdiction over them.

Rational self-interest has also been linked with the operation of markets. The non- or anti-cosmopolitan features of some of the most open (in the sense of unregulated) markets, is seen most graphically in illegal arms, drugs and people trading sectors, which while transnational, are nonetheless founded on cynical disregard for the effects of such transactions on the welfare of other human beings. Trust is basically non-existent, while cheating, opportunism, violence and abuse are rampant, creating an unstable high-risk environment. In this way, unenlightened self-interest offers a poor sociological (as well as moral) solution to the problem of action.

Most markets, however, are not quite so anarchic or amoral as this, and might better be thought of in terms of enlightened self-interest, capable of sustaining continuing and more commercially sustainable relationships. In this somewhat different logic of social action, co-operation and loyalty capable of stabilizing social interactions are supported. From this viewpoint, a cosmopolitan stance, in which actors trust and support others, might provide a route to more sustainable ways of conducting trans-national business and other kinds of activities. The enlightened trust each other and do better thereby over time, while the unenlightened do worse by cheating. This however does not necessarily lead to an all-embracing moral cosmopolitanism, for as we have seen in previous chapters, much that is termed cosmopolitanism involves relations with those closest to us in terms of ethnicity or religion, rather than all others. Such 'closeness' is often sustained through global kinship, migrant, religious, and political networks (Holton, 2008), even where the aim is largely commercial. This incomplete cosmopolitanism may not match up to moral and ethical standards of cosmopolitan philosophy, but it might come closer to 'actually-existing' forms of social or cultural cosmopolitanism.

At the most general level, nonetheless, any kind of rational self-interest theory – enlightened or unenlightened – flounders because of the failure to provide any secure solution to the problem of action. This, as both Weber (1978) and Parsons (1937) emphasize, requires direct scrutiny of the ends of action, and not simply the strategic means for achieving such ends. Rational self-interest in this account relies on impoverished utilitarian assumptions about the mainsprings of action grounded in maximizing pleasure over pain. This is a world without moral ties and binding rules of action. Those who think this way have few intellectual resources with which to explain the orderliness of society and the logic behind action, except by appealing to the spontaneous co-ordination of self-interest, as in Adam Smith's 'invisible hand' guiding the market. Even Smith, however, appealed also to moral sentiments and the institutions of civil society as further bases for social co-ordination (2002).

Utilitarian appeals to self-interest neglect norms and values which may be followed in and of themselves, rather than being necessarily reducible to self-interest. Religious or cultural rules and sanctions may both curtail or limit self-interest, as well as pre-dating many of the more modern forms of individualism, and thus functioning as traditions from a less individualist past. More modern rules and norms may be linked with forms of co-operation, solidarity and loyalty, which incorporate individuals as moral as much as self-interested beings. Whatever mechanisms are involved, it is clear that normative influences on social action may engage even more directly with cosmopolitanism than those founded on self-interest, because they apply to collective action that involves others.

Having said this, it is equally clear that such normative influences may take both cosmopolitan and profoundly anti-cosmopolitan forms. Religious, political and cultural values and passions may be relatively open in form, as in Christian and Islamic cosmopolitanism, or be closed, as in primordial forms of ethno-nationalism or tribalism. Communitarian alternatives to cosmopolitanism also rely strongly on norms as crucial elements in action, but these are seen as grounded within the strong ties of particular cultures rather than broader cross-border form of life (see MacIntyre, 1981; Miller, 1988). In this sense cosmopolitanism is not the only logical alternative to weaknesses in rational choice arguments seeking to provide answers to the problem of action.

Cosmopolitanism as a Normative Response to the Problem of Action

Moving then to specifically cosmopolitan norms, the most influential strand of argument here is derived from the work of Immanuel Kant. For Kant, very much under the influence of ancient Roman Stoics like Seneca and Cicero, the core to cosmopolitanism lies not in political regimes so much as regulative moral ideals that arise in everyday experience (Nussbaum, 1997). Political community for Kant rests upon 'a kingdom of free rational beings equal in their humanity' (*ibid*: 12). It is through the community of reason that we share with each other that we discern the inter-dependence of our various worlds such that 'a violation' of such ideals in one place 'is felt everywhere' (Kant, 1991 [1784]). While this ideal of cross-border cosmopolitan law subsists independently of actual political institutions able to exercise such law, it nonetheless relies on them for its implementation. In his writings on *Perpetual Peace*, Kant goes on to call for political institutions, such as a League of Nations, to be constructed, such that 'a communal possession of the earth's surface' is possible.

What is interesting in Stoic and Kantian accounts of cosmopolitanism is not simply lofty ideals, but their grounding in social action, that is rational but not narrowly self-interested. Morality represents right action and this can be redeemed by rational evaluation of the extent to which cosmopolitan ideals are reached. Stoics typically reflected on social situations in which the cosmopolitan might find themselves called upon to act. These included hospitality to strangers, self-education in relation to unknown peoples and ways of life, and limits to aggression in warfare achieved through rule-bound regulation, including humane treatment of the vanquished. Such situations were however directed not only at what ethically minded individuals should do, but also to larger challenges facing peoples and states.

At this broader level of social institutions, a further distinction between substantive moral principles and norms or rules of procedure is important. Cosmopolitanism in the tradition of the Stoics and Kant, and as recently updated by Habermas (1996, 1997), typically takes the liberal view that human rights, a core cosmopolitan doctrine, do not morally prescribe a particular version of the good life. While such rights can only ultimately be grounded in morality, they become instituted within social life through regulative norms of procedure that are indifferent to particular versions of the good life. In this sense such norms rely on legal enactment rather than moral consensus. Thus as Douzinas (2007: 166) points out, human rights 'unlike morality… retain their status as actionable legal claims; their enforcement is entrusted to legal remedies and courts of law…. In the cosmopolitan order, human rights violations are…criminal actions similar to war crimes against humanity.' Following the discursive logic here, interventions to defend gross violations of human rights are not so much 'just wars' as 'police action against criminals'. This analytical distinction may nonetheless be blurred in current practice, as in NATO's intervention in Kosovo, insofar as a 'full' cosmopolitan order separating norms from moral assertion is yet to be constructed (*ibid*: 166).

The Kantian tradition offers one example of linkages between cosmopolitanism and social action. A rather different example may be derived from feminist arguments from a micro-level point of view. Rational action theories tend to ground social life in micro level interactions, which are seen as generating more macro social structure, as in the paradigmatic liberal conception of markets. Normative approaches, as developed by Parsons and Durkheim, tend to set norms within structures, into which individuals are socialized. These in turn stabilize values into patterns rather than looser more free-floating forms of activity. Most work on cosmopolitanism is macro rather than micro in character, in the sense that it has sought to identify the underlying conditions and structural settings within which cosmopolitanism has emerged. This is very evident in the historical sociology of cosmopolitanism elaborated in Chapter 2.

Discussion of the theoretical potential of a stronger micro level focus can usefully start with Jeremy Bentham's travels in Russia and Turkey in 1785 (see Binney, 2006: 8). At one point Bentham writes home to his father about an incident during a visit to a Bulgarian family in which Bentham distributed gifts to most but not all family members, omitting for example a younger sister, out of what he referred to as 'habit'. This omission, however, turned out to be offensive, and Bentham saw that he would have gained a reputation for injustice through it. He therefore came to realize that his particular 'English' habit was inadequate in this setting, and that his action should be regulated by regard to 'Bulgarian' notions of honour.

For Binney this incident is interpreted as an example of friction arising between universalistic notions of virtue, on the one hand, and 'localized conceptions of right action'. Bentham comes to see that what he had tacitly treated as universal in his own habits was particularistic in certain respects, and needed to be made accountable to other particularistic senses of right action. For Binney, this kind of encounter is crucial to social action on the cosmopolitan stage, and may lead over time to the inter-penetration of different cultural ideals. For this to happen, further qualities such as sympathy are necessary. Yet the danger remains with this model that action is somehow monologic, meaning that it is confined within the consciousness of individuals, rather than dialogic, that is co-produced within social interaction and engagement.

Some recent feminist work on cosmopolitanism provides some tangible ways of deepening a micro perspective. We have already seen in Chapter 2 the ways in which Mica Nava (2002, 2007) in particular has provided a more elaborated discussion of the modalities of cosmopolitanism, involving desire, pleasure and the imagination, as well as freedom and hope (2002: 89). This is applied to inter-personal relationships, through cross-cultural sexual and intimate attractions, including the desire of white women for men of colour. These are seen not so much in terms of a 'reflexive and intellectual stance of openness' and more in terms of 'the non-rational and affective aspect of ourselves' (*ibid*).

If we ask how a larger cosmopolitan appreciation of humankind arises, then at least one kind of answer may be sought in emotional as well as intellectual actions by individuals, directed against racial exclusion and other contemporary forms of prejudice often connected with family conventions. Nava draws on psychoanalysis in general and feminist psychoanalysis in particular, as it affects desire for others in a context of what she calls 'psychosocial dislocation and non-belonging' (*ibid*). Freud and most other thinkers working in this tradition, as she points out, say little about unconscious dynamics connected with the allure of difference. Julie Kristeva (1993), however, is one of a few who have. In a manner similar to Adam Phillips' notion of conventional behaviour that offers the 'dull security of sameness' which kills desire (2000: 340), Kristeva identifies the local or national as offering a kind of limiting security in the precarious separation from mother(land). Cosmopolitan imaginaries by contrast offer ways of living with strangers, as well as ways of recognizing the stranger within oneself.

Added to this is a sense of women's subordinate social position encouraging a transgression of conventions of cultural femininity in choice of partner and sexual preference. This may link with a sense of solidarity with subordinate racial others including Black or Asian males. For Kristeva, as Nava goes on to point out, women are seen as more likely to be 'boundary-subjects' than men (1993: 35). This may give them an ambiguous position in relation to nation and the world, which Kristeva speculates may make them more likely to be either more 'nationalist' or more 'world-oriented' than men.

There is much that might be said about this line of thinking. It offers a gendered analysis of cosmopolitanism going beyond most other constructions of the problem of action, which are gender-free. It also takes us some way towards a more micro-perspective on cosmopolitanism, though it is one in which the unconscious rather than conscious deliberation plays a significant role, and may therefore not push the search for dialogic communication far enough. It is also one that is strong on theoretical speculation and long chains of reasoning, both of which require further empirical elaboration.

If Nava offers ways of understanding cosmopolitanism in personal relationships in terms of some women's greater generosity towards the culturally repudiated, Kathryn Mitchell (2007) offers another feminist-informed line of argument, which again relates to the problem of action. This draws initially on Bruce Robbins' (1999) discussion of novels such as Ondaatje's *The English Patient* and Ishiguro's *The Remains of the Day* (see especially 164–71). Mitchell interprets Robbins' argument as an attempt to link cosmopolitanism with 'erotic love built on a mutually affirming quest for knowledge and expertise that crosses familial and national boundaries, yet is embodied and passionate' (Mitchell: 706).

This sense of cosmopolitan love is linked with two further sources of cognitive and ethical practice as the basis for cosmopolitanism as practical ethics. The first of these involves educational practice, and in particular pedagogic strategies that encourage tolerance of difference at local levels rather than top-down global initiatives. The second concerns feminist discussions of the ethic of caring as it might be applied cross-culturally. This draws on McRobbie's elaboration of an argument by Judith Butler on the impact of mourning as a process involving profound loss that encourages relational ties with others. This may find expression in various kinds of caring. McRobbie shows how this may be extended across borders in contexts of war, conflict and dislocation, which, it may be added, are highly reminiscent of the setting of *The English Patient*. The result is a feminist-inspired cosmopolitan ethics of care.

Underlying this ethics is a very different logic of action to the emphasis on liberal-democratic choice making that Mitchell argues is inherent in Beck's (and for that matter Kant's) cosmopolitan politics. In this feminist alternative we have a cosmopolitanism from below centred on value commitments institutionalized into norms of care and careful knowledge. In this respect we may say that debates over cosmopolitanism and the problem of action yield at least two types of normative solution, both of which stand in contrast to the various rational self-interest approaches.

Cosmopolitanism and the Problem of Order

The problem of order, as conceived by Alexander, is different from what many understand by debates over social order. As developed in post-war sociology, order was twinned with conflict to generate two opposing views of the social structure. Either one accepted (so-called) structural-functionalist views of society developed by Parsons that emphasized a tendency to equilibrium through social consensus. Or one was drawn to Marxist (or possibly Weberian) accounts which took social division, conflict and revolution to be the most salient social processes.

In marked contrast to this debate between order and conflict, Alexander conceives the problem of order in a different manner, which refers, as it were, to the social articulation and co-ordination of individuals and institutions. This is a 'higher-order' theoretical question than that of order versus conflict, in the sense that both positions in this debate have to tackle a common question to do with the articulation of social arrangements. In a 'conflict theory', order may be imposed by force and/or ideological manipulation, whereas in so-called 'order theories' the emphasis has often been placed more on value consensus. In either case there is a higher-level problem of order to be resolved, namely how social articulation and co-ordination is achieved.

Another way of elaborating this problem is through the language of integration. This is a much used and somewhat ambiguous term, sometimes used to connote co-ordination and sometimes stronger forms of value-based or normative integration. One significant distinction here, developed by Lockwood (1964) in his critique of Parsons' contributions to the problem of order, is between system integration and social integration. The former entails no more than institutional co-ordination and a measure of individual compliance, often consistent with conflict and social schism. The latter pertains to value consensus. For Lockwood, individual national societies might display system integration without social integration.

Updating this through world system theory, Wallerstein's (1974, 1990, 1991) work suggests both system and social integration within the capitalist world-system. Order in Alexander's sense is secured in the first place through structural imperatives toward system integration. These include global capital accumulation and a hierarchical international division of labour between metropolitan 'core' and exploited 'periphery', enforced in large measure by state power. Beyond this, social integration is achieved, according to Wallerstein, through the ideological dominance of liberalism (1990). This argument converges with those that see global consumerism as a basis for global social integration, symbolized in the phrase 'McDonaldisation of the world' (Ritzer, 1998).

Cosmopolitanism is not included as a major strand within such thinking. This applies whether we are talking of cosmopolitanism as a version of liberal dominance associated with metropolitan economic power as an argument amongst those groups which dominate, or, on the other hand, as a form of resistance to it. This absence rules out the possibility raised by Mignolo (2000), in which cosmopolitanism is distinguished from globalization through its connection with expansive forms of social emancipation, whereas globalization is seen as connected with managerial control through imperialism and colonization.

Mignolo is one of a number of writers who question the assumption that the achievement of order under conditions of globalization necessarily requires both system integration and social integration. Whether or not one accepts his contrasting definitions of globalization and cosmopolitanism, there is a distinction to be made, whatever terms are used, between structural sources of order associated with political economic processes and socio-cultural sources of order that require not simply voluntary compliance but more active forms of social solidarity and integration through values such as global peace and justice, together with legal regimes based on human rights and transparent governing principles. From this viewpoint, cosmopolitanism is potentially a source of social integration for a world in which economic forms of system integration have failed to deliver social integration. Evidence for failure would include mass protests against global corporate power and the consequences of free trade for the world's poor, ubiquitous violations of human rights and endemic warfare across political and cultural borders.

Contemporary calls for cosmopolitanism in politics and law may be seen, in Held's (1997) terms, very much as calls for cosmopolitan democracy (see also Archibugi, 1998). This idea is both an ideal and, it may be claimed, an emergent feature of global politics and law. It is reflected in the ways in which cosmopolitan values such as human rights have been institutionalized, at least in part, in global processes which limit the autonomy of nation-states. Berman (2004–5), in his systematic survey of 'international law' and globalization, notes that cosmopolitan, as distinct from international, law offers a way in which to articulate recent trends towards legal pluralism. These reflect a shift from a classical model linking law in a unitary way with territoriality, to 'a more fluid model of multiple affiliations, multiple jurisdictional assertions and multiple normative statements' (*ibid*: 537). Legal pluralism also entertains the possibility that emergent norms may stem as much from transnational or sub-national 'forms of community', may sometimes exert more influence on debates than officially sanctioned rules. Norms of cosmopolitan law are not then a model of 'international citizenship' centred on standardization and harmonization, but rather 'a recognition of multiple refracted differences where people acknowledge links with "the Other" without demanding assimilation or ostracism'.

The resurgence of Islam stands as a further symptom of the failure of liberal market-based liberalism to deliver global social integration, as well as the projection of a religion-inspired alternative. How far radical Islam is intrinsically cosmopolitan is highly debatable in terms of high levels of violent intolerance and use of terrorist violence. Nonetheless, in a religious sense the *dar al-Islam* projects the idea of a singular cross-border world integrated through devotion to God and through a strong sense of the community of believers. Religious cosmopolitanism – whether Islamic or Christian – may be reviving precisely because secular individualism and liberalism have not so far succeeded in solving the problem of order.

Table 4.1 **Cosmopolitanism and the Problem of Order**

	Order profile	*Examples*
Option 1:	System integration and social integration with cosmopolitanism	(a) Cosmopolitan democracy and law (b) Religious cosmopolitanism (c) Wallerstein's liberal world-system (d) Global consumerism
Option 2:	System integration and social integration without cosmopolitanism	Westphalian system of orderly relations between nation-states, with high levels of domestic order associated with democracy and welfare
Option 3:	System integration without social integration	Unequal system based on markets, corporations and core of strong states Integration through system power not social solidarity System power: examples (a) Cold War balance of power (b) Geo-political alliance against terror (c) Corporate capitalism with global regulatory bodies, e.g. IMF, WTO NB: Cosmopolitanism from above as managerial control and below as resistance
Option 4:	Neither system nor social integration	Global social fragmentation separating 'tribes', nations or cultures

The discussion of cosmopolitanism and order is, therefore, rather complicated. This is both because order has two analytical dimensions – the systemic and the social – which may logically combine, be at variance, and because cosmopolitanism itself has different modalities, which may or may not contribute to order. One way of making sense of this complexity and the strong feeling of indeterminacy that it generates, is suggested in Table 4.1. Here, four analytical options are presented as to possible relationships between system integration, social integration and cosmopolitanism.

These, it should be emphasized are analytical constructs or ideal-types in a Weberian sense. Given the normativity that adheres to the topic of cosmopolitanism, it is worthwhile emphasizing here that such ideal-types are not meant to be normative or ethically recommended. They may be as readily viewed as 'cosmopolitanism without emancipation' (Rorty, 1992) as with it. Similarly, they are not meant as simple mutually exclusive descriptions of reality, though they are designed to guide empirical analysis. Whether, to what degree or in what combinations they may be taken to approximate to empirical processes, remains to be established.

Option 1, the search for cosmopolitan forms of social integration, appears very often as a response to the limitations of the state-centred option 2 in preventing anarchy as envisioned in option 4. The onset of anarchic conditions is threatened where global solidarities and obligations are fundamentally undermined by chronic processes of warfare, genocide and injustice. Kant's vision of perpetual peace was written in 1784 in an epoch of European war and expanding colonial rivalry, as were the Geneva Conventions on the conduct of war dating from the early 20th century, while the United Nations Declarations on Human Rights in the late 1940s again followed war and holocaust.

Equally option 1 has also arisen as a response to more integrated circumstances, outlined in option 3, where states and markets are powerful but not able, within their own resources, to generate secure, prosperous and just global arrangements. Complications enter here because of the variety of forms that cosmopolitan option 1 may take. Option 1(a) dealing with cosmopolitan democracy and law, for example, is more concerned with problems of injustice and inequality, while option 1(b) focusses on the weaknesses of secular individualism in creating the ties of solidarity that are sometimes possible within cross-border faiths. Options 1(c) and 1(d), by contrast, generate top-down managerial and corporate cosmopolitanism that are not so much radical alternatives to option 3 as evolution within international or regional organizations that move beyond national sovereignty. Conflicts between these variants of option 1 are also clearly widespread, such as that between democratic and corporate cosmopolitanism (option 1(a) versus option 1(c)), or between religious and consumerist versions (option 1(b) versus option 1(d)). In this sense, rival cosmopolitanisms may turn out to be sources of disorder as much as order, unless such disputes can be institutionalized in cosmopolitan institutions. The extent to which this has occurred is discussed in Chapter 6.

Of all the versions of option 1, the Wallersteinian picture of a highly integrated world-system in both structural and social terms generally runs against theorists of modernity who typically emphasize the differentiation or loose- rather than tight-coupling of economy, polity and culture under contemporary conditions (Robertson, 1992; Beck, Giddens, and Lash, 1994; Habermas, 1976). Loose-coupling is not however the same thing as post-modern fragmentation, one possible version of option 4. Lyotard, for example, in diagnosing the post-modern condition, deployed some of Wittgenstein's analysis of language to claim that 'a universal history of humanity' is lacking in feasibility (Lyotard, 1985). Incommensurable and untranslatable linguistic discourses stand in the way. Following his particular interpretation of Wittgenstein, Lyotard suggests this is because 'there is no unity of language, but islets...each governed by a system of rules untranslatable into those of the others' (Lyotard, 1984: 61, also cited in Rorty, 1992: 64).

Rorty, however, takes issue both with this interpretation of Wittgenstein and its implications for cosmopolitanism. While agreeing that there is no single 'commensurating language known in advance' (*ibid*) which provides a resource into which any cultural product may be translated, this is not the same as saying that unlearnable languages exist. Wittgenstein's islets are not entirely separated behind boundaries. The problem here is not incommensurable systems of rules, but inadequately developed skills, which may over time be developed, according to Rorty, through 'curiosity, tolerance, patience, and hard work'. To insist on incommensurability, since to perceive other systems of linguistic rules, is already some way toward being able to achieve some kind of causeway between islets. And while Lyotard may be justified in rejecting any transcendent metanarrative or set of rules, upon which secure forms of translation are possible, this does not rule out provisional and multiple engagements from different viewpoints, very much in keeping with the multiple modalities of cosmopolitanism discussed in previous chapters. It follows then that the post-modern version of option 4 lacks epistemological credibility.

Such considerations assist in mapping the complex theoretical location of cosmopolitanism within diverse accounts of the problem of order, in a manner that remains analytical, but which is less general and abstract than Alexander. Translation of the problem of order in a way that engages with more concrete social processes may lead in several further directions. One of these represents the familiar socio-logical dichotomy of structure and agency, around issues of struc-tural determinism and the autonomy of social agency. Rather than re-describe debates around cosmopolitanism in these terms, this study takes a somewhat different tack, focussing on the problem of order in relation to two other questions. The first is the issue of co-ordination through organization, the second refers to the order in relation to the multiple scales of social life.

Order and Organization

The sociology of organization examines how social activities become institutionalized within regular patterns of interaction that may be called organizations. They may be formal and informal, local or global. Such organizations may be seen as contributing to resolution of the general problem of order formulated by Alexander, insofar as they co-ordinate social action, whether through coercive power or co-operation, persuasion or the satisfaction of some kind of interest, whether mater-ial or symbolic. Organizations also contain *within* them some of the problems of structure and agency that surround generic issues of social order. That is to say organizations are both individual and collective phenomena, rather than necessarily to be regarded as one or the other. Even states, which may be seen as highly authoritative collective actors, are composed of sets of actors with varying interests, capacities and resources. While organizations can from a different viewpoint be regarded simply as sets of self-interested individuals, it is just as impor-tant to avoid reifying the autonomous individual as it is the collective actor.

So what has all of this to do with globalization and cosmopolitanism and the problem of order? One way of answering this is to consider the relationship between these two processes, with their multiple modal-ities and organizational form. What in particular can be learnt about the contribution of cosmopolitanism to social order from consideration of variations in organizational form?

The most promising way of pursuing this question is through debates stimulated by organization theorists on markets, hierarchies and net-works (Powell, 1990; Thompson, 2003). The basic argument here is that each of these represents a different way of organizing social trans-actions. Markets are flexible and efficient ways of co-ordinating action across multiple sites, but their vulnerability to short-run self-interested behaviour creates problems for the construction of trust and enduring institutions. By themselves they lack trust and social solidarity. Hierarchies whether private or public create longer-term more formal institutions able to surmount individual self-interest and opportunism, and encourage learning and the accumulation of human capital assets. They may nonetheless become over-bureaucratic and inflexible. Networks, meanwhile, may combine the flexibility of markets with the enduring qualities of hierarchies, maximizing trust over self-interest, and be able to deploy knowledge more quickly. This may give networks a significant role in generating social order, especially when harnessed to new information and communications technologies. Thus for Castells (1996), networks represent the dominant future organizational form in an epoch of globalization, where network businesses interact with network states.

There is by now sufficient evidence to adjudicate this claim and to clarify the relationships between global networks and cosmopolitanism (for a systematic review see Holton, 2008). To take the Castells thesis first, there is no compelling reason to believe that networks are now taking over. They are important cross-border processes in many spheres from governance policy advocacy and terrorism, to business, migration, knowledge and the arts. But they have not replaced markets and hierarchies, so much as augment or assist in their more effective functioning in some way. Inter-personal business networks help create trust by restraining self-interested opportunism in market transactions, while within and between hierarchies, interpersonal networks are also important ways of surmounting rigidity and improving learning and information flow. Networks contribute to order in Alexander's sense by creating improved macro-micro links between sets of individuals and sets of institutions. Yet this in no way privileges consensus over conflict, insofar as both advocacy and terrorist networks deploy conflict in rather different ways to achieve their aims.

Cosmopolitanism, as we have seen in previous chapters, is often seen as an elite or top-down phenomenon. This accords with Castells' (1996) argument about the advantages of the mobile socio-spatial forms of network capitalism, compared with prior nation- and place-based enterprises. 'The space of flows' as depicted by Castells is thereby very similar to Calhoun's notion of cosmopolitanism as the 'class consciousness of frequent flyers', detached from social bonds and hence indifferent to social inequality. For Castells, the contrasting socio-spatial constellation is the 'space of place' a more immobile world inhabited by the dis-privileged. To the extent that the cosmopolitan space of flows is pre-dominant over the space of place, and thus unchallenged, we would clearly be in the presence of something like option 1(c) rather than 1(a).

There are nonetheless problems with any theory which limits cosmopolitanism and global networks in this way. One key problem is that many different social groups, not simply dominant elites, inhabit the space of flows, whether physically, including migrants, activists and protesters, or symbolically as consumers, religious groups and utopians. Each, as we have seen in Chapters 2 and 3, may be seen as a form of cosmopolitanism. Many though not all such examples do involve challenges to current forms of system integration, whether seen as founded on markets, capitalism, strong states, power, secularism, or individualism. Such challenges may come from below, whether from the space of flows or the space of place, but also from above, since many elite members are not themselves content merely with system integration without social integration. Options 1(c), 1(d), and 3 are therefore under severe pressure and relentless challenge from below whether directed at market failures, recourse to war, or lack of global democracy and justice. Pressure from below is however ambivalent with respect to the various options canvassed being compatible with localist communitarian versions of nation-centred option 2, as with radical activist supporters of option 1 (a). Further empirical analysis is therefore required as to the organizational dynamics of such complex processes in relation to markets, hierarchies and networks.

In an immediate sense we may say that under a broad definition, cosmopolitanism may be a characteristic of markets, hierarchies, and networks. While exclusively ethical or legal versions of cosmopolitanism may have looked to public hierarchies, i.e. international institutions, to create cosmopolitan democracy and law, this attribution is now insufficient where other modalities of cosmopolitanism deal with 'open' ways of life, cross-border competencies and solidarities. In this broader sense, cosmopolitanism may be located within markets and networks as well.

Markets, in almost every case except for one-off short-run transactions, are embedded in various kinds of social arrangements. These may include legal or customary forms of regulation, but they may also involve networks of traders searching for information or aiming to create trust as a basis for continuing trading relationships. Trust is especially important where trading conditions are uncertain. This may be for reasons of market volatility, but uncertainty may equally arise where trade is conducted across borders, within multiple jurisdictions, and by traders from differing cultural backgrounds speaking different languages. Global business networks have formed both to gain more reliable information, reduce uncertainty, and better co-ordinate complex transactions. Where they are primarily inter-personal, they are often based on shared cultural backgrounds whether ethnic or religious, as seen in Jewish or Chinese trading diaspora. But they may equally be based on more expansive inter-cultural relations within trading cities, whether land-based or maritime. All this has a long history rather than being a mere prelude to Castells' contemporary network society.

To qualify as cosmopolitan, such inter-personal milieux need to exhibit some sense of inter-cultural openness. This raises questions about the sense in which those kinds of trading diaspora that have an exclusively inward-looking orientation, such as the Senegalese Murid traders (Diouf, 1999) discussed in Chapter 3, qualify as cosmopolitan. Diasporas may include 'locals' as well as 'cosmopolitans'. Even where 'locals' have trans-national or trans-local connections, as the Murid have in New York, Paris and Hong Kong, they may remain embedded within a set of enclaves for all purposes apart from trade. It is arguable that even within trading cities, cosmopolitanism depends on interconnection and engagement of some kind with other groups, rather than the simple co-presence of different cultural groups linked only by thin ties of commerce.

The theoretical point here is that markets may, through the operation of networks, exhibit cosmopolitan features, and where such features exist, they draw attention to the capillary-like micro-structures of cosmopolitanism operating within civil society. This contrasts with the more formal institutional focus of cosmopolitan articulation of politics and law.

Micro-macro-micro interactions between networks and hierarchies are of course significant, warning us against treating these modalities as separate mutually exclusive entities. There are plenty of global networks other than those linked with markets which may display cosmopolitan features. This is, for example, an explicit focus of many global advocacy networks (Keck and Sikkink, 1998; Holton, 2008) which aim precisely to enhance human rights and which promote cosmopolitan law above the national sovereignty of states. The shift here is from nationally focussed citizenship rights to human rights which somehow stand above the self-interest of states (Turner, 1993). For many, the successful institutionalization of option 1(a) as the only socially just and sustainable form of global order depends upon the success in creating cosmopolitan norms of this kind, norms that national institutions will either implement and comply with, or at least take into account in a more diffuse way in political and legal processes. Macro-change, in such cases, depends in large measure on an accumulation of micro-level pressure to create macro-level change, as well as subsequent micro-level action to monitor successful implementation.

Other global networks which may have a cosmopolitan connection include those connected with religious movements. Like trading diaspora, these may be inward-looking and, in the case of some religious networks, intolerant as well. Intolerance may also be projected outwards in a fundamentalist manner that excludes dialogue. However religious networks have also been important in more open outward-looking cross-border activities whether within different branches of the same faith or between them.

This discussion of networks and cosmopolitanism emphasizes the significance of organizational form for various modalities of cosmopolitanism. This in turn contributes to an understanding of the problem of order in relation to micro-macro interactions under conditions of globalization. Within this discussion, diffuse references have already been made to questions of scale when referring to global, trans-national or international as well as national and local social entities. The relationships between such 'levels' or 'scales' of activity are now tackled more explicitly.

Order and Scalar Complexity

A crucial issue in the understanding of social order as co-ordination under conditions of globalization (and what Beck calls cosmopolitanization) is scalar complexity. This complexity arises from the simultaneous co-presence *and* inter-penetration of global, regional, national and local scales of activity. These include the global or trans-national, the international, the national, and the local. Regional scales may also matter too, whether conceived in supra-national fashion (e.g. Western Europe, the Middle East) or in a sub-national sense (e.g. Brittany, Anatolia). They implicate structural processes, institutional evolution and social action.

Many of debates around globalization are debates about problems arising from this multiplicity of scales. Questions include:

- whether globalization is undermining national, regional and local institutions and activities, leading to their demise or radical weakening, and the creation of new neo-liberal solutions to problems of order
- whether globalization is necessarily in conflict with nations, regions, and localities or whether harmonious or mutually supportive relationships are possible through interactions between scales

- whether the distinction between scales is blurring rather than sharpening through the interaction and interpenetration of scales, creating glocal fusions of the global and local
- whether political identities and institutions can take an effective global form, or whether particular bounded nations, regions and localities remain more suited to the expression of identities and the functioning of democracy.

Such questions implicate individuals and social groups, as well as institutions. They are also paralleled in debates over cosmopolitanism and the way it should best be studied. Questions here include:

- whether there is a trend towards cosmopolitanism which is undermining national, regional, and local identities and institutions
- whether cosmopolitanism is necessarily in conflict with nations, regions and localities, or whether harmonious or mutually supportive interconnections are possible between the two
- whether cosmopolitanism is a feasible and thus desirable basis for identity and institution-building
- whether methodological cosmopolitanism provides a more adequate way of studying cross-border relationships than older forms of methodology based on bounded nation-states.

There is no consensus among scholars on any of these questions. Clear answers are not immediately to hand. This is largely because they require further theoretical elaboration, conceptual refinement, and sustained empirical enquiry. It is also because the urgency of normative challenges on how to create a more just, secure and sustainable global order sometimes conflict with caution arising from the complex analytical issues involved.

The particular line of argument developed in this book nonetheless offers some preliminary judgements if not definite answers around the following propositions. The first and most important of these is that *global processes take place through multiple intersecting and interpenetrating scales of activity*. To this may be added a second proposition, namely that *relationships between scales of activity may conflict, but may equally be mutually sustaining* (Robertson, 1992, 1995). Accordingly the trans-national and inter-national, the global and the national, the cosmopolitan and the local are not necessarily in conflict. And even where conflict is present, or where global-local relations are not understood as complementary by social actors, most attempts at creating order aim to find ways of articulating global and local institutions, activities and ways of life, rather than opting fundamentally for one rather than the other.

Such propositions may be sustained in a number of ways. First, the point may be made that it is very hard to find complete and absolute localism or complete and absolute globalism. Autarky based on social isolation of peoples or states is scarcely feasible except as a utopia, while context-less one-worldism (the kind of caricature that sees cosmo-politanism as devoid of any particular reference point) is unfeasible and very hard if not impossible to locate empirically. Second and more important is the key point that the global and national, cosmopolitan and local, while often experienced and understood as in conflict, both draw on each other and are, as Robertson points out, mutually self-constituting. Examples include multi-level governance in politics which links different scales of governing institutions; corporate business stra-tegies that seek to combine global outreach with local knowledge; cultural fusions of the global and local, such as world music, as well as cosmopolitan patriotism that applies trans-contextual ethical commit-ments to particular settings.

When assessed against the problem of order, each of these examples can be used to demonstrate challenges associated with attempts to secure order within a single scale alone. Multi-level governance, for example, arises from difficulties faced by nation-states in responding simultane-ously to challenges of global economic competition, technology transfer, social inequality and social cohesion. Under conditions of intensified global inter-connectedness it is no longer feasible, if it ever was, for indi-vidual nation-states to resolve all these challenges alone. Inflows of cap-ital, labour, new technology and ideas create opportunities for economic development, but raise new problems of social inequality and cohesion, alongside those inherited from the past. Multi-level governance in set-tings like the EU pools markets and resources to facilitate enhanced global competitiveness while addressing regional inequalities. Even so, democratic politics and social identity is in many though not all respects still linked with particular nations.

To say all this is not meant to suggest that multi-level governance in the EU has succeeded in resolving all these challenges in an effective manner through functional specialization of tasks at different levels of scalar complexity. To imply this would be to revive a structural-functionalist model in which order is taken to be the typical outcome of social differentiation. This rules out the possibility that social differ-entiation across different scales may defy effective co-ordination. How to generate social cohesion in a globalizing world of rapid economic change, market instabilities, mass migration and virtually instant-aneous globalized communications, for example, remains unclear. Yet taking all this into account, the example of multi-level governance remains significant as an example of the attempted inter-penetration of scales of governance.

Another very important example is provided by various attempts to fuse cosmopolitanism with liberal-democratic as distinct from ethno-cultural types of nationalism. Whether conceived as 'cosmopolitan patriots' (Appiah, 1996), exemplars of national cosmopolitanism, as Beck (2006: 11) describes the writer Thomas Mann, or 'nationalist cosmopolitans' (Malachuk, 2007), such fusions speak to the relativ-ization and inter-penetration of political cultural traditions associated with nations and wider trans-national orientations. Cosmopolitanism and nationalism are not in others words always and invariably contra-dictions. While some ethno-national traditions may be introverted or xenophobic, others may contain commitments to values such as liberty, freedom, community or good government which are translat-able beyond the immediate context in which they originated.

Both the French republican traditions and European Marxism, to take two examples, contained within them elements that could at least be imagined in operation in other contexts. These elements have sometimes been referred to as inter-nationalism in a very general and diffuse sense, rather than as a strict alternative to cosmopolitan trans-nationalism. Such translations are significant even if they proved inadequate to the development of internationalism or cosmopolitanism in other contexts. As Appiah points out, it is not simply from the West that proto-cosmopolitan ideas such as equality, concern for others or good gov-ernment arise. They are imaginable in other non-European contexts too, such as his own West African background. And as such they may themselves be circulated elsewhere as part of a global repertoire of cosmopolitan ideas with multiple origins.

The inter-penetration of scales of activity, addressed in these two examples, is a familiar argument in recent sociology (Robertson, 1992, 1995; Holton, 2005; Beck, 2006), though not necessarily one that has made much impact on wider public debates or policy discourses. This may in part be due to the terminological contortions that have arisen in attempts to come to terms with scalar complexity and inter-penetration. In Robertson's case, this involved the idea of glocalization (1992, 1995), applicable within economy, polity (see also Brenner, 1998) and culture. In Beck's case, by contrast, the discussion is framed in terms of the concept of 'methodological cosmopolitanism' as distinct from method-ological nationalism. In the concluding section of this chapter we ask the question as to whether social theorists should, as Beck suggests, take up methodological cosmopolitanism, or whether Robertson's notion of glocalization is a more plausible or productive option.

Methodological Cosmopolitanism or Glocalization?

Methodological cosmopolitanism is, for Beck, the required social science perspective to make sense of contemporary globalization. It is contrasted with the methodological nationalism that is seen as dominating social science since the 19th century (for a useful commentary see Wimmer and Glick Schiller, 2003). Whereas methodological nationalism centres on analysis of nation-states as the dominant social reality, methodological cosmopolitanism centres on the global arrangements which now predominate. This argument is clearly linked with Beck's two stage theory of modernity. Whereas methodological nationalism is appropriate to the first modernity, methodological cosmopolitanism is seen as more appropriate to the second.

The general argument in favour of a global or world-level focus is a familiar one, based on the realization that nations are profoundly influenced by processes that lie outside their borders, including transnational processes rather than simply the activities of other nation-states. A version of the argument was powerfully advanced in the 1970s by Wallerstein (1976), who wished to replace nation-focussed analysis with a world-system perspective. So what is distinctive about Beck's version?

Three immediate features stand out. One is rejection of hyper-globalist theories which assumed the imminent death of the 'nation-state'. Like many earlier theorists, including Robertson (1992), Hirst and Thompson (1996) and Holton (1998), Beck argues that the nation-state and national scales of activity remain significant. The point is not that nation-states or nationalism are disappearing in any general sense (clearly individual states may collapse for a variety of reasons), but rather that they no longer monopolize the core institutions of social life capable of engaging with the problem of order. The challenge is henceforth to recognize the 'national' as one of a number of scales of activity. The cosmopolitan outlook does this because it '...retains a reference to the nation-state but situates and analyses it within a radically different horizon' (Beck, 2006: 33).

A second feature of Beck's approach is the theory of the two modernities. This as we have seen is historically dubious. The contrast made between the two is grossly exaggerated and misleading. Since globalization and cosmopolitanism have longer histories that cannot be merely acknowledged in passing (Beck, 2006: 68), the case for methodological cosmopolitanism might better be re-formulated as a long-term one. To accept this Beck would have to rethink his theory of modernity, either projecting it back in time as many writers from Wallerstein (1974) to Frank and Gills (1993) have done, or accept that globalization and cosmopolitanism have, as it were, traditional or archaic variants, as Hopkins (2002), and his collaborators have done in the case of global history. In this sense cosmopolitanism challenges prevailing theories of social change which somehow foreshorten complex long-run historical processes in the rush to delineate broad abstract schema that require little historical work.

The third and more interesting element in Beck's argument is the choice of terminology. If the question is asked 'why methodological *cosmopolitanism*?' rather than *globalism*, or *glocalism*, the answers get to the core of Beck's distinctive approach.

Beck prefers cosmopolitanism as a quality of his methodology because globalism is somewhat discredited as a term. It is often vague. But it has also developed connotations of top-down managerial control of the global system. Beck prefers a term like cosmopolitanism because it can simultaneously refer to global phenomena while carrying a stronger (and for Beck positive) normative connotation than globalism. To think in terms of methodological cosmopolitanism is thus to have both an analytical and normative anchorage in contemporary processes and change and debates about the good society.

This brings us to issues to do with the philosophy of history. Beck is clearly not starry-eyed or unduly romantic about cosmopolitanism, which he acknowledges may be banal or despotic as much as emancipatory. Cosmopolitanism may potentially offer imagined futures that differ from current arrangements, but cosmopolitan politics needs realism as much as ideals to be effective. Nonetheless, for all these reservations there remains a strong sense of a cosmopolitan philosophy of history echoing themes in Kant and especially Hegel and Marx.

Philosophies of history typically draw strong links between what is and what ought to be. They also invoke the idea of struggles of humanity to in some sense become freer, more just, or closer to God. Beck deploys Hegel's concept of reflexivity, that is an emancipatory sense of greater self-consciousness as the direction in which history is moving (for the following account of Hegel, see Hart, 2006). This arises in Hegel through the disjuncture between feelings of human autonomy that seem frustrated by human institutions. Through the dialectical conflict between the two, Hegel sees the emergence of a world of Spirit or consciousness that restores the unity between autonomy (subject) and the external world (object) through a higher reflexive understanding.

In Beck's case this reflexivity is grounded in more concrete social processes.

Within Beck's philosophy of history the movement from cosmopolitanization to a cosmopolitan outlook draws on Marx's philosophy of history. Here objective circumstances generate subjective possibilities that create a third set of processes grounded in the emancipation of social actors from exploitation, leading to new creative possibilities. Class struggle becomes the vehicle for social change and historical progress. The story begins with class-in-itself, or objective social conditions, which generate class-for-itself, embodying new forms of social consciousness, and a dynamic leading to radical change in institutions and human possibility. Very much on this model, Beck refers to cosmopolitanism-in-itself (or cosmopolitanization), and contemporary challenges in how this may generate cosmopolitanism-for-itself (Beck, 2006: 95–6). He also, like Hegel before him, sees Europe very much as the key site of historical advance, though in Beck's case it is the European Union rather than the Prussian state and Germanic Christendom.

Beck is nonetheless less optimistic than Marx and Hegel, and thus his parallel philosophy of history is not projected with all that much confidence. This is in part because of the difficulty in establishing who will be the equivalent agents of change to Marx's proletariat. The most clear-cut agents are the global political advocacy movements discussed above. And this involves a loose parallel with Castells, for whom it is the global environmental movement that he sees as able to transcend ties of particularity while maintaining links with place and community.

Philosophies of history typically assume what analysts try to prove or test through theoretical clarification and empirical analysis. For Beck, such philosophies are not enough. Tensions between philosophical and sociological elements, as he points out, are very strong in discourses on cosmopolitanism. An alternative approach to that of methodological cosmopolitanism linked with Roland Robertson – namely glocalization – is possibly more fruitful, in part because it is relatively free of philosophies of history.

Robertson's influential earlier response to the problem of scalar complexity under conditions of globalization (1992) is to think in terms of the inter-penetration of the universal and particular, and the global and national or local, rather than their separation and necessary mutual antipathy. The terms 'glocal', and 'glocalization' stand here as hybrids of the *glo*(bal and the lo)*cal*. Robertson sees globalization not as a system, but pursues questions of order and articulation in terms of the idea of a global 'field'. This contains individuals and nation-states, the *dramatis personae* of Beck's first modernity, but also conceptions of the world as a single space and sets of international and trans-national institutions. These interact in complex ways, but one immediately striking difference with Beck is the greater emphasis given to conceptions of the world as a single space drawing on religious as well as secular sources of imagination. The world religions, as we have argued above, represent many of the leading cosmopolitan imaginaries, but they fail to feature as such in Beck's foreshortened historical discussion of modernity and cosmopolitanism.

Robertson's idea of the glocal contains with it a way of demonstrating linkages between the global and the local at any point in time and space. It is not thereby restricted to modernity or to Europe. It is grounded, unlike Beck's cosmopolitanism, in an ontological pre-supposition rather than in a philosophy of history. This pre-supposition concerns the human condition seen in social context. Robertson's social ontology features the mutual dependence or sense of our particularity and that of those around us, with more general and in some sense universal reference points. To be able to compare particulars requires some sense of commonality as well as difference. This does not require a single privileged and lofty universalistic viewpoint as in a number of cosmopolitanisms from above, whether Western or non-Western. Rather there are many ways of constructing universal-particular or global-local relationships, as Robertson's sociological work points up. His use of the term glocal, for example, draws from Japanese business discourses that spoke of a selective fusion of elements both from Japan and beyond, an insight he also developed in relation to the syncretic sources of Japanese religion.

Beck acknowledges Robertson's contribution in making 'outlook' an important indicator of cosmopolitanism, but avoids any real engagement with the concept of glocalization. This term has advantages, nonetheless, not simply for the substantive understanding of global-local fusions, but also as a methodological standpoint. Like methodological cosmopolitanism it provides a way of surmounting the limitations of methodological nationalism, without dispensing with nation-states and nationalism altogether. Unlike methodological cosmopolitanism, however, it is detached from positive normative concerns linked to any particular philosophy of history. As such it is both more sociological and more able to resolve some of the tensions between sociological and philosophical issues discussed by Beck. Its social ontology is also relatively bare of substance and hence capable of including a variety of substantive ways of linking the global and local, not simply those connected with Europe.

Conclusion

The methodological considerations on which this chapter ends are not simply methodological in the sense that they prescribe modes of empirical analysis. They include this vital work, but they also refer back to large issues in social theory to do with the problems of social action and social order. In this sense they are a bridge between the two parts of this study, the first dealing more with theoretical and conceptual issues, and the second which will look more closely at evidence. There is always a danger that sociology divides into theorists and empirical researchers, each specializing in one dimension with little regard to the other. This book is founded on the opposite presumption, namely that each needs the other. In this study, theory and evidence are really co-present throughout. Theorists should not therefore stop reading here, while those empirical researchers who may have flicked through the first part anxious to get to the data might do well to go back to the beginning and start again.

Part II
Empirical Research Issues

5

Cosmopolitanism: Social and Cultural Research

In Part II of this study the focus shifts to a systematic review of evidence about cosmopolitanism. This addresses a number of important issues. How significant is cosmopolitanism, for example, for an understanding of contemporary identities, ways of life and institutional processes? This question requires that attention be given to the scope of and limits to cosmopolitanism. Is cosmopolitanism expanding or contracting in importance, and how even are such trends across the range of modalities of cosmopolitanism identified in previous chapters? Establishing patterns of this kind also requires attention to the orientations and activities with which cosmopolitanism may be contrasted or with which it is in competition. How far is the world becoming more cosmopolitan, tolerant and hospitable to social and cultural difference, and how far, by contrast, is the picture one of inward-looking nationalism and a new intolerant tribalism?

As it turns out, the answers that can be given to such questions are complex ones. This is partly because the evidence is not clear-cut, but more fundamentally because cosmopolitanism is not easy or straightforward to define for purposes of empirical analysis. The reasons for this, some of which have been identified in Part I, deserve considerable attention if the sifting of evidence is to produce meaningful results.

Problems in Interpreting Evidence of Cosmopolitanism

The underlying objective of this study is to provide a sociological rather than exclusively philosophical analysis of cosmopolitanism in both past and present. This sociological focus is designed to incorporate philosophical modalities of cosmopolitanism alongside more everyday modalities. In this sense, empirical analysis of cosmopolitanism does not depend on the presence or incidence of philosophically elaborated forms of cosmopolitanism, though their continuing importance for intellectuals such as Nussbaum (1997), Appiah (2006) and Rorty (1992) is significant. What is even more significant, as Appiah points out very powerfully, is the wider presence of cosmopolitanism in a range of social, cultural and political settings, whether or not the term cosmopolitan is used by those involved.

Even so, some clear sense is needed of what *both* formal and explicit *and* less formalized and implicit expressions of cosmopolitanism hold in common. Some of the problems in producing an operational or working definition of cosmopolitanism stem from ambiguities in conventional definitions. As discussed in Chapter 1, cosmopolitanism is usually defined in terms of openness to others, in many modalities from thought and identity to action, whether conducted by individuals, groups, communities, philosophers or travellers, political and legal institutions. This may involve ethical commitments to others, but it may equally be free of ethical intentions or qualities, and be more a matter of curiosity, personalized consumption or sociability. Yet openness in and of itself is rather too vague for purposes of working definition.

How open, for example, does a cosmopolitan have to be? Open to all others in all their rich diversity or only some? And if openness is qualified, are we not shifting back into non-cosmopolitan closure? It is not easy to give a clear answer here. If cosmopolitanism was restricted to complete cultural relativism, tolerant and accepting of all kinds of others, the violent and immoral as well as peaceable or ethically responsible, then the term would cease to have much practical purchase, largely because there are few if any souls around who practise this kind of openness. A working definition is then based on relative openness. This may be procedural rather than substantive in the sense that cosmopolitanism entails support for rules, laws or institutions that are inclusive of all the world's peoples and citizens. Openness may be limited by law and cultural preference, but still involve meaningful cross-border engagement. This in more concrete terms involves notions such as *tolerance* of what one may not personally like or support, or *hospitality* to others, the latter point being a major theme in Kant's discussion of cosmopolitanism.

Openness and closure are thus extreme positions on a spectrum that includes many intermediary positions. Since cosmopolitanism may well involve qualified openness, there is considerable scope for empirical research to illuminate the complexities of partly open and partly closed relations.

Working definitions of cosmopolitanism pre-suppose the possibility of delineating what cosmopolitanism is and what it is not. The existence of a spectrum of positions on the dimension of openness and closure makes the formulation of a definition more complicated. This can be illustrated in relation to the relationship between cosmopolitanism and nationalism, including cosmopolitan and national institutions.

The question here is whether the 'cosmopolitan' and the 'national' are mutually exclusive. There is no agreement among scholars on this question. This is evident in the volume *For Love of Country* (Nussbaum and Cohen, 1996), produced to broaden debates around Nussbaum's positive philosophical evaluation of cosmopolitanism. While some contributors presumed that if one is a patriot, one is therefore not a cosmopolitan (Himmelfarb, 1996; Glazer, 1996), others found ways of combining them (Appiah, 1996; Falk, 1996). In a more institutional context, many national politicians and citizens reject political or legal interventions from international bodies, such as the United Nations, because they are taken to undermine national sovereignty and be harbingers of world government or federalism. National sovereignty in this view is indivisible by supra-national commitments. If such mutually exclusive options settled the matter, empirical investigation of the scope and limits of cosmopolitanism would be far easier than it is.

The reason that mutually exclusive definitional options don't work is precisely because individuals can and do combine cosmopolitanism and patriotism or nationalism, as explored in empirical depth by historians like Kleingeld (1999), and because nation-states in practice pool or cede sovereignty to supra-national institutions, such as the European Union, for certain purposes. While nation-states (or at least their leaders) have to agree to this, once they have, complete national sovereignty becomes very much an ideal, rather than a practical reality. It is a reality that can in theory be reversed, though this becomes harder as supra-national institutions create on-going institutional arrangements that are hard to unravel.

Such examples support the argument that the cosmopolitan and national are opposite ends of a spectrum, not mutually exclusive options. Elements can be combined from either end. The positions of individuals, groups or institutions upon the spectrum are also dynamic and subject to change over time. There is no underlying compelling philosophy of history which guarantees a long-term shift to cosmopolitanism, nor any clear reason why nation-states and nationalism are the default setting for social organization and cultural identity. Such considerations accord well both with

Robertson's concept of glocalization and Beck's methodological cosmopolitanism.

Openness is a crucial defining feature of cosmopolitanism, but one where a number of ambiguities need resolution before it can be built into a working definition. Attention now turns to a second element of such a definition, which involves the extent of the stage upon which openness is exercised.

Openness may be practised on a micro-scale within a school yard or village, and it was in rather closed settings of this kind that Merton (1968) deployed a distinction between 'cosmopolitans' and 'locals' to distinguish those whose relations were conducted according to what they knew, and those drawing on who they knew. This metaphorical extension of the cosmopolitan/local distinction is not typical of more conventional usages. These have included a further additional sense of the *breadth of the stage* upon which relationships and institutions operate. This breadth requires that cosmopolitanism involve a sense of bridge-building across cultural or political difference. This can be direct in terms of face-to-face relations with other people depicted metaphorically by Appiah in terms of 'living with strangers', it may be mediated through communications technology, such as television, the press or the internet, which bring us into contact, directly or more indirectly with others, and/or it can be expressed more symbolically through the imagination in utopian or visionary imaginaries.

But how broad does the stage have to be to qualify here? The pragmatic answer here involves a strong sense of the trans-national at work, bringing physical, cultural or more virtual strangers in contact with each other, albeit in a range of settings which include nations. Focus on the trans-national means movement, whether of people, ideas, cultural practices, media representations or political and legal inter-connection. Trans-national movement does not however mean that cosmopolitanism is restricted to people who are physically on the move as managers, diplomats, migrants or tourists – important though they are. One can sit still, but nonetheless engage with the world in a cosmopolitan manner, often, as we shall see, through powerful communications media. Nor do all who move do so in a cosmopolitan spirit, since it is possible to move with a closed mind, keeping very much to one's own people or sense of national interest. This means, firstly that the physical or symbolic sites of cosmopolitanism may be within particular nations or localities as much as on the road, and secondly that mere movement across boundaries is not sufficient for cosmopolitanism to be present.

In unravelling these complex issues, a working definition of cosmopolitanism may be built around the following propositions:

1. Cosmopolitanism involves inter-cultural openness on a transnational stage. This may be face-to-face, or mediated through communications technologies and discourses.
2. Openness may be combined in practice with elements of cultural or institutional closure, but the more closed the less cosmopolitan.
3. Not all trans-national activities qualify as cosmopolitan, since some may be conducted in a closed manner.
4. Trans-national openness does not require personal cross-border movement, but it does entail some kind of mobility whether of the imagination, or through activities (including political advocacy, consumption, the arts or religion) that engage with the wider world.

A final category of problems concerns limitations in existing evidence. There is a wide body of relevant evidence, both quantitative and qualitative, though as in other areas of sociological research, those working on the two kinds of evidence do not talk with each other as much as they should. Quantitative evidence exists both on patterns of movement of migrants, tourists, and commodities across boundaries, as well on individual attitudes and identities, including national and cosmopolitan identities. Most of this has been collected through national surveys allowing comparisons of attitudes across different nations. Qualitative evidence, mainly in the form of institutional and cultural case-studies, is probably even more widespread, much of it spread across disciplines of anthropology, history, geography, political science and law, as well as more applied fields of consumption, travel and networks.

Much research, as indicated in previous chapters, was designed more to open up the field, taking it beyond philosophy and into the social sciences and humanities. This opening up exercise introduced a wide range of modalities and cases of cosmopolitanism, but at the price of loose definition and theoretical indeterminacy. Some research has nonetheless been designed in such a way as to test theoretical issues around cosmopolitanism.

A good qualitative example is provided by Nowicka's (2006) in-depth study of mobile professional workers employed by international organizations. Working for long periods away from home countries, this group is seen as an important test-case for assessing whether hypothesized connections between cross-border mobility and mobile cosmopolitan ways of living are evident. A good quantitative example is provided in Norris (2000, 2006) and Phillips (2002), who use World Values survey data to explore nationalist and cosmopolitan attitudes . These data were collected in such a way as to allow respondents to mention more than one dimension from a list of global, regional, national and locally focussed attitudes. This permitted Norris and Phillips to pursue a research design in which complex combinations of attitudes, e.g. national + local or global + local, can be established and attitude scales created, thereby broadening an appreciation of global-local interactions and relationships, as well as oppositions and conflicts. Well designed research similar to the types indicated here is not widespread.

As things currently stand then, there are at least two problematic features of the literature. The first methodological problem is the proliferation of largely unconnected studies that are not generally designed in a way that gets directly to questions of the scope and limitations of cosmopolitanism. A second, more substantive problem is what might be termed a lack of micro-level interactional work relevant to cosmopolitanism, whether within conversations, community and neighbourhood life including interactive media, relations between professionals and clients, or within institutions. There is comparatively little work of this kind. Elijah Anderson and his colleagues' (2004) urban anthropological fieldwork observation in Philadelphia are one notable exception, as are some of the empirically-informed network analyses published in the journal *Global Networks* (see for example Ferguson (2003); Batnitzky *et al.*, 2008).

Within the definitional parameters and problems outlined here, this study now turns to the question of an elaborated empirical research agenda for cosmopolitanism.

The Empirical Research Agenda

Until recently no systematic identification of an empirical research agenda around the topic of cosmopolitanism had been attempted. With the shift of focus away from philosophy one might have expected social science to pick this up. The revival of interest in cosmopolitanism during the 1990s, however, emerged in large measure from cultural studies and anthropology, many of whose practitioners were more interested in pluralizing conceptions of cosmopolitanism and deflating what they saw as the pretensions of Western universalism with which it was previously associated. Conceptual advances and some important qualitative case-study research ensued (Werbner, 1999; Pollock, 2000). But it was not until the early part of the following

Table 5.1   Beck's Research Agenda for Cosmopolitanism

1. Consumption of global cultural commodities
2. Dual citizenship
3. Political representation for cultural minorities
4. Language diversity
5. Cross-border mobility
6. Global communication patterns
7. International travel
8. Transnational initiatives and organizations
9. Criminal activity
10. Transnational ways of life
11. Transnational news coverage
12. National identities and their relationship to cosmopolitanism
13. Ecological crisis responses

Source: adapted closely from Beck (2002a): 79–80.

decade that Beck proposed a more systematic empirically focussed agenda.

As outlined in Table 5.1, Beck (2002a: 79–80), has listed 13 sub-areas that require detailed research. These cover a wide range of topics, some of which, like cross-border mobility and international travel, are familiar indicators, others, like criminal activity, are not. This is, as Beck points out, very much a provisional list, with items not ranked, and including a range of macro and micro elements.

It is also a list with some striking omissions. Foremost of these is cosmopolitan law. This theme has become increasingly central to Beck's recent work (Beck, 2006) as a key element in the institutional implementation of cosmopolitanism as distinct from its cultural expression. While possibly subsumed within 'transnational initiatives and organizations', it is arguable that cosmopolitan law deserves more explicit attention. This is because it clearly demarcates supra-national norms that represent something both beyond and additional to national and (strictly defined) inter*national* law.

It is not proposed to offer within this study a revised and more extensive empirical check-list, rather to work more closely from Beck's check-list. Nor will each and every item be discussed separately with relevant research assembled under the 13 headings, supplemented by law. This is partly because many of the items are so closely inter-related that it seems arbitrary to separate them out. Cross-border mobility, for example, is crucial in its own right, but is also intimately connected with trans-national ways of life and closely involved with issues like consumption of global commodities, the political representation of cultural minorities and global communication patterns.

Taking the example of post-war Italian and Greek migration to popular immigration destinations such as Australia (Bottomley, 1992; Castles, 1992), it is clear that this was not simply a matter of cross-border movement. It also involved extensive mobility of migrants, relatives, commodities, religious and political practices to and fro, linked with forms of communication such as letters and phone calls. Attempts were also made to make a mark in Australian politics, while retaining as close as possible an interest in politics in the home country. This in turn connects with issues like language use and possibilities of dual citizenship. Such patterns of thematic inter-connection may be repeated with many other migrant groups in many different settings.

An alternative approach to investigating each item in the check-list separately is to group items under broad headings, which emphasize inter-connections between them. In the following discussion, four broad themes are identified from the literature for further analysis, namely:

1. Inter-cultural engagement
2. Communications media
3. Personal attitudes
4. Politics and institutions (incorporating cosmopolitan law)

The first three of these are dealt with in this chapter. The fourth is discussed in the chapter that follows.

Inter-cultural Engagement

This theme encompasses inter-cultural relations – that is, what people do – as distinct from what their attitudes are when asked by researchers. Cosmopolitanism as action has many potential modalities, embracing the worlds of paid employment, consumption, mobility and community relations. These may be conducted through face-to-face relations with people and are typically mediated through cultural discourses that identify 'others' and modes of interaction with them. Cosmopolitanism typically involves bridge-building, whilst its obverse involves creation of strong borders and boundaries. While such encounters may also be connected with the mediating role of various communications technologies, processes which have received more widespread attention (Szerszynski and Urry, 2002, 2006), it is important not to foreclose on questions of direct engagement.

Contemporary evidence drawn from the world of management and paid employment has been used to explore linkages with cosmopolitanism. Garsten (2003), notes that managerial discourses which invoke corporate social responsibility might be seen as examples of the 'cosmopolitan organization', especially where these rise above the kind of public relations rhetoric that Naomi Klein has criticized in *No Logo* (Klein, 1999). It is not clear, however, how far more institutions like Business for Social Responsibility make any kind of tangible difference to cosmopolitan goals like human rights or higher labour standards within the global economy.

Most of the relevant work on paid employment, with the exception of Werbner's (1999) work on working-class cosmopolitanism among Pakistanis in the Gulf, deals with trans-nationalism among mobile professional and skilled workers. Although they may be mobile, such workers may remain largely embedded within ethnic (Biao, 2005) or class-based communities (Batnitzky *et al.*, 2008), or where employment is shorter in duration, among expatriates (Kennedy, 2004). There is a contrast in class focus here with historical research where mobile workers such as seamen or pirates have been seen as generating cross-border openness (Rediker, 1987; Gilroy, 1993). Class themes of any kind are generally less prominent in contemporary work, consistent with the contested view that social class is no longer the most salient or defining social relationship (for debates on this question see Lee and Turner, 1996).

Waxer (2001) is one of the few to pursue class themes within cosmopolitanism through a study of the spread of salsa musical styles from their origins of Cuban and Puerto Rican musical styles in the mid-20th century, through Cuban and Puerto Rican cultural diaspora in New York City, to Venezuela (Caracas) and Columbia (Cali). She sees this as aspects of working-class cosmopolitanism (*ibid*: 221) that somehow transcends regional or national musical styles. Not at first available through local distribution networks, salsa came in through black Caribbean sailors (222–3), linked with codes of dress, physical bearing, talk and dancing. Whereas the Latin middle class looked to British and North American rock music, salsa spread through the mobile world of seamen to urban, working-class black and *mestizo* Venezuelans and Columbians. In this sense she sees it as 'a sort of musical lingua franca' for Latin working-class communities (*ibid*: 223). In this example, however, it is not so much direct relations within the workplace as the link between working-class mobility and class-based consumption that is central to discussions of class and cosmopolitanism.

Nowicka's (2006) study of professional workers in international organizations within the UN system is more typical of research that explores linkages between skilled employment and cosmopolitanism. She asks how far trans-national mobility within employment detaches individuals and families from homeland affiliations, creating new trans-national spaces and (in the words of the book's sub-title) cosmopolitan universes. Founded on a case study of less than 20, this research is a departure from the many studies of diaspora, where employment relations are usually subsumed in issues of family, kinship and community. But it is equally distinct from work (or more usually speculative comments) that treat cosmopolitanism as a 'thin' veneer of managerial openness designed for fleeting cross-cultural engagements of frequent flyers crossing the globe.

Nowicka's argument cautions against any facile assumption that long-term residence outside country of origin for purposes of work necessarily leads to a liquid detachment from particular places. Rather mobile professionals exhibit a more ambivalent combination of activities directed both to current place of residence and country of origin (using communications technology). Even within the new setting, moreover, whatever connections with others take place within the workplace, outside of work expatriates do not necessarily go very far in exploring wider cultural connections. One option is to develop networks with other fellow expatriates from one's own country or other expatriates, but not with the locals. Thus 'networks of foreigners and expatriates, English-speaking television, cinemas, and bookstores etc, but also...supermarkets, translations, translators and interpreters, and fitness studios which support individualized, delocalised practises...enable any foreigner to decide whether or not to encounter the unknown, and the specifics of a place' (*ibid*: 233).

More outward-looking engagement through consumption of local products and services is discussed by Thompson and Tambyah (1999) in a paper called 'Trying to be Cosmopolitan'. This is based on a sample of 14 professionals working in Singapore in fields like information technology, health care, education and journalism, and drawn from American, European and other Asian backgrounds. The study is framed in terms of those with an explicit desire to broaden their horizons during a period of employment outside the country of origin, often of a shorter duration than Nowicka's group. 'Our participants', they report, 'profess a love for travelling and a passionate desire to move beyond their familiar cultural surrounds in order to live in and experience a new culture' (*ibid*). This, however creates tensions, similar to those discussed in Nowicka's work, between new settings and positive feelings for home. This may result in trips home, and certainly involves long phone conversations. But these are combined with forms of consumption and sociability, not simply of privatized commodities seen as 'exotic' mementoes, but also through clubs and hobbies that link with others and are ways of building up networks (*ibid*: 230ff). While Thompson and Tambyah see this very much on the model of cultural tourism, derived from writers such as Urry (1990, 1995), their evidence has a broader significance where it moves beyond privatized touristic experiences into attempts to create some kind of local community.

In any case consumption may be regarded as a free-standing modality of cosmopolitanism that need not carry any particular relationship with employment. This is how it enters into Beck's check-list, in relation to consumption of global commodities. Consumption may have distinct class and gendered profiles that may tend to fracture any sense of cross-class cosmopolitan solidarity. Equally though, consumption is a socially ambivalent category, having both privatized individual and public collective elements. While consumption is often seen an exclusively private matter, as it were internal to the individual consumer (and then criticized by some for narcissism or privilege), it may equally be linked with common or collective cultural expressions. This is often associated with the public life of cities and urban amenities, such as parks, theatres and other cultural pursuits that go well beyond personal shopping. It is this kind of collective consumption that is referred to when cities or urban spaces are described as cosmopolitan or multi-cultural. Such terms are also ambivalent, however, as to their precise meaning in terms of actual patterns of social interaction. When real estate companies describe urban locations as cosmopolitan they may be referring to cultural mixtures of people as much as opportunities for the consumption of commodities from diverse cultural settings.

The relationship between cosmopolitanism and cities is not simply a matter of collective consumption but may also be usefully linked with broader patterns of mobility *per se* (including travel as well as cross-border migration to take up employment) and explored in terms of inter-cultural or community relations. There are of course many distinct aspects of cities that may be interpreted as cosmopolitan milieux, from city centre palaces of global consumption like Gordon Selfridges's famous central London department store selling the merchandise of the world (Nava, 2002, 2007), through centres of performance like the theatres and nightclubs of Shanghai in the 1930s (Yue, 2006: 228–9) to cosmopolitan media like Berlin's SFB 4 'Radio Multikulti' (Vertovec, 2006) and multicultural or cosmopolitan quarters that may be identified in global cities from Vancouver (Hiebert, 2002) to Melbourne.

There is a potential problem of exaggerating the scope of the cosmopolitan city, especially where the co-existence of different cultural groups is taken, *ipso facto*, to represent cosmopolitanism. Zubaida (1999: 15) illustrates this with reference to his experience of visiting Toronto for the first time in the mid 1970s. 'I was struck', he recalls, 'by the city of Toronto...here was a wide mix of nationalities; Chinese, Indian, Polish, Hungarian, Portuguese, and many others, yet it was distinctly provincial...home-centred, hard-working, and culturally monochrome'. Whether this verdict was entirely true then or now, his point – one which has been encountered earlier in Chapter 3 – is that 'multi-cultural co-existence' is not a clear-cut indicator of cosmopolitan openness. Just as diasporic migrant communities may be trans-national but nonetheless inward-looking, so the ethnic or cultural diversity of much urban life may again far too readily be taken as cosmopolitan in character, with little regard for the necessity of evidence of inter-cultural engagement.

There are many studies of global migration and settlement across the globe, but comparatively few of them ask searching questions about the scope and limits of cosmopolitanism. Debates about settlement trajectories raise an inter-related set of questions about outcomes over time, which may include assimilation, integration, acculturation, melting pots and multiculturalism as well as cosmopolitanism as outcomes. Many such terms, such as integration and acculturation, seem to overlap, while others, such as melting pot or multiculturalism, are defined in different ways. Melting pot is often taken to be synonymous with the assimilation of migrants to a common culture, yet in Zangwill's original (1914) formulation, the term meant something akin to cosmopolitanism, in terms of the sharing of cultural differences in American cities, where New World and Old World interacted. Multiculturalism for some means celebration of cultural difference, even cultural separatism (a position common in the US), where for others it refers to a more integrative respect for and interaction between different ethnic groups within a new common core of enlarged citizenship rights (as in some Australian formulations, see Australian Council on Population and Ethnic Affairs, 1982; Zubrzycki, 1987). Conceptually, therefore, there are difficulties in clarifying *both* cosmopolitanism *and* what may be taken as alternative approaches.

This problem is further complicated by the time factor. Settlement is typically thought of as a process that takes place through different phases over time. In one simple model, early on-arrival relations tend to be conducted within the migrant group, as people look to those closest to them for help with somewhere to live and work. Subsequently greater outward contact may emerge with a greater security. This may be greatest for the second generation who either migrate as younger children or who are born in the new context and are more likely to be functionally bi-lingual. Their circles of friendship, influenced by schooling and the transition from school to work or further education, are typically cross-cultural in form. They may be more likely to marry outside the migrant group than the first generation. In all such ways they may be more likely to develop cross-cultural connections and possibly cosmopolitan inter-actions. At any rate identities become increasingly hyphenated, for example as Italian-Americans, or Vietnamese-Australians.

But what happens beyond these first two generations? Here work by Gans (1979) based on the US experience creates a further twist to the generational time-sequenced settlement model. The point here is that ethnic ties, while not disappearing altogether, become weaker. Once they become less crucial to survival, such ties become symbolic in form, to be celebrated episodically rather than lived everyday. What this means for cosmopolitanism is however difficult to determine. Does it ebb away as ethnic traditions weaken and third and fourth generations assimilate to a mainstream? Or does the mainstream itself change in more cosmopolitan directions, by becoming more hospitable of differ-ence and more open to new waves of migrants? The latter focus on initiatives from the side of the 'host nation' is crucial, because it has the power and capacity to be more or less open and more or less inclusive. Racist exclusion would stand at one end of the spectrum, while active welcome and inclusion would come at the other. The dynamics of cosmopolitanism in global cities may then be very strongly influenced by the characteristics of the reception settlers receive, rather than being determined by the settlement strategies of new migrants alone.

Hiebert's (2002) work on the culturally diverse city of Vancouver draws together the threads of cosmopolitan urbanism, migration and ethnicity and change over time. This work accomplishes two impor-tant tasks. First it breaks free of the association of cultural co-existence with cosmopolitanism, using micro-level evidence of interaction. Second it produces a more subtle sense of the situational dynamics of relatively open or closed interactions, rather than assuming that milieux that have the potential for cosmopolitan interaction actually achieve this. Vancouver, like Toronto, is a Canadian city marked by recent culturally diverse migration. Whereas Zubaida gained an impression of provincial separation of migrant groups from different ethnic backgrounds in Toronto, Hiebert (*ibid*) shows that closer atten-tion to micro-level interactions tells a more complex story for Vancouver.

Here recent mass migration of Chinese from various mainland and South-East Asian settings, overlaid upon older European migrants, has created a city with high levels of residents born in another country – reaching 70% in some areas. Migrants from similar areas tend to congregate together but this has not led to tight territorial segregation by ethnicity. In some cases members of different groups keep to themselves, more likely in the immediate context of migration or where negative experiences in the new setting have undermined the confidence to mix. In other cases, interaction is evident in a neighbourhood setting. Hiebert cites the example of back-yard gardening using plants associated with the country of origin, but also the exchange and often sale of produce. The presumed cross-pollination of varieties, is paralleled here by interaction across cultural divides. Over time, Hiebert finds many migrants prefer to live in mixed surroundings, in part because enclaves tend to be controlling. Such general findings are supported by other work on Canadian cities (Rose, 1997).

Moving beyond the immediate context of migration and settlement, there is another way in which the presence or absence of micro-level cosmopolitan sentiments may be determined. This involves choice of marriage partner. Under conditions of globalization, there are a range of circumstances under which this may arise. It may be an issue in relation to cross-border migration and settlement, but it may equally arise in the context of other kinds of cross-border movement including travel, war or through the global market for wives. As with any other set of social relationships there are complex inter-connections to be made in this case between opportunity, choice and inequalities of power, and these are set within further variations in cultural practices including those conducted and enforced through social institutions.

Two immediate empirical observations may nonetheless be made. The first is that where connections of kinship and ethnicity are strong, marriage partners are most often found within the group, and this applies whether the group is settled or highly mobile. Trans-national ethnic diaspora practise in-marriage (endogamy) in a similar way to many settled groups, providing another example of the lack of fit between trans-nationalism and cosmopolitanism. A number of pieces of evidence support this conclusion including Werbner's (1999) work on Pakistani kinship connections in Britain, Biao's (2005) research into gender, dowry and marriage amongst Indian information technology professionals, and Beck-Gernsheim's (2007) study of the marriage patterns of Turks living in Germany. In such cases, it is inadequate to regard continuing in-marriage as necessarily traditional or patriarchal. There may be strong elements of both. The necessity of this connection with tradition is incompatible with the highly modern lives which many in-marrying trans-national professionals live. The assumption that continuing in-marriage simply represents unbroken traditions is also brought into question by the economic rationality inherent in choosing marriage partners from those in well-paid employment, whether in country of origin or country of migration. Such rationalities may emerge even where certain traditional cultural moves persist (Beck-Gernsheim, 2007: 243ff).

The second empirical observation that points in a rather different more cosmopolitan direction is that there are contexts in which cross-cultural marriage patterns become more significant. Nava (2007) speaks of contexts where sexual relations and marriage take place across divides of cultural difference and social inequality. A clear example involves relationships between white women and black men, arising during the Second World War and the stationing of US soldiers, many of them African-American, within the UK (*ibid*: 75–94). While a number of observers have spoken of racial prejudice in the UK as a historical constant in the periods immediately before, during and after the war, Nava argues for a more nuanced understanding of 'inter-racial' connections which vary across time and space. Unlike the older Orientalist and often racialized constructions of the East, America in the 1930s and 1940s – through its popular culture in which White and Black were present (however unequally) – was received symbolically in a more positive manner. Idealized fantasies about the 'US' seen through Hollywood movies, American dance styles, musical innovations in swing and jazz meant glamour and opportunity, modern symbols that contrasted with English class-bound conservatism.

Beyond this, Nava offers a strikingly gendered analysis of women's interest in sexual relationships across line of cultural difference and 'colour prejudice'. Such interests were more than a fascination with 'abroad' or a wish to escape the 'constraints of Englishness'. They were also in her view 'a self-reflexive act of defiance in a social climate in which the repudiation of prejudice towards cultural others [including Jews] was increasingly widespread' (*ibid*: 90). While much attention has rightly been given to prejudice against and hostility towards difference as sharp limits to cosmopolitanism, finding their extreme expression in genocide and the holocaust, Nava sees the emotional and affective attractions of difference as possibly under-explored. In the example of 'white women and black men' that she analyses, it is plausible to think that white women may find black men desirable in part because romance with an excluded other helps the white woman to diminish her own social marginality, and in this way assert a kind of 'proto-feminism' (*ibid*: 91–2). In the case of black men, on the other hand, she believes such marriages to white women may enhance their status among men, though this enhanced status may not be sufficient to overcome the deep insecurities among many white men about sexual competition. Whatever the precise consequences may turn out to be, this work clearly opens up the empirical exploration of cosmopolitanism on further dimensions of inter-cultural engagement beyond the more familiar themes of trans-national migrant mobility and top-down forms of privileged global consumption.

Communications Media

The topic of inter-cultural engagement and cosmopolitanism has still further dimensions to explore, connected with the mediating role of communications processes and technologies. If we focus on direct inter-cultural engagement alone, a somewhat distorted picture emerges, because so much engagement takes place through the mediating influence of culture industries and discourses. Inter-cultural engagement should not then be treated simply as if it emerges spontaneously through the situational logic of everyday life – even though this is a significant and often neglected dimension of life within the context of globalization. Rather what we think of others, and how we act towards them, will be profoundly influenced by patterns of media representation through various communications technologies, and institutional processes and policies affecting areas like citizenship rules and education. Bringing such influences to bear raises further questions about the distribution of cultural power as it affects what messages are sent 'from above', how these may be received, processed and acted on from 'below', and how far a diversity of popular cosmopolitan and anti-cosmopolitan constructions of the world and its peoples emerge from whatever source.

Szerszynski and Urry in two very important joint papers (2002, 2006), provide some far-reaching insights into this range of issues, in ways that are both theoretically and empirically informed. The empirical scope of their enquiries includes printed books, print journalism, radio, television, film and the internet. They note that much research on culture industries is concerned more with institutional indicators, such as ownership patterns and programming, than on the cultural consequences of global media representations of the world. Their own focus then is on 'how these mediations of "other" peoples, places, and environments are folded into our daily lives' (2002: 464). Whether representations of others evoke pity, compassion, identification or active solidarity (or indeed hostility, boredom or repulsion) are very salient to questions of the scope and limits of cosmopolitanism. This line of work engages with a number of Beck's research agenda checklist items including 'global communication patterns', 'transnational news coverage', 'ecological crisis responses', 'transnational ways of life' and 'consumption of global commodities', while transforming the category of 'international travel' to include modes of 'inhabiting the world from afar'.

An important theoretical proposition underlying this work is that specific communication technologies may make considerable differences to the way that social life is imagined and acted upon. Benedict Anderson (1983) famously argued for the significance of the print media in creating senses of nationhood as communities of like-minded people who would never meet face-to-face. Bruce Robbins (1999) has asked why the process should stop there, since print media may also be significant for cosmopolitan imaginings and activity. Szerszynski and Urry (2002, 2006) focus rather on television as a source of images and representations of the world. They show how TV is saturated with global images, from representations of the earth as a generic 'global' environment, through images of wildlife as indicators of the state of the environment and images of 'the family of man' sharing global commodities, to images of global people, whether as celebrities or experts (2002: 466–7). All of this can be interpreted as a kind of 'banal globalism' or cosmopolitanization in Beck's terms. But it may equally be of wider significance for the emergence of what Szerszynski and Urry call mediatized 'cultures of cosmopolitanism'. Such cultures arise in other words through media representations rather than the kind of inter-cultural engagements discussed earlier. Further questions arise, nonetheless, as to how far such cultures are simply privatized or banal exercises in the consumption of commodified images, and how far aspects of an emerging public culture that may connect with cultural politics and cosmopolitan democracy.

Urry (2000), drawing on work by Hebdige (1990), has previously argued that contemporary cosmopolitanism developed through 'imaginative travel' by means of the TV. Szerszynski and Urry (2002: 472–7) report the findings from focus groups conducted in North West England to elaborate further what this might mean. The evidence they review tends to support views which link local, national and global concerns, and in concrete rather than abstract ways, informed by exposure to TV images. While few claimed to be citizens of the world, many of those who identified with their nation also thought there were moral obligations, such as to the welfare of the world's children, that went beyond it. These commitments were, in other words, not to some abstract ideal of cosmopolitanism, but to more mundane or personalized symbols and activities. These included global moral exemplars, such as Nelson Mandela or Mother Teresa, special organizations, such as the Red Cross, or events, such as Band Aid (*ibid*: 474).

The connection with TV and the idea of visuality is extended further in Szerszynski and Urry (2006). Here the idea is developed of 'inhabiting the world at a distance', which can be linked with the idea of cosmopolitanism at a distance. Physical travel has for many centuries been seen as a crucial aspect of inter-cultural engagement relevant to cosmopolitanism (Binney, 2006; Euben, 2006). It continues to grow in scale. Yet there are two additional forms of mobility that may be equally or possibly more significant for cosmopolitanism. These, according to Szerszynski and Urry (2006: 118) are imaginative travel and virtual travel.

The significance of virtual travel through TV is extended in several ways. First questions are raised, drawing on the work of Ingold (2000) and Cosgrove (1994), about the relationship between televisual images of Planet Earth, such as the NASA image Earthrise, and the projection of worldly power over nature. If such images pertain to a cosmopolitan image of the world as a single place, they seem to render cosmopolitanism, according to Szerszynski and Urry, as positioned outside any immediate context. They do not however explore this very far through empirical evidence, and there remains doubt as to whether images that look down on the earth need presume an all-powerful technological vision of society dominating nature. This may be the NASA view, but it is not necessarily the spiritual or environmental view.

In any case, their argument is more to do with changes in the nature of the visual under conditions of globalization than the reception of certain kinds of image. A contrast is drawn here between visualization through televisual tourism and the more embedded visualization that may come from dwelling in a locality (Szerszynski and Urry, 2006: 124). Using focus group evidence they also point to a contrast between the ways in which locality is discussed. The official or professional view deploys a language of abstraction and comparison drawing on surface-based cartographic constructions of where a locality is, while a denizen's view is more deeply connected with experience of being within a locality overlaid through memory. This suggests not simply a tension between the local and the cosmopolitan, but also an incompatibility, entailing the pessimistic conclusion that as cosmopolitanism advances, senses of locality become transformed into touristic visualizations.

This line of argument converges with Castells' sense of a polarization whereby the space of flows comes to dominate the space of place. Castells has somewhat relaxed this line of thinking, and this is welcome in the sense that any such polarity tends to erect an unsustainable dichotomy between the system 'up there' and the life-world 'down here'. In Szerszynski and Urry's version of this dichotomy, abstract cosmopolitanism encounters embedded localism. One way of deconstructing this is to show that cosmopolitanism is not necessarily an abstract way of looking down at the surface of one set of phenomena, before moving on to the next. It may indeed have abstracting features, but empirical analysis is always required to show how these may be related to more concrete features of life.

The issue of cosmopolitanism and memory offers crucial insights here. Levy and Sznaider (2002) in particular argue that collective memory does not simply adhere to nations or ethnic groups, but can also take cosmopolitan forms. In the case of the Holocaust in Nazi Germany, they show how subsequent media representations of the event have developed a trans-national trans-contextual character. This draws on Assmann's (1991) distinction between communicative memory requiring group-specific bearers, and a wider cultural memory that can exist independently of its carriers. The construction of a cosmopolitan memory of the Holocaust takes the latter form, represented through films such as Spielberg's *Schindler's List*, memorials such as the Holocaust Museum in Washington DC and media constructions of events such as trials of Holocaust perpetrators. While aspects of the communicative memory among Jews may be particularistic, they argue that the wider cultural memory can be trans-contextual. This is because emergent cosmopolitan norms of human rights become associated with the Jewish Holocaust, while also being extended on a wider scale to other events such as Balkan atrocities around the war in Kosovo. By 2000 the Stockholm Intergovernmental Conference on the Holocaust was able to deterritorialize and institutionalize memory of the Holocaust. The cosmopolitan tone of its subsequent declarations took it as a future civilizational premise that no similar event should ever be permitted to occur again (Levy and Sznaider, 2002: 101).

This argument about cosmopolitan memory is interesting because it combines a kind of abstraction from the immediate context of group-specific memory among Holocaust survivors, but together with constructions of particular moments, processes, and symbols. This is an interesting example of the way that cosmopolitanism can be connected with glocalization – the inter-penetration of global or trans-contextual and local.

Such global-local connections and relationships are also the stuff of media genres such as film. The predominance of Hollywood in world cinema for most of the 20th century, coupled with the insistence of the US on cultural free trade rather than national rights to protect cultural industries, may be seen as consistent with theories of cosmopolitanism as cultural Imperialism (Schiller, 1976). This interpretation may not however tell the whole story, for several reasons. First the allure and glamour of Hollywood may also, as Nava (2007) suggests, be consistent with a more visceral or utopian cosmopolitanism from below. She interprets the success of Hollywood in Britain during the 1930s and 1940s as a result of 'its idealism, its depictions of glamour and affluence, and its democratic story-lines which featured ordinary men and women in a sympathetic light' (*ibid*: 88). These contrasted with the more stilted class-bound narratives of British cinema. In this sense the impact of Hollywood and its connection with cosmopolitan sensibilities is multiform rather than unitary, dependent on reception as much as delivery.

A second complicating aspect of world cinema in the contemporary post-colonial world is the rise of Bollywood, the Indian film industry based in Mumbai (Bombay). Jigna Desai (2006) has pointed out the many complex ways in which the appearance of Bollywood on the world stage alongside Hollywood intersects with South Asian cosmopolitanism, the worldwide Indian diaspora and cultural constructions of what it means to be Indian. Indian film has reached a worldwide audience not simply in minority art houses, but in a broader sense. This has three elements. The first is 'cross-overs' reaching out to non-Indian audiences, as in Global Globe nomination for Gurinder Chana's film *Bend it Like Beckham*, and nomination of the film *Lagaan* for an Oscar. The second is the importance of Indian film (and diasporic films like *American Desi*), for the Indian diaspora in North America and Britain. The third is references to Indian film genres in Hollywood productions like *Mississippi Masala* and *Fire*.

Desai also shows how the theme of global-local connections and dislocations appears within Indian film, illustrating the senses in which diaspora may be said to be cosmopolitan or non-cosmopolitan. Within the film *Dilwale Dulhaniya Le Jayenge (The Lover Takes A Bride)*, for example, Desai shows how different characters represent cultural shifts in relations between diaspora and homeland. These include the older patriarch, feeling alienated from Britain where he has settled and reminiscing about the homeland, and the younger suitor for his daughter, who is able to remain loyal to Indian cultural practices, while equally integrated into his British home, where he plays rugby and rides motorbikes. These appear as cosmopolitan competencies that contrast with the nostalgia of the older generation, and yet remain oriented to India as much as Britain. They also help to specify the ambivalence of diaspora groups to cosmopolitanism, a point stressed in the first part of this chapter.

There are many other ways in which mass media and cosmopolitanism intersect. One is the development of international news services depending in part on foreign correspondents that Hannerz (2004b) has associated with cosmopolitanism. In one sense the international reporting and delivery of news may be seen as a top-down form of control over information associated with primarily Western news agencies. This was certainly how critics of the 'new information order' have approached the global organization of news. News itself, as a range of sociological work has argued, is not simply the straightforward delivery of obvious 'facts', but the selection and packaging of certain types of information into 'stories' that are tailored in length and content to fit conventions of news programmes.

Having taken all this into account, it is also evident that the globalization of news media has widened rather than restricted sources of information. While Voice of America and BBC World in the Cold War period served ideological as much as reporting functions, the global media picture has changed in the post-Cold War period. Ideological management of stories is still there. But the range of providers has expanded with the development of initiatives like Al Jazeera, the Arab world's news service. This is delivered in a cross-border manner in Arabic and English, using a network of reporters in London and Kuala Lumpur as well as the Middle East. The net effect of this has been to widen access to world news, and hence, in a very diffuse way, to extend the possibility of wider potentially cosmopolitan linkages with others.

News gathering has also been influenced by new communications technology such as the internet and satellite phone. These have made it less difficult for alternative voices to challenge official news services.

Is the internet intrinsically cosmopolitan, whether in the hands of activists or citizens going about more mundane everyday encounters?

The internet has been associated with many broad social trends from globalization and the rise of network society (Castells, 1996), to democracy and cosmopolitanism. One of the difficulties with general arguments of this kind is that they often over-simplify what are far more complex and contradictory processes. It would certainly be tempting to argue that major new communications technologies create fundamentally new worlds, full of new cultural, political and economic possibilities. Just as the print media (and print capitalism) spawned the nation as an imagined community (Anderson, 1983), we might want to say, so the internet has spawned the possibility of a new virtual democracy that could be world-wide and thus finally realize the philosophers' and activists' dream of a cosmopolitan world community.

The evidence unfortunately is not strong enough to sustain this interpretation. This is primarily because the internet is used for a variety of purposes. Some of these are concerned with hate and racial exclusion, using, as it were, global 'means' for very particular anti-cosmopolitan 'ends'. Others are very mundane rather than world-transforming, such as diffuse everyday searches for information or routine exchanges with friends. Most commentators now emphasize the variety of internet usages rather than any unitary impact, whether corporate or personal (Sassen, 2002; Castells, 2001).

One way of thinking about cosmopolitanism and the internet is to ask whether cosmopolitan people are more likely to use it than non-cosmopolitans. Much empirical research on particular countries or localities notes that internet users are more likely than non-users to travel and have wider more dispersed circles of personal contacts outside immediate family and friends (Katz *et al.*, 2001: 413–14; Chen *et al.*, 2002: 95). This effect held taking variations in income into account, though it is not clear what kind of travel was involved, and how far travel and internet use were connected with employment requirements. In any case such data do not make clear whether greater cosmopolitanism as measured by increased travel and wider circles of friends was cause or effect. A further problem, clear from comparison with the far richer cultural markers of cosmopolitanism discussed in qualitative studies reviewed above, is that quantifiable markers of cosmopolitanism are very thin on substantive content.

Guillén and Suaréz (2005) have attempted a more systematic 118 country survey on internet use, which asks what drives internet use using data from the International Telecommunications Union. Cosmopolitanism is taken to be one driver, but measured again rather thinly in terms of the value of travel abroad measured as a proportion of the GDP of each country. Using this measure they find little association with cosmopolitanism, the drivers of internet use lying elsewhere in terms of income levels, easier access in democratic countries, and higher levels of privatization of telecommunications. Whether this operationalization of cosmopolitanism is adequate is debatable, nonetheless the significance of other drivers suggests that cosmopolitanism, however measured, is unlikely to be a major causal factor.

Most attention therefore concerns effects of new information technology. Here the association of usage levels with travel and wider interpersonal ties is of limited significance. It cannot tell us whether levels of cosmopolitanism were greater as a result of internet use, since we do not have comparable data on patterns of social life before and after. If people who once corresponded with others abroad now do so via the internet, nothing much has changed. And the mere fact of such cross-border exchanges tells us little about attitudes or behaviour. It cannot distinguish between Nazis planning political events and members of Greenpeace planning such events. It is also striking that researchers find rather weak links between internet use and increased use of other media such as newspapers, books and radio (Chen *et al.*, 2002: 91; Robinson *et al.*, 2002: 255).

The net effect here is to downplay the more extreme linkages that are often popularly made between internet use and radical social changes. Debates over the role of the internet, reviewed here, are methodologically interesting nonetheless because they introduce quantitative methods into a discussion that is often exclusively qualitative. We turn in the remainder of the chapter to primarily quantitative work on cosmopolitanism at the level of individual attitudes.

Personal Attitudes

Attitude surveys which quantify the distribution of attitudes within a population have an important bearing on issues about the scope and limits of cosmopolitanism. Because they deal directly with variations in attitudes to the world as a whole, as well as nations, regions and localities, they seem very well placed to answer questions as to whether the world is becoming more or less cosmopolitan. This is especially true in relation to measures of identity, but they can also be extended to cover actions – what people do – as well as what they think. Nonetheless attitude surveys are rarely discussed in most of the qualitative research reviewed above (for a partial exception see Szerszynski and Urry, 2002: 462, 474). In the case of historical work, this is primarily because such surveys are unavailable. But in the case of contemporary research, this neglect appears to stem from methodological objections, though these are not usually articulated.

The standard objection of qualitative researchers to quantitative attitude surveys obtained through structured questionnaires and interviews, is that this material is often superficial and easy to take out of context. Instead of exploring the complexities of experience, the meanings of the language people use and the connections between thought, behaviour and their consequences in interaction with others, quantitative research tends to use very crude measures abstracted from the empirical richness and complexity of life. The counter-argument is that to exclude such evidence is to exclude important empirical data that cannot be obtained using qualitative research strategies. Such strategies make considerable use of individual case studies – like those dealing with particular instances of cosmopolitanism in space and time – but which are hard to use as a basis for generalization. Breadth is needed as well as depth.

What then can quantitative research tell us about contemporary cosmopolitanism? First and most important it offers measures of identity whether to nation, locality and the cosmos or world as a whole. Second it may be used to examine the bridges or walls which people may construct in their dealings with others, notably migrants. This kind of data may be used to test for cosmopolitan tolerance. The most important source for this purposes is the World Values Survey conducted periodically (1990–1, 1995–7, and 1999–2000) in dozens of countries across the world (together with the European Values Study, which is a sub-set of the whole). These sources were not constructed primarily as measures of cosmopolitanism, but they do contain valuable information relevant to it. They also collect data upon nations alone, and as such ignore cross-national or cross-border evidence. Yet in spite of their clear relevance to critical assessments of cosmopolitanism, they are noticeably absent from the work of theoretically inclined writers such as Beck and Urry.

The first conclusion to be drawn from this research is that nation and locality are far stronger sources of identity than the world as a whole (Norris, 2000, 2006). Using WVS data from two points of time in the 1990s, nearly half the respondents (47%) identified as belonging primarily to locality or region, while over one-third identified with nation (38%), leaving only one-sixth (15%) identifying with 'the world as a whole' (2000: 162). This kind of distribution is also relatively even across different types of post-industrial, post-communist and developing societies. This, as Norris points out, runs contrary to Inglehart's (1997: 303–5) speculation that cosmopolitanism might be strongest in post-industrial societies most affected by globalization. This may not however rule out the impact of globalization, since this may arguably be a presence everywhere, not simply in post-industrial countries like the US, UK and Germany.

A methodological strength of the WVS data is that it asks about both the first and next most important source of identity, allowing therefore for richer multi-dimensional approaches to cosmopolitanism, nationalism, and localism. This is important in view of the global-national or glocal inter-actions and fusions noted in previous chapters, together with the notion of methodological glocalism. The evidence on first and second choices, analysed by Norris, suggests that there are very few (2%) 'pure cosmopolitans', measured in terms of commitments to world first + continent second, but a significant (15.5%) number of 'pure localists', who identify with locality first and sub-national region second. The most common mixtures are those that link nation and locality (35.5% – composed of 18% who place nation first and 17.5% locality first). Linkages between world and nation comprise 12% (with around equal numbers putting world and nation first), and between world and locality 6.1% (*ibid*: 164).

These data converge with much of the qualitative research in emphasizing the importance of mixed (or hybrid) identities. Cosmopolitanism where it exists is situated in place and time, rather than context-free. What they add to the qualitative work, if taken at face value, is a sense of the limits of a 'world' or cosmopolitan perspective, which, at best, features in only 15–20% of choices, with only 12% putting world first. (For further elaboration of these data in the Australian case, see Phillips, 2002.)

These findings on the distribution of attitudes suggest that Beck's optimistic scenario of advances in both cosmopolitanization and the cosmopolitan outlook is overdrawn. Most people do not have cosmopolitan outlooks, if the measures here are credible. Rather they maintain distinctions and boundaries between where they belong and the world outside. Globalization has not created a boundary-free world, yet the exploration of the robustness of boundaries within that world has only recently revived amongst scholars of cosmopolitanism (Delanty, 2006a; Rumford, 2007). The data also suggest that it would be premature to take up methodological cosmopolitanism and preferable to analyse mixtures of identity through the alternative more nuanced idea of methodological glocalism.

Norris's analysis of WVS data also points to generational effects in cosmopolitan identity. This is strongest amongst the younger cohorts born after the end of the Second World War, and weakest amongst the oldest generations born around the turn of the 20th century. The former are three times more likely to be cosmopolitans than the latter. These data very much support Beck's argument about increasing cosmo-politanism, at least among the young. What is not clear is whether the older non-cosmopolitans who have lived through two World Wars have always been more oriented to nation, or have come to be so, perhaps in reaction to insecurities arising from recent phases of globalization. In any case the young emerge as more at home in the world. Not surprisingly cosmopolitans are also found most of all among the educated, with those in higher education twice as likely to iden-tify this way than those with the least education, and amongst city-dwellers. The strong association with education once again draws attention to a class effect, and to the issue of a greater sense of security amongst those who feel able to be outward-looking.

Other dimensions on which attitudes relevant to cosmopolitanism may be measured include attitudes to cultural others such as immigrants. These represent one of the manifestations of globalization that are often said to induce insecurity and calls for barriers against cross-border movement. At least two issues are at stake here, namely attitudes to policies of economic openness or protection of trade and employment, and tolerance or intolerance within community relations. In the WVS data from the 1990s, Norris found that while around one-third of respondents favoured free trade, the majority favoured some regulation of trade to protect employment. Meanwhile, only 7% agreed with borders open to anyone, while 43% believed in strict immigration controls and 12% wanted no immigration at all. The 7% 'no borders' group include many of the cosmopolitans, especially since they are also likely to be in the younger cohort, but may also possibly include small business people looking for cheap labour. Other cosmopolitans may also be found amongst the remaining 38% who favour immigration if jobs are available (*ibid*: 171–5).

Rother and Medrano (2006) have looked at tolerance levels within and between European countries using EVS data on 11 countries including the US at three points in time – 1981, 1990, and 2000. They find no general decline in attitudes to tolerance during this period of intensifying globalization, but they do find some slight aggregate increase of intolerance towards 'foreigners' during the 1980s but not the 1990s and a sustained increase in intolerance to those perceived as 'political extremists' across the period – which significantly predates 9/11. From the viewpoint of cosmopolitanism, these data do not show a marked swing towards or away from an open outward-looking orientation, though they are aggregated averages, from which social groups and individual nations may vary. Once again the 'young', born since 1940, come out as more tolerant in general and in relation to particular groups. Yet of course any such inferences come up against the problem of knowing how far attitudes are replicated in behaviour. Do the intolerant behave accordingly in uncivil and violent ways to others, such as migrants, or just keep their views to themselves?

Staying for the moment with attitudes, Rother and Medrano (*ibid*: 164–5) see some cross-national convergence in terms of general tolerance, but individual national variation in terms of specific intoler-ances. In Spain, Denmark and Italy, a steady increase of intolerance to foreigners is evident, while the reverse is true in West Germany (as it then was) and the Netherlands. In most of the remainder, the position was more volatile, as in Ireland and Great Britain with greater toler-ance of foreigners in the 1980s succeeded by greater intolerance in the 1990s. Such national variations may in turn be linked to variations in national experiences and events. In Ireland, immigration expanded for the first time in nearly two centuries during the 1990s when attitudes to foreigners became less tolerant. Events such as 9/11 in the US, or the killing of Pym Fortuyn, the Dutch opponent of immigration, which fall outside the scope of this study, have nonetheless adversely affected community relations in both settings. In this sense both processes and events matter in the analysis of cosmopolitanism and its limits.

A final study of methodological significance here is the attempt by Phillips and Smith (2008) to link what people do and what people think. They have analysed data from a study of Australian national identity conducted in 2001 to compare measures of cosmopolitan attitudes (or outlook) with cosmopolitan practice (or behaviour). The former were measured in terms of willingness to have members of different cultural groups (e.g. including Asian and Middle Eastern migrants and aboriginal people) living next door, the latter in terms of five items including extensive overseas travel, internet use, overseas friendship networks, and watching explicitly multicultural TV (SBS). The most striking finding is that cosmopolitan outlook did not necessarily mean very much cosmopolitan practice. Put another way, for the 1,000 or so in the sample who would have no problem with members of any of the various cultural groups as neighbours, around 40% exhibited none of the five examples of cosmopolitan practice, while another 30% scored only one.

These may indicate that cosmopolitan outlook is not followed through in active cosmopolitan practice, suggesting a thin rather than thick cosmopolitanism. It could also mean that non-cosmopolitan locals can be hospitable to others. Nonetheless, Smith and Phillips confirm the findings of other studies that those who scored high on both outlook and practice were more likely to have higher education credentials and be younger, though in this case they also found that being non-religious also mattered. Interestingly they single out the expansion of higher education, rather than globalization *per se* as an important driver of cosmopolitanism, a finding somewhat at variance with Norris' argument that level of socio-economic development makes little difference to cosmopolitan attitudes.

Conclusion

This is the first of three chapters dealing with empirical research findings concerning cosmopolitanism, organized in terms of inter-cultural engagement, communications media, and personal attitudes. These deal more with socio-cultural dimensions of cosmopolitanism, as distinct from the normative aspects that will form the core of the following chapter on politics and institutions. In this chapter, emphasis has been placed on many of the 13 aspects of the cosmopolitan research agenda offered by Beck, most notably consumption, trans-national mobility and travel, communications media and global news, and attitudes. These have been discussed, as far as possible, taking account of interactions between them.

The overall picture that emerges is one in which cosmopolitan open-ness is widespread, but circumscribed to a degree by national and local orientations. These occur both within processes of mobility and toler-ance rather than simply external to them as oppositions and resis-tances. Although much of the recent literature has sought to open up the field to multiple modalities of cosmopolitanism, this has occurred at the cost of seeing aspects of the particular, local or national within cosmopolitanism. There is very little evidence for cosmopolitanism pure and simple, but this scarcely closes debate. Rather it makes debate more complex.

Methodologically the balance of work reviewed here remains focussed on finding new processes and phenomena to which some kind of label of cosmopolitanism might be attached, rather than find-ing instances of non- or anti-cosmopolitanism. Genocide and ethnic cleansing have not yet been taken into account, nor has a final balance been struck on relations between nations and the world, tasks for the remaining chapters. Yet the attitude data reviewed here have begun the process of asking more challenging questions designed to establish limits to cosmopolitanism, rather than piling up yet more qualitative case-study evidence of its presence. It is in this more scep-tical spirit that politics and institutions are approached in the follow-ing chapter.

6

Cosmopolitanism: Legal and Political Research

The empirical scope of cosmopolitanism extends well beyond socio-cultural ways of life and institutions, and beyond individual attitudes. In this chapter attention shifts to political and legal institutions and activities, often seen as the main location of normative dimensions of cosmopolitanism. This focus brings to the fore debates over the nature of political obligations to others, human rights, questions of war and peace and conflicts over the best way to organize political and legal relationships and institutions in an epoch of globalization. The emphasis is less on cosmopolitanism as consumption or as a way of connecting with others across cultural divides, and more upon political and legal organization, the relationship of states with each other, as well as between states, non-state actors, and global civil society.

This is not to say that socio-cultural ways of life do not influence politics and law, nor to deny the significance of political and legal processes for inter-cultural relations. Such interactions are very important, a historical example discussed in Chapter 3 being the role of empires in providing conditions of political stability that have sometimes proven conducive to inter-cultural engagement and co-operation. Other examples include recent public policies in human rights and citizenship affecting community relations, immigration and settlement. Such policies may encourage inter-cultural mobility and engagement, or at least channel such engagements in particular officially approved directions. While the major analytical focus of this chapter is political and legal, particular attention will be given to interactions with the socio-cultural processes already discussed in previous chapters.

In pursuing this focus it is necessary to consider dimensions to Beck's research agenda for cosmopolitanism other than those discussed in Chapter 5. These comprise items drawn from the original list such as citizenship (including dual citizenship), political representation for cultural minorities, trans-national initiatives and organizations and ecological crisis responses (Beck, 2002a: 79–80). But they also go beyond it to embrace global governance and cosmopolitan law, missing from the 2002 check-list, but a major feature of Beck's more recent work (Beck, 2005, 2006; Beck and Grande, 2006). The approach in this chapter as with the previous one is to explore both the scope and limits of cosmopolitanism.

States, Nations and Cosmopolitan Challenges

Much of the modern context for cosmopolitan politics and law is set by conditions of international connection and trans-national interdependence. These two conditions affect both the capacities (and incapacities) of states and their moral standing as political and legal entities.

The concept of international connection presumes a world of nation-states who engage in relations with each other. Such relations may be orderly to varying degrees, but they may equally see endemic conflicts which lead to war. For Kant, the purpose of politics is not utilitarian, with the aim to produce happiness, but normative, to produce right, as a basis for freedom, equality and the autonomy of citizens. (The argument here draws on Reiss, 1991, see also Fine, 2007: 22–58.) The sovereignty of states ultimately rests on peoples, even if Kant believed this was exercised on their behalf in the non-democratic states of the late 18th century when he was writing. While this ideally means a republican constitution within each state, on an international level it requires arrangements that protect freedom, equality and autonomy from the action of other states.

Warfare violates this requirement both in Kant's day and our own. Some states have a superior capacity to inflict war on others, we may say, while losers' capacities are further impaired leading to further entrenchment of inequality and stronger senses of injustice. Political expediencies which recognize unequal power and the underlying premise that 'might is right' cannot in his view resolve such problems, nor can ideas of a 'balance of power' which only gives temporary relief. Colonial conquest and rule is also unacceptable. Kant (1991 [1784]) sees perpetual peace based on cosmopolitan principles as the only way of resolving such challenges. Such principles mean some relaxation of state sovereignty, in that states must accept external arbitration of disputes between them, which would otherwise lead to war. This view may be seen from hindsight as rather restricted. As Habermas (1997: 115) points out, it is cast in terms of experience of spatially limited wars between states, rather than world wars or civil wars. Nor does it think in terms of war as a crime. It has nonetheless, for all these limits, helped stimulate an expanding discourse of cosmopolitan law over more than two centuries that have elapsed since it was written.

Trans-national interdependence also enters into this discussion in the sense that Kant presumes some kind of universal moral basis for perpetual peace. 'The peoples of the world', he writes in a much-quoted sentence, 'have entered in varying degrees into a universal community, and it has developed to the point where the violation of laws in *one* part of the world is felt everywhere' (Kant, *ibid*: 107–8). In an anthropological sense this universal community is fostered through increased exchange between nations, an argument which invokes the familiar linkages between trade, travel and cosmopolitanism.

The evaluative yardstick here for judging states' capacities to deliver perpetual peace is thus not states themselves but autonomous individuals capable of reason and moral responsibility. In a philosophical sense this moral dimension is a pre-supposition associated with Kant's belief that the purpose of nature and reason is to maximize our freedom. In an empirical sense though, such diffuse and somewhat elusive trans-national moral phenomena are capable of exploration and assessment with evidence. They raise issues about both cosmopolitan justice and cosmopolitan democracy. Cosmopolitan justice relates to the creation of institutions able to resolve instances of injustice, whether created by war or some other process, by reference to cross-national cosmopolitan standards, such as human rights. Cosmopolitan democracy involves popular democratic consent to global acts of government and the processes by which decisions are made and implemented. Such processes for Kant included publicity, which may be interpreted to mean some kind of world public opinion. This itself, as Bohman (1997: 182–3) points out, requires some kind of institutionalization in deliberative processes where 'the success of public actions depends on their public acknowledgement' (*ibid*: 182). Overall these two dimensions – justice and democracy – are joined together by Kant, though they may be regarded as analytically distinct insofar as cosmopolitan justice is possible even in the absence of cosmopolitan democracy (Caney, 2005). This however requires some kind of alternative mechanism, such as normative pressure on elites, to realize more just institutional action.

Underlying the discussion so far is an analytical distinction between states and peoples. This distinction is both reflected but somehow elided in the widely used idea of the nation-state. This is an aggregation of two entities, the connections between which may be close but which are far from organic. Thus whereas 'nation' refers to peoples as a political-cultural entity, 'state' refers to political institutions. While peoples have sought their own political institutions, especially when ruled autocratically by internal or external powers, the tightness of fit breaks down under a number of circumstances.

First under conditions of globalization and population movement, individual states are not the sole arbiters of who peoples are and what rights they should have. This is very obvious in the case of migrant diaspora spread across different national territories, a phenomenon often overlaid by trans-national religious commitment and identity. Second the peoples within particular state boundaries are often far from homogenous culturally or in terms of political preferences, and may contain secessionist elements, as well as migrants with dual citizenship rights in country of residence and country of origin. State sovereignty and national citizenship rights confined within a given territory are not necessarily congruent with the terms upon which peoples think of popular sovereignty. Thirdly new institutional developments beyond the nation-state, such as supra-nationalism within Europe, also engender changes in the character of public spaces within which democracy and citizenship may be expressed.

Such distinctions matter when exploring evidence about cosmopolitanism and its limits in the political arena. In particular the lack of tight fit between the territorial state and cultural allegiances raises questions about possible trends towards post-national forms of identity, politics, citizenship rights and state organization. An example of this kind of thinking is Soysal's work on 'new modes of belonging and patterns of participation' within Europe that suggest 'multiple arenas and levels on which individuals and cultural groups enact their citizenship'(2001: 160). The focus here is on Islamic migrants to Europe and the existence of connections between Muslims in different countries around controversial issues such as rights for young women to wear veils in schools. Appeals to the European Court of Human Rights by umbrella organizations indicate a Europe-wide cultural politics, rather than one contained within individual polities.

Commentators have approached these growing complexities in several analytically distinct ways. One is to reassert the centrality of the territorially bounded nation and state to the mainstream of social and political organization (Mann, 1993, 1997). This option often depends on arguments about the weakness, incoherence or exaggerated scope of post-national alternatives (Smith, 1990) or on perceived difficulties of institutionalizing democracy beyond nation-states (Görg and Hirsch, 1998; Urbinati, 2003). However it may also be linked with rather different ways of re-structuring national polities.

One option is to replace ethnic nationalism with civic republicanism and secular patriotism (Habermas, 2001; Pettit, 1997) as a more inclusive mode of democracy. In Habermas, this is connected with the potential for a European *demos* to emerge that would transform the older non-democratic Europe through greater citizen involvement in politics. This kind of option depends on the contested assumption that civic republicanism could be enough to create a viable mode of politics (Canovan, 2000). For Habermas, supra-national republicanism might be fostered by a sense of dual allegiance to nation and to Europe. However it remains unclear how feasible this prospect really is, especially where mass culturally diverse immigration creates a lack of consensus on political values, rights, and obligations. French conflicts over bans on wearing the Islamic headscarf in schools are symptomatic of this problem. A second variant of re-structuring national politics may be labelled liberal-culturalism. It is often connected with various ideas of multiculturalism, in the sense that attempts are made to accommodate cultural differences within a liberal-democratic order. These may take the form of special policies to recognize minority rights, or acceptance of group rights. Such policies are nonetheless charged with fossilizing cultural differences, undermining inter-ethnic linkages, and downplaying economic causes of inequality and exclusion.

A final option is to subordinate the particularistic loyalties to nation to cosmopolitan democracy in a supra-national global or at least regional sense. This applies both as a moral orientation and through the construction of new institutions (Held, 1995, 2005; Jones, 1999). This depends for its plausibility on convincing some sceptics that cosmopolitanism can be expressed in sufficiently substantive terms to overcome problems of abstractness, that states can be persuaded to pool or otherwise limit such sovereignty as they claim to possess, while convincing others that this would not skew cosmopolitan democracy to narrowly conceived Western models.

We will return to these questions below.

Further cosmopolitan challenges arise insofar as nation-states do not have absolute sovereignty to do what they like within their own borders and have a tendency to intervene in the affairs of other nation-states. The so-called Westphalian system, developed after the highly damaging Thirty Years' War in the 17th century, was supposedly constructed on the twin principles of nation-state sovereignty and non-intervention. In the standard interpretation, the Treaty that ended the war in 1648 asserted the sovereignty of states against the Holy Roman Empire, and is thus a turning-point in the achievement of modern nations of national sovereignty (Bull, 1977; Boucher, 1998). Yet as Osiander (2001) points out, this interpretation is very wide of the mark. The Empire by this stage was more a symbolic rather than powerful actor. The war was not a conflict between the principles of Empire and national sovereignty but a jostling for power between European actors and an occasion for various states to seek aggrandisement in relation to each other.

Meanwhile the Treaty did not deal explicitly with sovereignty but with continuing relations between the Empire and European states. The political influence and the symbolic claims of the Holy Roman Empire as head of Christendom continued into the 18th century. The Empire had not been a state prior, during or after the War, and was not in the position to challenge the effective autonomy of nations. Such continuities, according to Osiander, were subsequently written out of history by the increasingly national focus used by historians of the 19th century. The turning-points in the more gradual shift in the direction of the modern system of sovereign states are rather the American and French Revolutions and industrialization. The former revolutions clarified notions of popular rights-based sovereignty linked with democracy as distinct from dynastic state sovereignty, while the latter process equipped nation-states with the resources to conduct expansive foreign policies, including Empires with a strongly economic rationale.

So over the next 300 years from 1648 to the establishment of the United Nations in 1945, the linking of sovereignty with non-intervention was more often an ideal rather than reality, as states continued to go to war with each other. Meanwhile on the economic front, markets and firms developed cross-border trans-national activities that by the 20th century were increasingly able to transcend national controls by states. By the second half of the 20th century, economic globalization was joined if not by political globalization, then by the re-structuring of political norms in international relations, whereby new forms of pooled sovereignty between states limit their individual sovereignty. This in turn has resulted in a variety of new forms of intervention in the affairs of particular states. Beck (2005) regards this process as a shift from a world order based on nation-states to a world order that has become cosmopolitanized, even while operating through groupings of nation-states. Added to this, however, is a sense in which moral responsibility has also been globalized through the elevation of human rights above such basic rights as existed within particular nations (Honneth, 1997). This was reflected in the Universal Declaration of Human Rights passed by the General Assembly of the United Nations in 1948.

This empirical chapter has begun with Kant's argument for cosmopolitanism, in part because such arguments lie behind attempts to develop cosmopolitanism in international relations, politics and law in the period since the late 18th century. In testing how far these developments have proceeded we are in a sense testing the plausibility of Kant's observations and presuppositions. Two key questions here are (a) the extent to which state sovereignty has been relaxed in the direction of cosmopolitan norms, and (b) the extent to which a transnational democratic politics of cosmopolitanism may be detected.

Cosmopolitan Governance

Governance according to cosmopolitan norms can be seen as a feature of both public and private law. In the public domain it may be associated both with international organizations like the United Nations, regional bodies like the European Union, and with individual nation-states both in their external and domestic policies – though the distinction between these two spheres has been largely overtaken under conditions of globalization. In private international law it may be seen in largely autonomous rules-based processes like *lex mercatoria* within which many trading disputes are privately resolved (Appelbaum *et al.*, 2001). Other examples of this kind of governance include debt-rating agencies that assess the risk inherent in different types of sovereign and corporate debt (Sassen, 1996) and processes of technical standardization and professional self-regulation (Teubner, 1997). Together with *lex mercatoria*, such legal processes occur, as Teubner points out, without the direct involvement of states. They remain invisible, unaccountable and thus, as Benhabib (2007: 257) observes, may more easily violate human rights. An example here is the suspension of human rights in special zones of economic and business privilege, as in the unregulated *maquiladoras* on the Mexico/US border and Central America.

The very distinction between public and private international law which has probably been exaggerated for a long while (Berman, 2004–5: 519–20) has been further problematized by globalization. Public and private activities may seem more sharply differentiated from the standpoint of cosmopolitan democracy and human rights, but in another sense have become profoundly embedded in each other. This is true both in the sense that economic globalization has made the functioning of markets the subject of new kinds of 'lighter' regulation, and in the sense that corporate activities have become the stuff of state to state relationships (Braithwaite and Drahos, 2000). Global governance now involves both public and private interests together, whether in the regulation of banking and finance, the lighter regulation of labour law or the favouring of corporate interests within intellectual property rights.

Against the background of connections between economic globalization and challenges to strong cosmopolitan standards, it is also worthwhile to investigate claims of progress toward cosmopolitan law in the light of the realist objection that nation-states remain the key players in international relations (Waltz, 1979; Morgenthau, 1992). This continuing and active presence for states may be true at the level of political capacity, but, as Berman (2004–5) points out, it may not be the case in relation to the normative principles, or institutional processes of regulation and standard-setting actually used in international relations. The robustness of nation-states as political actors is not necessarily a fatal objection to the idea that cosmopolitan governance is a significant empirical phenomenon, only to the idea that the form of cosmopolitan governance must necessarily be cast in terms of some supra-national world government. Even Kant felt that nation-states would remain key features of the institutional architecture of perpetual peace (see also Beck, 2006: 46).

In reviewing the scope for cosmopolitan law and democracy then, the task is to identify political and legal spaces between private economic globalization, on the one hand, and nation-state sovereignty on the other. In the remainder of the chapter, we look at evidence that sheds light on the scope, dynamics and limits of this space, drawing on evidence dealing with norms, attitudes and institutions.

War and Peace in Relation to Cosmopolitan Order

In a broad sense the continuing ubiquity of war between states suggests, at first sight, a strong limit on the scope of cosmopolitanism as 'perpetual peace'. Ethnic cleansing with which states collude as seen in Serb policies in Bosnia during the late 1980s and early 1990s, would also add to this sense of limits (Donia, 2006). Yet on the other hand, two important counter-arguments exist. The first observes that wars do not typically take place between liberal democracies (Doyle, 1983, 1986, 1993). The second is that the scope of cosmopolitan institutions is expanding, though not in a smooth uncontested 'ever onward and upward' curve.

The end of the Second World War, the Nuremburg trials, and the UN Universal Declaration of Human Rights of 1948 mark a significant cosmopolitan moment, where cosmopolitan ideals became institutionalized to practical effect. The case against the Nazi leaders invoked ideas of human rights in support of peace and justice, principles that stood above the rights of nation-states and their leaders to do what they liked free from intervention from other states. Winners in such post-conflict processes often cloak their own violent and often self-interested actions in ideals that may not seem enormously different to the actions of the defeated. However, even discounting for this, the appeal to human rights has since 1945 represented a cosmopolitan norm of widening trans-contextual significance (Cover, 1992: 199–201).

There are two inter-related aspects to this. The first is some sense of shift from international law, that is law between states assumed to be following their own national interests, to cosmopolitan law, based on some kind of supra-national norm. The second is the parallel extension of the actors recognized in law and global politics to include individuals alongside states.

As Berman (2004–5) points out, the processes whereby legal norms and processes have gone beyond the jurisdictionally bounded worlds of nation-state are manifold. Law has ceased to be seen purely as official rules and more as ways of imaging and constituting social relationships (*ibid*: 493–4). What is at stake here is not so much jurisdiction in a narrow territorial sense, but in its wider sense in Latin, namely to 'speak the law', captured in the term 'jurispersuasion'. This implicates culture and everyday life as much as formal and official procedures in courtrooms, parliaments and international organizations. While the latter are obvious and egregious, the former have often been largely invisible. Both are important in constituting law, and their effects need to be considered in an interactive manner within relations between states and civil society, rather than as separate influences. Berman also links this more sociological conception of law with processes of globalization. Here the emergence and diffusion of legal norms, as well as conflicts between them take place within cross-border relations within multi-level forms of governance reflecting the co-existence and inter-penetration of national, regional, and global regulatory regimes. This incorporates processes such as 'hybrid' models where international legal regimes such as that of the International Criminal Court can support local prosecutions (Concannon, 2000), and 'choice-of-law' models, where courts might draw from a wide set of norms developed in a number of jurisdictions (Dinwoodie, 2000). This of course requires a very widely drawn empirical research agenda.

One feature of the shift from international law to cosmopolitan world order, identified by both Beck (2006) and Fine (2007) is the increasing external intervention of sets of states, sometimes with UN blessing, into particular states where fundamental social breakdown and violence are so endemic as to be interpreted as violating human rights. Two examples may be cited. The first is the moral and financial pressure brought on the white racist South African regime, initiated by UN sanctions in 1962 – a struggle which the US government eventually joined – to effect fundamental constitutional change in the direction of citizenship rights for all (Beck, 2005: 67). The second is the so-called 'military humanism' of the 1999 intervention by NATO in Kosovo to prevent the genocide of Albanians by the Serbian state (*ibid*: 17, 40). Similar interventions elsewhere in Africa and the Middle East might also qualify under this heading insofar as defence and promotion of human rights are used as a justification.

The sense in which such activities might be seen as cosmopolitan is, however, somewhat controversial, as is their desirability. There are three major objections here. One is that such international ventures involve self-interested behaviour by nation-states, notably the US and Britain acting in an increasingly unilateral manner (Habermas, 2003), rather than according to some higher multilateral cosmopolitan purpose. The second is that the use of military force or even its threat is either un-cosmopolitan or at least morally dubious. The third is that notions of human rights used to justify such activities are a largely Western construction that downplays issues of obligation and community, felt outside the West, in favour of the social arrangements dominated by the rights of secular individuals. The net effect is to render ideas of ostensibly humanitarian military intervention as more ambivalent and equivocal products of complex and conflicting pressures (Fine, 2007: 82–3).

In relation to the first objection, Beck (2005) implies that such interventions may indeed display 'cosmopolitan' and self-serving 'national' elements. The existence of national self-interest does not however exclude the deployment of cosmopolitan rights-based norms. The implication that parties to influence or intervention may gain economically or strategically by so doing does not necessarily rule out the cosmopolitan significance of such events. Nonetheless a sense of balance is required here, since ethical cosmopolitanism would require that processes of intervention and longer-term forms of political restructuring meet the normative standards invoked as justification of involvement. Failure to observe Geneva Convention rules of war (as in the Guantanamo Bay torture camp) or the US removal of 'national personnel' in Iraq from the jurisdiction of the International Criminal Court are inconsistent with such norms. In this sense Beck (2005: 17) argues that an analytical distinction is necessary between false and genuine forms of cosmopolitanism. Here the attribution 'false' depends on a wide gap between ideals and reality, as in cases where cross-border intervention is a cloak for super-power pretensions. The examples Beck gives range from Stalin's 'false' internationalism within the Soviet-dominated Communist International, to contemporary US activity in the War on Terror.

Second, and closely related to this, the conjoining of cosmopolitanism with 'military humanism' is not easy to square with most senses of cosmopolitanism as a liberal-democratic philosophy. As Carenti (2006), has argued, Kant himself was deeply ambiguous as to whether states could make war on each other in the name of perpetual peace (*ibid*: 342). The dilemma here is how far illiberal measures are justified in pursuit of liberal ends. The standard argument here is to say that this would only be so where it would be a greater evil to do nothing.

Whatever positive justifications are used, Beck indicates that such action gives to cosmopolitanism a necessarily authoritarian character. This may however be required if the cosmopolitan ideals developed by Kant are ever to be implemented. Yet at what cost is this approach to be sustained? For Waltz (1959: 113), writing in the Cold War context, the spectre was raised of 'perpetual war for perpetual peace'. This spectre remains even within a post-Cold War context. Further problems also arise from the selectivity of the invocation and application of human rights, such that there are some state violations of rights which are pursued (e.g. in Sadam Hussein's Iraq) and others in a range of African, Asian and Middle Eastern settings which are not.

Third, there is the idea that human rights doctrines are skewed to Western perceptions and traditions and thus not universalistic in some transcendent sense, but rather post-colonial ways by which Western interests still seek to dominate the global order. This argument was made in the 1993 Bangkok Declaration by a number of Asian governments, including China, in the lead up to the 1993 UN World Conference on Human Rights held in Vienna. The claim was that purportedly universal human rights do not and should not take precedence over unique 'Asian' values and the national sovereignty of Asian countries.

Underlying such challenges is the philosophical question as to what exactly is human about human rights. For Bernard Williams (1995), this has two dimensions, the first pertaining to the human species, the second pertaining to conceptions of what qualities are regarded as human. While the first of these raises fascinating questions of the relationship between humans and other species around issues such as the value of bio-diversity (Maris, 2005), it is the second that has provoked more attention within mainstream debates on cosmopolitanism (Bohman, 2005). Are the qualities referred to when human rights are invoked primarily moral (e.g. respect for others' autonomy and dignity, or personal security) or political (e.g. democracy, freedom of speech and assembly), or do they extend beyond this to socio-cultural qualities (e.g. purported community values)? If so, does the idea of universal applicability to all members of the human species fall apart in a clamour of difference, or is it possible to think in terms of the human rights of different groups, such as women's human rights, which are somehow particular instances of a more generic principle?

How far then do these problems and objections weaken or render incoherent any sense of expanding cosmopolitanism?

The claim that human rights doctrines are not of universal validity and may reflect their Western origins is not, following the argument of this study, a fatal objection to purported examples of human rights cosmopolitanism. This is because it is an illusion to suppose that any kind of cosmopolitanism abstracted from time and place can exist except in the conceptual imagination. All cosmopolitanisms are then influenced by context in some sense, as well as requiring some basis of support in particular local or national settings to be sustainable. Yet having said this, it would indeed be a major empirical limit to the scope of cosmopolitanism if its key elements were to be so culturally specific to the West as to make them intrinsically foreign to other cultural contexts. To argue in this way would be to accept the theory of profound divides between civilizations evident in the Bangkok Declaration or regarded as a very real possibility in Huntington's (1996) 'clash of civilizations' thesis. While this kind of conflict is widely believed to be self-evident, this presumption is rarely tested with evidence.

A preliminary point that needs to be made here is that there are elements of self-serving special pleading on both sides of the political debate over human rights. Just as Western interests may benefit materially from the appeal to defence of human rights within interventions in non-Western countries, so too may authoritarian governments in Asia and Africa benefit by denial of the suitability of human rights to their own cultures, in terms of being better able to repress and destroy political dissent when human rights are absent. Such self-serving features apply even if states on either side of the debate feel they are acting for the best of motives, whether these be Western civilized values or authentic Asian values.

In any event the key question to be pursued further here concerns the idea of a civilizational divide with respect to cosmopolitan politics. A number of points may be made here. The first is that cosmopolitan doctrines of democracy and human rights were developed in elaborated form in classical Greece and Rome and subsequently with the European Enlightenment and subsequent commentaries on it. This current of thinking did not develop a sustained or universal long-term historical trajectory. To say this is not however to prove the civilizational divide thesis. To assume that it does is to make two further generally unexamined presumptions. The first is that political values and traditions are homogenous on either side of the divide. The second is that openings to cosmopolitanism are only to be found on the one side – the side of the West.

The first of these presumptions obscures vast differences within what are conventionally referred to as Western and non-Western civilizations. The 'West' has exhibited authoritarian as much as liberal-democratic values at many points in its history, while in Asia (and elsewhere) processes and episodes of public debate and pluralism exist alongside authoritarianism. Meanwhile the second presumption forecloses on the extent to which ethical and political modalities of cosmopolitanism are evident outside Europe and North America (conventionally referred to as the West). There are two further possibilities here. One is that certain cultural values in Asia and Africa generated practices and institutions that approximate to political and ethical forms of cosmopolitanism and did so prior to the Western impact. The other less ambitious claim is that such practices and institutions may at least be receptive to explicit cosmopolitan senses of rights and obligations even if not originating them.

The edited collection entitled *Human Rights and Chinese Values* (Davis, 1995), written in the immediate aftermath of the Bangkok Declaration, brings together a number of strands of argument relevant to these possibilities, at least in relation to China. While noting attempts to discern human rights values in traditional Asian cultures (Tai, 1988), more emphasis is given here to a more diffuse sense of openings and receptivity within Chinese political and ethical traditions to human rights ideas. Gangjian and Gang (1995), for example, argue that notions of benevolence and resistance within the work of Confucius and other scholars in the Confucian tradition are conducive rather than inimical to modern notions of human rights, human dignity, openness to dissent and constitutional government. These contrast with what they call the 'human rights nihilism' of the state.

Sen (2005), writing on India, identifies other kinds of openings in what he sees as the plural rather than unitary traditions of Asia. Critical of the homogenizing anti-democratic thrust of the Bangkok Declaration, Sen notes the widespread historical Asian discussions on politics and participatory government in Sanskrit, Pali, Arabic and Chinese – few of which seem to have been consulted in Euro-centric literature (*ibid*: 135). Public reasoning over political and ethical as well as religious questions has a long history in India, with some of the earliest open general meetings in the world organized by Buddhists (*ibid*: 15). He refers also to traditions of openness and tolerance among rulers such as Ashoka in the 3rd century BC and Akbar in the 16th century. It was the Buddhists also who did most to connect India with China in the first millennium AD.

In the case of Africa (like Asia a very diverse continent), much emphasis has been placed on traditions of communalism and how far these either inhibit or encourage a sense of outreach to others. Is communalism simply authoritarian or does it contain within it a stronger individualized ethical component (Mbiti, 1990; Njoroge and Bennars, 1986)? Some writers like Diawara (1998) give greater weight to the nexus between communalism and tribalism and hence look outside Africa for modernist inspiration. Others like Kigongo (2002) consider the possibility of synthesis between the ethical side of communalism, entailing responsibility for others, and imported ethical traditions, provided the latter are shorn of colonial pre-suppositions. 20th-century African socialism represents one example of synthesis. The actual impact of personalized notions of ethics from outside Africa is however seen as largely damaging to African traditions. Ake (1991) meanwhile points to historical evidence for democratic values as distinct from democratic institutions.

Drawing on historical evidence, Bhebe and Ranger (2001) argue for a more cautious position that is sceptical both of Western universalism that downplays African democratic traditions and what they call African relativism which overplays their democratic potential. They cite the work of Vansina (1991) on Central Africa both to warn against reducing African traditions to a unitary status and to warn of the difficulties (though not impossibilities) in reasoning from traditional notions of rights and forms of governance, on the one hand, to democracy and human rights on the other. Such traditions contain a tension between equality and the idea of government by the Big Man, which may lead in a range of directions, not simply to democracy.

What this evidence suggests is not cosmopolitan traditions in Asia and Africa similar to those developed by the Stoics and Kant. Rather the emphasis is on cultural openings outside the Western canon which provide some kind of fertile soil for political and ethical cosmopolitanism. Appiah (2006: 135) adds to this the point that it is not just that we have some things in common that matters in creating dialogue. It may sometimes be ways in which we are different that can be most salient, provided that we have a commitment to dialogue and, one might add, some kind of ethical interest in the fate of others as well as ourselves.

Such considerations suggest that arguments about profound civilizational divides may be exaggerated and misleading if they remain focussed solely on conflicts over colonization or religious fundamentalism. Such openings encourage a wider cross-cultural search for evidence of ethical and political cosmopolitanism than the conventional grand narrative of great European minds provides. Taking this into account the question remains as to how far political and ethical senses of cosmopolitanism are currently expanding. To answer this we turn to examine a range of institutions and networks.

Cosmopolitan Democracy in International, Regional and National Settings

Analyses of cosmopolitanism in law and politics focus on two broad issues. One is the significance of processes that somehow extend beyond bounded national or local political and cultural settings to trans-national or trans-contextual norms and relationships. The other involves assessment of the contemporary possibility of cosmopolitan democracy. In the discussion so far most emphasis has been given to the first of these, focussing on how the dynamics of inter-state relations are changing. The argument here is that the normative expansion of cosmopolitan ideals in international relations cannot be seen simply as the outcome of self-interested behaviour by states. It also requires some acknowledgement of jurispersuasion, including some explanation as to the new legitimacy of ideas of human rights. We have looked at some powerful objections to this process including its underestimation of the robustness of inter-state relations and its possible cultural skewing to Western cultural traditions. Neither of these, however, presents insurmountable obstacles to the normative reality of contemporary human rights cosmopolitanism.

At this point in the discussion it is important to bring the second of the two issues, namely cosmopolitan democracy, into the analysis. This is because the legitimacy of human rights is closely bound up with ideas about the necessity and desirability of creating a rights-based global polity characterized by greater openness, transparency and accountability to global opinion. This is very much in line with Kant's arguments that a cosmopolitan order of perpetual peace depends on some kind of informed consent by the peoples of the world. Its normative urgency is not simply a matter of the priority of peace over war, but also to do with the inability of states or markets by themselves to create stable systems of justice and economic security (Held, 2002: 317–21).

A bridge between these cosmopolitan principles and the actual world of international organizations was made in 2001 by the then European Commissioner for Trade, Pascal Lamy. In a speech on harnessing globalization for practical benefits, he argued that a greater emphasis was needed on reforming political institutions and processes (see Charnovitz, 2002: 299–300). Orthodox politics he felt was unable to achieve the needed reforms. These required new organizational forms to mediate between different economic and political interests and to reflect public opinion by linking with new cosmopolitan constituencies. The term cosmopolitics (*Weltordnungspolitik*) he felt captured this new requirement.

This argument is interesting for a number of reasons. First there is the vast expansion of international organizations over the last 150 years (Boli and Thomas, 1999), from the International Postal Union and International Red Cross to multinational companies like Microsoft and BHP Billiton, and such bodies as the World Bank and World Trade Organization, European Union and North American Free Trade Association, Amnesty International and Greenpeace. Long and complex scholarly debates have ensued as to how far this set of state and non-state organizations operate autonomously from nation-states and might therefore be seen as trans-national or cosmopolitan (Hirst and Thompson, 1996; Braithwaite and Drahos, 2000).

There is no general answer to this question of autonomy. What is clearer is a sense that however international or trans-national these organizations may be, there are no effective cross-border mechanisms of democracy by which they might be regulated. National constituencies are only represented indirectly in most of the organizations such as the World Bank that have nation-states as members. Even in the EU where representatives are elected to the European Parliament, it is unclear how far this body has effective control over policies which are largely determined by officials or by leaders of nation-states with little direct recourse to electorates. Meanwhile for private bodies, whether corporations or non-government organizations, there is, by their very nature, no direct elected democratic mandate. NGOs may enhance democratic discussion by adding voices from below to those of the powerful. Yet when an overall balance is struck, the verdict on this complex web of organizations is, by comparison with liberal nation-states, one of democratic deficit. The existence of this formal organizational deficit, which is simultaneously a deficit for cosmopolitan democracy, is the first reason why Lamy's argument is important.

A second reason for interest in cosmopolitics as a response to the global democracy deficit, is in relation to the uncertain state of international public opinion towards this plethora of international organizations. Widespread criticism of the United Nations as ineffectual, the World Bank as over-bearing and neo-colonialist, the European Union as bureaucratic, corporations as unethical profit-maximizers, and NGOs as unelected, raise doubts as to whether there is a pro-cosmopolitan public constituency. Perhaps the global media amplify the pervasive sense of international organizational failure that characterizes the contemporary world. Yet even if so, their messages fall on fertile soil and the reasons for this are ambivalent with respect to support for cosmopolitanism. Perceptions of failure might equally stem from cosmopolitan disappointment with lack of progress as from anti-cosmopolitanism. In the former case, it would be frustrated cosmopolitan dreams that fuel the litany of criticism as much as nationalist sentiment.

Cosmopolitanism and Public Opinion

One way of sustaining the former hypothesis is to examine evidence of public opinion. Norris (2000, 2006), drawing on systematic data from the 1990s up to and including 2005–6 collected by the World Values Survey, found trust and confidence in bodies like the UN involved the majority of the populations of the countries involved. In Norris (2000), reporting on the 1990s, the figure was 57%, with rather less support for regional bodies like the EU and NAFTA (44%) and lowest for one's own nation-state (34%). Such divergencies were widest for non-Communist countries and narrowest for the developing world. In Norris (2006), including data from 2005–6, the majority of countries reported support for the UN, though there were considerable variations in support (from 88% in Bangladesh to 13% in Morocco), as well as shifts over time in individual countries (*ibid*: 168–9).

This evidence is not consistent with some key elements in the litany of criticism approach, such as the idea of the UN as too remote or ineffectual. It also suggests that however nationalist people may or may not be, they are even more strongly critical of their own political leaders than the leaders of supra-national bodies. Nation and state in this sense are two different entities when it comes to attitudes. Yet while the evidence indicates that cosmopolitan attitudes, as measured by support for the UN, are quite high, there is no evidence that the level of support is on an upward trend. Rather levels fluctuate, often it appears in response to particular issues, crises and events (Norris, 2006: 11). In terms of specific issues, respondents were generally more positive towards the role the UN, plays in relation to refugees than human rights. In the latter case the role of national governments was often seen as more crucial. Whether the latter finding is evidence of nationalism or cosmopolitan realism or pragmatism is unclear.

In both studies the younger, urban and more educated were more likely to take a stance in favour of the UN than the less educated, rural and older generation. Interestingly the proportion of women supporting the UN was greater than men, possibly indicating a greater peace-orientation among women. Nonetheless, the particular historical context matters too, with post-communist countries struggling to effect a stable transition most committed to global and regional organization from which resource benefits were flowing at this time while national governments typically remained weak and ineffectual.

Similar data were not available for private organizations, but there are some data on attitudes to policy which shed at least indirect light on economic globalization. Here only around a third of the public supported free trade as such, with many supporting trade limitation to protect jobs. Immigration too was a concern with only 7% supporting completely open borders and the most popular options being support for strict limits (43%) or entry solely for those with jobs (37%) (Norris, 2000: 170). While political cosmopolitans were more likely to support open borders, such data suggest that positive attitudes to the UN are not inconsistent with only qualified support for openness. As we have seen throughout this study, a combination of cosmopolitan and national attitudes or concerns is not uncommon. Cosmopolitics, we may infer from this, may have some basis of mass support, but this is likely to be qualified, rather than unconditional and absolute.

A third reason for interest in cosmopolitics, though not one discussed by Lamy, arises from the uneven incidence of cosmopolitics across political organizational cultures. The attitude data discussed previously suggest that support for the UN over national political processes is higher in developed than developing countries where UN and national level politics scored similarly. The position in developing countries may be a post-colonial effect where loyalty to recently independent states is still strong even where delivery of social development is lacking. In any case the net effect may be that cosmopolitical advance or at least potential is indeed stronger in the West and possibly strongest in Europe, which Beck and Grande (2006) have singled out for particular attention. This controversial claim deserves greater critical attention.

Cosmopolitan Europe?

Europe may be seen both as a set of institutions and as a symbolic entity represented in terms of a long history and cultural continuity. Cosmopolitanism may be linked with one or both of these. Symbolically, the claim that cosmopolitanism is rooted in the liberal-democratic soil of the European Enlightenment is redolent of an older sense of cosmopolitanism as a universalistic moral philosophy, part of the civilizational legacy of the West to the rest of the world. Such purported universalism as we have seen in this study is untenable, as is the assumption that cosmopolitanism takes a single form deriving from one set of origins. So where does this leave the relationship with Europe?

Symbolically, it is certainly possible to imagine Europe as the historical and cultural home of many strands in normative conceptions of cosmopolitanism, providing the context for Christian cosmopolitanism, the Enlightenment and Kant's major contribution to thought and political action. To be sure, Europe is also simultaneously a collection of nation-states with their own senses of history and cultural identity and language. At this institutional level, nevertheless, there is plenty of evidence of Europeanization. This includes the establishment of the Council of Europe (1949), European Convention of Human Rights and Fundamental Freedoms (1950), European Community (1957), later European Union, with its Council of Ministers and European Parliament, the European Court (1959) and the European Court of Human Rights. A core cosmopolitan principle underlying these institutions is that European law takes precedence over national law in cases of conflict, and it is through European institutions that such conflicts are resolved. This gives the EU a clear supra-national character, even though it may not qualify as a state in terms of lack of independent revenue-raising powers.

Such supra-national institutions emerged after a half-century of European war that extended onto a global stage, and may in this sense be seen as an alternative to war in parallel with the United Nations. Yet the sense that supra-national co-operation between nation-states, whether in Europe or elsewhere, is unambiguously cosmopolitan is again problematic. While resting on an agreement to limit the national sovereignty of each participating nation-state, EU politics also has a strongly inter- rather than supra-national quality in which states retain considerable autonomy, giving regionalization the character of an alliance of the self-interested. This argument appears stronger if co-operation is not matched by a strong sense of European, as distinct from national, identity able to transcend sectional interests.

One manifestation of the persistence of competing national interests was the disarray following the December 2003 summit of the EU at which the adoption of a new European constitution was under discussion in the context of EU enlargement. Major difficulties arose because the European nation-states were unable to resolve conflicts over key issues such as national voting rights, foreign policy-making, budget deficits and whether reference to God should be included in the constitution. Such disagreements, together with some adverse national plebiscites, resulted in the shelving of a formal constitution.

As Kokaz (2005) notes, that such measures were even considered suggests how far processes of regional institution-building have gone. Yet their failure also suggests limits to the process, as well as to any arguments about the intrinsic commitment of governments in Europe to boundless projects for cosmopolitanism.

Against this, the existence of pro-European elites might be able to offset at least some of this self-interested sectionalism and create a more detectable trend towards a stronger sense of Europe. That such elites exist and have aims of this kind is revealed in Shore's (2000) work on Brussels policy-makers and senior administrators based on intensive fieldwork conducted during the 1990s. The implication as Delanty (2003: 476) points out is that cosmopolitan Europe is not a pre-formed cultural good handed down through the generations, but rather a possibility that might be created through policies and strategies for change. The difficulties though remain, namely that 'there is no European demos as such, [and] no common European language' (*ibid*).

Eder and Giesen (2001), in more optimistic vein, see in citizenship the possibility of a European foundation myth. Europe has never had centralized political unity, though it did develop unified nation-states in the modern period. European integration is nonetheless better seen not as the continuation of national state-building, but in terms of two alternative strands. One is 'a continuation of the self-organization of European society' where older cross-border models of the Church and Holy Roman Empire of the first millennium, based on a union of souls, are being replaced through the EU as a union of citizens (*ibid*: 263). The other scenario is a continuation of the cosmopolitan forces that produced the Enlightenment and modern science, but with a new widening emphasis on self-creating political activity within a widened democratic public sphere.

All this makes for a very interesting projection of Europe's historical sociology into the future. It is not however clear quite how it connects with cosmopolitanism or with observable social trends within institutions.

One of the main analytical problems in interpreting the scope and limitations of European cosmopolitanism is the prevalence of either/or thinking. Europe in this approach is either cosmopolitan or it is dominated by national interests and thinking. This way of putting the choice of perspectives rules out the possibility of the complex interpenetration of regional with national attitudes and institutions. Beck and Grande (2006), writing in support of the idea of cosmopolitan Europe, expand here on Beck's (2006) arguments on the outdated assumptions of methodological nationalism and the need for an analytical shift to methodological cosmopolitanism (see Chapter 4 above). Their argument is that nationally focussed approaches to institutional change in Europe misinterpret the robustness of national interests and feeling, by asserting these as the dominant realities. The 'national delusion' (*ibid*: 21–2) as they put it fails to see genuine evidence for supra-national changes and more importantly, the simultaneous integration and inter-dependency of regional and national institutions and processes.

Considerable conceptual ingenuity is required on their part to characterize this inter-dependency. In the first place, there is the problem of the grave weakness of cosmopolitan democracy in the EU. A European Parliament exists but exerts little real power. The Council of Ministers and the Commission of bureaucrats are far more powerful in determining policy, which itself tends to operate through technocratic mechanisms. This Beck and Grande refer to as 'deformed cosmopolitanism' (*ibid*: 5–6). Second, there is the problem of the complexity of institutional arrangements within the EU, in terms of multiple levels of political and legal power and authority. This they characterize in terms of the notion of empire (*ibid*: 50–93). This implies a bounded entity constituted through top-down supra-national politico-legal institutions that is not itself a nation-state nor a simple collection of such states. Nor is it an empire on the model of Hardt and Negri based on the affirmation of cultural differences within 'an effective apparatus of command' (2000: 200). It is seen rather as a post-Imperial empire founded on cosmopolitan 'openness', involving the 'creation and expansion of free space' (Beck and Grande, 2006: 71). Political openness here means openness to the overcoming of its supposed deformation, through enhancement of its democratic potential from below. All this is however rather more programmatic rather than secured through empirical analysis of social trends.

Beck and Grande have pursued a line of argument that is ingenious, but one suspects too charitable to the cosmopolitan character of Europe. While methodological cosmopolitanism does assist in interpreting the inter-penetration of complex political and legal scales, there is a strong suspicion that recourse to the device of Empire whisks away the reality of limits to cosmopolitanism through conceptual sleight of hand. Meanwhile the argument that deformation might be corrected by a larger dose of democratic politics from civil society seems grounded more in teleological hope than fine-grained analysis. The bureaucratic deformation of European cosmopolitanism, rather than a transitory stage in the historic struggle for democracy to be realized on a wider and wider political canvas, may rather be the typical institutional form that large-scale cosmopolitanism takes. This would also bring into question Beck's linkage between cosmopolitanism and a second reflexive stage of modernity (see Chapter 4).

Beck and Grande (2006), nonetheless, rightly focus on the problem of multiple scales of institutional activity within regionalization processes, including the global scale, alongside the local, national and regional. Regionalization in Europe and elsewhere, is clearly an important part of contemporary changes in global political arrangements alongside globalization and the robustness of the nation-states. The context is neither one of the withering of the nation-state, nor one of the unilateral dominance of the system of nation-states. It is rather one of multiple complex intersecting scales of social activity as recognized in Robertson's glocalization theory and Beck's conception of cosmopolitanization.

This phenomenon of multiple scales is nowhere more apparent than in Europe. Here the emergence of institutions like the EU is at once a response to economic globalization (especially that emanating from North America) in terms of promoting Europe's global competitiveness and a further stimulus to it (Rumford, 2002). European interests are a key part of global political and regulatory institutions, including NATO, the IMF, World Bank and WTO, as well as a host of standard-setting institutions (Braithwaite and Drahos, 2000).

But the EU and Council of Europe are also equally concerned with social cohesion within, both in terms of addressing regional inequalities and responding to the greater cultural diversity created by mass immigration into Europe. All of this creates interlocking scales of activity from the global arena, where the EU, its national members and organized interests participate in global economic, political and other regulatory institutions, to regional initiatives within Europe itself, which involve interaction between European institutions and nation-states, sub-national regions, and cities.

Another example of multiple scales of activity concerns questions of immigration, citizenship and social cohesion. Migration takes place both into the EU and within it. Immigration to the EU over the last three decades has been on a scale that has been seen by all policy makers as well as public opinion to require controls. The Schengen border controls to which a number of European states within and around the EU have signed up represent a restrictive regional means of engagement with global flows of people. Although free internal movement of citizens of EU countries is a regional policy objective, individual nation-states may choose to erect further controls on immigrants whether of non-EU or EU origin.

Processes of migrant settlement that lie beyond immediate intake also raise questions of social cohesion, and this leads to further questions about the relationship between citizenship, cosmopolitanism and multiculturalism. Each EU member has its own conceptions of what citizenship means as well as regulations regarding access to citizenship rights and obligations. These rules have in general become less restrictive over time by limiting citizenship criteria based on ethnicity or 'blood' (*ius sanguinis*) and building on some notion of territorial residence (*ius soli*). Whether the term multiculturalism is an analytically helpful way of describing these processes of inclusion of culturally diverse migrants is however debatable.

In a demographic sense multiculturalism might simply mean many cultures in the one setting, region, nation or city. In a policy sense, by contrast, the meanings of multiculturalism range from cultural preservation with cultures existing unchanged alongside each other, to a more dynamic regime of inter-cultural engagement within a core of shared democratic institutions. The former, it may be argued, is incompatible with cosmopolitanism, insofar as it privileges particular cultures within individual nation-states. Waldron (1995) takes this view in his discussion of political rights for cultural minorities. The reason these may not count as cosmopolitan is that they involve a 'thick' view of minority culture as a unified way of life, a position often associated with the idea of separate cultures as totalities that reflect 'natural' distinctions between different human groups. Policies which simply promote the preservation of such groups say nothing about engagement with cultural others, nor anything about different modalities of culture that may be unconnected with minority status or ethnicity, nor again anything about the possibility of multiple cultural affiliations.

Evidence discussed at a number of points in this study suggests that cultural life is not as unitary as this, whether for reasons of class, gender or religion. There is no tight fit between nation, territorial community and identity, while many who identify with nation or locality also identify with region or the world as a whole. Such evidence supports Waldron's argument that cosmopolitanism is more consistent with thinner views of culture which require no special public policies in favour of minority rights for cultural groups. Having said this there may be a cosmopolitan defence of human rights policies that have the consequence of protecting particular sets of victims of abuse. But this is however rather different from special rights for particular groups. Such considerations mean that political rights for minorities are not an unambiguous empirical indicator of the presence of cosmopolitanism.

Sub-national regional and urban scales of activity also matter in the complex institutional interactions of European cosmopolitanism. Vertovec (2006) demonstrates this in his case study of the inter-relationships between Council of Europe policies on cultural diversity and media cosmopolitanism in the city of Berlin. Having initially supported a 'liberal-culturalist' cultural rights perspective aimed at the preservation of immigrant cultures, the Council's position shifted in the late 1990s to support 'transverse' inter-cultural linkages between groups (*ibid*: 286). In terms of media policy this lent influential support to multicultural media in this 'inter-cultural' cosmopolitan sense.

In cosmopolitan Berlin, a city priding itself on world-openness (*Weltoffenheit*), and with support from federal German and city-based sources, radio SFB4 'Radio Multikulti' merged in the late 1990s as a media experiment in fostering cosmopolitanism of this kind. Vertovec measures its impact in terms of the integrative rather than assimilationist policies of the station, examples of inter-cultural programming and a significant share of the migrant listeners. Even so, it is not clear how far and to what effect this kind of broadcasting penetrates wider audience categories.

The general notion of multiple intersecting scales of political activity within Europe is a useful one, provided the scales are not regarded as fixed or given territorial entities. The reality has more flexibility and dynamism than this. One way of getting at this is through the idea of Europe as a network. Following Castells (1996), Europe may be seen as a polycentric network of flows of capital, labour and governance in which the transmission of information is crucial (Rumford, 2007). Network thinking has informed both information and information policy and has been linked with enhanced forms of European democracy (Prodi, 2001). This emphasis on networked scales may also be linked with a growing complexity of borders, creating a complex variable geometry of cosmopolitanism.

Complex Scales and Complex Borders

In parallel with such multiple intersecting scales of global, regional, national and local activities is a growing set of borders or frontiers between the various political and regulatory arrangements that constitute Europe. These are relevant to the assessment of the scope of European cosmopolitanism, because 'hard' borders might be seen as evidence of the limits of cosmopolitanism, whereas 'soft' borders might be more compatible with a greater openness even amidst the continuation of national and sub-national political institutions and identities (Rumford, 2007, 2008).

One thing is clear. In contrast to the much-touted predictions of a borderless world (Ohmae, 1990, 1995) or a world of liquid social relationships (Bauman, 2003), boundaries still matter, both within and around Europe (Delanty, 2006a). Yet they do not matter simply in hard form as territorial markers of sovereign nation-states. Processes of globalization and regionalization have not simply rendered many borders permeable, but have multiplied the types of borders that exist. In the case of Europe, as both Delanty (2006b) and Rumford (2007) indicate, borders now include: the border around the EU which is an extendable rather than fixed line, the rather wider Council of Europe politico-cultural border around 40 countries regarded as Europe, the boundaries around the Euro-zone and the Schengen immigration zone, neither of which include all EU members, as well as the national borders around each country which are now far softer as Europe-wide rights to personal, trading and financial mobility extend internally across countries. Rumford regards all the borders mentioned so far, bar the last, as 'cosmopolitan borders', in part because they operate at some kind of European rather than national level (*ibid*: 3). At the same time there remains considerable symbolic sensitivity to permeable borders, as in opposition to large immigration flows, concerns about free trade and anxieties about EU enlargement. Hard borders, meanwhile, have emerged in relation to attempts to forestall terrorism in the aftermath of 9/11. In this sense the position is rather contradictory with elements of cosmopolitan institutional 'soft' bordering at variance with symbolic anti-cosmopolitan 'hard' bordering.

Overall then cosmopolitanism and cosmopolitan democracy, where they exist, are situated within this ambivalent complex of scales and the bounded political spaces they generate. These are ambivalent on the question of cosmopolitanism because institutional evolution does not match popular symbolic concerns. This is not immediately apparent from Beck's ringing declaration that the EU represents 'institutionalized cosmopolitanism' (Beck, 2006: 141), though he does somewhat grudgingly recognize Europe is also home to 'anti-cosmopolitanism' even if this is then dismissed as resting on 'a clinical loss of reality' (*ibid*: 117). Use of the term 'clinical' is somewhat disturbing here in that opposition to cosmopolitanism seems to be regarded as a political pathology, rather than a legitimate political option.

Moving on from the discussion of cosmopolitanism and Europe, attention turns finally to questions of cosmopolitan political activism on a global stage.

Trans-national Politics and a Cosmopolitan Public Sphere

What evidence might be drawn on to explore the sense in which a cosmopolitan public sphere may have been created? In Kant's world this depended very much on a reading public and the inter-connected world of letters and public debate involving networks of the educated and politically engaged. While this was in many respects a bourgeois and liberal aristocratic world, it is clear from the work of social historians like E.P. Thompson (1963) that movements of radical thought and action drew on wider sources of popular involvement from below. It is therefore important in any account of public spheres – then and now – to avoid stereotypical class characterizations that downplay popular sources of cosmopolitan awareness and action.

Since Kant's time, processes such as the growth of literacy, mass education, knowledge-based employment, increased low-cost opportunities for geographical mobility, together with mass communications media, have done much to encourage cosmopolitanism as well as influence the cultural and institutional forms which the cosmopolitan sphere might take. One widely used expression for this sphere is that of global civil society, comprised in part at least of cross-border networks (both virtual and inter-personal) of political activists. These include movements for human rights and for global environmental sustainability, which are between them the two major cosmopolitanizing forces within world public opinion. As Honneth (1997: 175) points out, 'there is hardly any region in the world that does not have church associations, scattered intellectual groups, and organised international groups calling for political support from the outside to help in the struggle for human rights'. Other bodies of scholarship have charted in great depth the movements and networks of advocates of global change both at the organizational level of bodies like Amnesty International and Greenpeace, and more informal networks of opinion and action (Keck and Sikkink, 1998; Trubek, Mosher and Rothstein, 2000; Rodrigues, 2004). Such bodies express, promote and re-formulate cosmopolitan norms, pressurize governments and international organizations to implement them, and monitor and evaluate subsequent actions and inactions. Environmental protection movements are an integral part of this world.

The Example of Environmental Crisis

Environmental crisis response features as a distinct item within Beck's original (2000, 2002a) empirical research agenda for cosmopolitanism.

Connections between environmentalism and cosmopolitanism may operate at several levels. First environmental issues such as global warming or pollution are cross-border, affecting the planet as a whole rather than in individual nations, and hence require cross-border political responses. Second environmental values, such as biodiversity or ecological sustainability, are oriented to humanity rather than a sub-set of the world's population. These are simultaneously environmental and cosmopolitan, a connection developed through ideas of environmental citizenship (Jelin, 2000) which, like human rights, apply to the world's citizens.

What then can be said about the empirical scope and impact of environmentalist movements? The mere presence of such movements is striking at the level of political activism, but what of their influence? If Beck and Grande are right that a new more democratic cosmopolitan Europe could emerge through the participation of civil society alongside 'the state and supranational actors' (2006: 157), then how detectable is movement toward such an outcome?

A considerable body of research has come to the conclusion that environmental NGOs have played a significant part in changing global agenda on environmentalism, influencing debate, the terms of agreements, and that key roles continue in monitoring and evaluation of environmental regulation. Keohane, Haas, and Levy (1993) and Caldwell (1988) emphasize their impact on policy change, while Braithwaite and Drahos (2000) provide a range of examples where NGO-based models for regulation have been taken up in the construction of regulatory regimes. In the 1990s, they note that both Greenpeace and the World Wildlife Fund had larger budgets than the United Nations Environment Programme (UNEP) (*ibid*: 272). This does not mean that NGOs are always the major players, since nation-states like the US and corporate interests, individually or in alliance with each other have succeeded, either in opposing change (see the US position on the Kyoto Protocol on global warming), or in influencing the ways in which change is organized (see the role of business lobbies in seeking market-based approaches to sustainability).

Maris' (2005) work on the Convention on Biodiversity, elaborated at the Rio Earth Summit in 1992, is a useful contribution to an analysis of cosmopolitan discourse on the environment even amidst the largely interest-based negotiations over the Convention involving nation-states and business lobbies. Rather than interpreting such deliberations in mutually exclusive terms as either processes dominated by nation-state *realpolitik* or as outpourings of cosmopolitan environmental values, Maris sees both as irreducibly present. This position offers discursive and institutional evidence in support of cosmopolitan impact, while also showing its limits in terms of hard-nosed bargaining conducted in the name of national interest.

There are however two strong cautionary notes that need to be made about the use of global civil society evidence to enhance arguments linking global public opinion with cosmopolitanism. One is the problem of cross-national incivility. As John Keane (2003) has pointed out, many components of civil society are racist or fundamentalist in temper, which involves the creating of barriers rather than cosmopolitan bridges between themselves and others. Hate rather than love of humanity constitute the worlds of such movements. A second problem is that even those political activists who aim to create a positive bridge to others through campaigns of global outreach act from moral and normative concerns rather than in most cases with the legitimization of election in a democratic forum.

Being unelected in a representative sense is not of course the only measure of democracy. If it were, then all pressure and interest groups, including powerful corporate lobbies, should be included as unelected groupings alongside human rights and environmental activists. Democracy, however, includes public deliberation of issues, beyond formal political institutions, and it is in this deliberative sense that the term democratic may be applied to activists and any other interest prepared to engage in debate as distinct from clandestine or unaccountably private modes of operation.

Earlier in this chapter, reference was made to Bohman's distinction between cosmopolitan justice and cosmopolitan democracy. The possibility was raised that the achievement of cosmopolitan justice may not require representative democratic procedures at a global level, processes which currently do not exist. In their absence, justice may better be achieved by other kinds of pressure on elites and parliamentary representatives (or perhaps a combination of such pressures with national electoral activity). Moral pressure and direct action are two weapons in the activist armoury that have assisted in effecting change in political agendas on human rights and especially environmentalism, without global democracy at an institutional level. In one sense such processes may be regarded as successful examples of cosmopolitan justice without cosmopolitan democracy. In another more deliberative sense, however, they may equally be regarded as combining cosmopolitan justice with cosmopolitan democracy. Even when this is recognized, there clearly remain very significant limits to the scope of cosmopolitan democracy.

Conclusion

In this second empirical chapter, political and legal measures of cosmopolitanism have been scrutinized. A number of substantive findings have emerged. The first is is that cosmopolitan norms have grown in legal and political importance since 1945. Their impact has been greatest in the human rights and environmental areas, and also arguably so in areas of cross-border business regulation which are not conventionally associated with cosmopolitanism. It is somewhat harder to assess the impact of cosmopolitanism in the sphere of war and peace, since recent military interventions in ostensible support of human rights are more ambiguous as an indicator of cosmopolitanism. Across this range of examples, cosmopolitanism has been seen as taking a variety of forms, rather than being the simple implementation of liberal-democratic values. They include initiatives from above as well as below, organized through pressure on elites as much as democratic politics.

Second, there is significant though not overwhelming public support for cosmopolitan political objectives and institutions, as measured by support for the UN in a number of areas, such as support for refugee populations. European regionalization has also received a degree of mass support, though being very far from constant across time. Set against this, areas of ambiguity of support, as well as outright opposition to supra-national institutions remain very important. Ambiguity is reflected in the situated character of cosmopolitan attitudes, which are often combined with more local or national allegiances, a point to be explored further in the case study of Ireland in the next chapter. It may also be a product of cosmopolitan disappointment with institutional failures, as in the case of much UN peace-keeping. Opposition is reflected in introverted forms of nationalism, and continuing support for strong borders around national territories, exacerbated by the recent shift to greater security concerns under the impact of terrorism.

Third, political and legal dimensions of cosmopolitanism are set within a complex set of interacting global, regional, national and local scales of activity and identity. As emphasized throughout this study, cosmopolitanism in its various modalities is typically situated in time and space, rather than a free-floating abstract universalism. This affects how political and legal evidence is interpreted. While the nation-state and political borders still matter, their continuing existence cannot be regarded as setting an absolute limit to cosmopolitanism. Rather evidence must be carefully sifted, as in the attitude data reported above, to assess ways in which the cosmopolitan and the local, the global and national, may sometimes be combined. To achieve analytical balance, however, it is important to avoid privileging evidence of cosmopolitanism, as if it were an inexorable trend. Beck's research agenda for cosmopolitanism, is very important, but his preference for methodological cosmopolitanism runs the risk of identifying the cosmopolitan scale as somehow more significant than other scales.

Fourth, the most significant limit to cosmopolitanism, identified in this chapter, is not lack of normative prominence, cultural opposition outside the West or absence of popular support, but rather institutional implementation at a global level. The networks and activists of global civil society may well be invoked as an indicator of greater deliberative democracy but in a representative sense, the highest scale that democratic cosmopolitanism has reached is the regional (i.e. European-level) and its articulation here is not strong. This raises the paradox that cosmopolitan justice may have emerged without cosmopolitan democracy and may thus be more dependent on elites and unelected activists than global democratic consensus.

7

Cosmopolitanism in Ireland

This chapter provides a case study of cosmopolitanism in relation to a single country: Ireland. The aim here is to explore many of the themes discussed previously in the book in more depth. It is of course a contradiction in terms to regard cosmopolitanism as operating within single nation-states, so the emphasis remains one of connections between global and local, regional and national scales of activity across a range of economic, cultural and political settings.

The Republic of Ireland has social characteristics which make it an interesting though somewhat paradoxical choice for a case study. Firstly it is a very small country with a population of around four million. Yet it is one that is well-known around the world, whether for its writers and poets, for products like Guinness, performers like U2 and Bob Geldof, as a tourist destination, and as part of the globally well-promoted English-speaking world, linked as it is with the United States, Canada and Australia, as well as Great Britain.

Ireland in fact ranks very high on measures of globalization. In the *Foreign Affairs* index it has recently been ranked either the most globalized or in the top five globalized countries. This reflects high levels of inward capital investment and labour mobility as well as economic deregulation during the fifteen years or so of the boom-time Celtic Tiger economic expansion. On the other hand, a strong sense of Irish cultural identity remains important, linked with nationalism and localism. This has been influenced, in part at least, by the historical legacy of a bitter war of independence against the United Kingdom, and by the creation of powerful nation-building institutions around church, education and sport. Meanwhile within the partitioned island of Ireland, conflicts in the North over the Union with Britain and preferred forms of local and regional government have also to be taken into account, whether as examples of intractable national and local conflicts or more recently as processes amenable to inter-cultural reconciliation. These are just a few of the important shifting indicators of paradox, when one begins the analysis of cosmopolitanism in Ireland.

Another instance of paradox occurs in the sphere of consumption and in particular consumer brands. Here worldwide brands such as Guinness and Jameson whisky, together with cultural products such as Michael Flatley's *Riverdance*, have a global cross-border and cross-cultural appeal, while also evoking seemingly localized images of Celtic Ireland (Kuhling and Keohane, 2007). Such phenomena clearly relate to the field of cosmopolitan consumption discussed in Chapter 2. But they also raise once again questions about the relative merits of the key concepts cosmopolitanization and glocalization as a way of making sense of paradox.

One possible explanation of paradox is that the elements that seem to be in tension are mutually connected, the one being a reaction to the other, prompting renewed tension. At least part of the contemporary revival of nationalism (Holton, 1998; Mann, 1993, 1997) may, for example, be a reaction to globalization, while cosmopolitanism in its turn may be a reaction to the seeming intractability of terror and violence caused by warfare justified in ethno-cultural terms as much as conversion to ideas of human rights. These general considerations may apply anywhere. What is striking in Ireland is both the immense importance of historical memory to the present, and the rapidity of recent social change, reflected in economic growth rates in excess of 10% per annum for around ten years beginning in the early 1990s. The contemporary co-existence of the two requires some considerable sifting of evidence to establish quite how they are connected, how far in tension, and with what implications for cosmopolitanism. Why then does history matter?

Historical Themes

A major argument in this study has been the importance of a historical approach to the analysis of cosmopolitanism. This is both because cosmopolitanism has a long history and because some influential theories, notably those associated with Ulrich Beck (2002a, 2005, 2006), advance strong propositions about cosmopolitanism and phases in the development of modernity. Within the case of Ireland, three important historical elements are: first the relationship with European Christendom, second the troubled and complex relationship with the English state and later British Empire, and third processes of Irish emigration and the creation of diasporas.

Well before the modern period, as indicated in Chapter 3, cosmopolitanism was connected with both religion and Empire. The religious connection operated for most of the last 1,500 years in terms of

Catholicism. Christianity, apparently brought to Ireland by St Patrick in the 5th century, subsequently saw in the next few centuries a flowering of Irish Christianity and its re-export to Europe. Mobilities within European Christendom by the 17th century saw many Irish priests trained within Irish colleges in Europe, while in the 19th century a reverse flow saw European religious orders establish many schools, hospitals and orphanages in Ireland (Inglis, 2008: 91–3). By the late 19th century, Irish Catholics, inspired in part by French missionary activity, had begun to play a larger missionary role both to Irish migrants in Europe and North America, and further afield within the British Empire (Hogan, 1990: 60–1). It has been estimated, for example, that around 10% of missionaries in Africa (both Catholic and Protestant) were Irish (Murphy, 2000: 526).

In what senses then does involvement in an outward-looking religious venture conducted worldwide in a myriad of local settings qualify as cosmopolitanism? One kind of answer connects religious and imperial types of cosmopolitanism, in that missionaries in Africa, South East Asia and parts of South America were part of a Western-izing mission centred on education as much as pastoral care and the saving of souls. Such processes may have created negative images of dour and aloof colonists who refused to learn the languages of indigenous people (Hogan, 1990: 8), but they nonetheless gave access to education, including education for girls (Inglis, 2008: 92). This is neither equivalent to 20th-century human rights cosmopolitanism, nor practical egalitarianism, which stands at variance with the private wealth of and social stratification within the Church. However the egalitarian religious message of equality before God has been a stimulus to cosmopolitan world-views and social movements in the contemporary world.

There remains, nonetheless, a problem of weighing global and local elements in the balance, in the case of religion as much as other political and cultural phenomena analysed in this study. While both the imagined space and institutional operations of world religions are clearly global, this has not inhibited a close nexus with very localized as well as national spheres of activity and operation. In the case of Ireland, the Catholic Church, was associated in a very practical way with the construction of Irish institutions including schools, hospitals and orphanages across the 19th and most of the 20th centuries. This contributed to a sense of cultural distinctiveness and confidence in contrast to primarily Anglo-Irish Protestant landowners and officials who organized British rule. Meanwhile at the parish level, as Inglis (1998) has shown, priests worked very closely with all elements of the community, men and women, young and old, helping to foster disciplined communal ties in the face of poverty, shortage of available land and urban decay. None of this is intrinsically cosmopolitanism. And yet the Church, because of its co-presence among Irish emigrants in North America and Australia, was also in a sense a trans-local cement for the Catholic Irish diaspora.

The historical impact of Empire and the British connection (with which religion and emigration are closely linked), is of major significance. This has a number of elements. First colonization meant political and cultural domination of the Irish including the dispossession of the traditional Catholic Irish ruling class, economic priorities including land re-distribution favouring British and Anglo-Irish interests. Second, this did not prevent significant elements of agricultural modernization from the 17th century onwards as sections of Irish agriculture were integrated into international markets and food-processing industries like brewing expanded (Tovey and Share, 2003: 52–3). A good deal of Irish agriculture modernized even if peasant farming was also widespread.

A third major historical issue connecting Empire and Irish development is the tragic and traumatic Irish Famine of the 1840s when large numbers died after the failure of the potato crop and many others left the country to find a better life. While emigration and a slowing of rates of population growth are evident before the Famine (Foster, 1988), the net effect of increased mortality, morbidity, and continuing emigration led to Ireland alone of European countries having a declining and then static population for over a hundred years. There remains on-going controversy as to how far to emphasize British culpability in mass starvation and death in the aftermath of failure in the potato harvest (Foster, 1988; Ó Gráda, 1999; Haines, 2004). Nonetheless this event has thereafter functioned symbolically as a dire consequence of colonial rule and the need to overcome it.

If Empire, like free trade globalization of today, has encouraged nationalist reaction, it has simultaneously encouraged some kind of shift towards cosmopolitanism in a number of senses. First it involved the Irish in the apparatus of Imperial power, whether as soldiers, pioneering settlers, or professionals, such as doctors and teachers. In this sense the Irish were beneficiaries as well as victims of colonization. While in the sphere of education and letters, Irish writers and intellectuals contributed to European processes of debate around the time of Enlightenment and Romanticism, and subsequently through the English-speaking world throughout the 19th and 20th centuries. James Joyce famously left Ireland in the early 20th century for exile in Europe, critical both of colonial domination and what he saw as repressive features of Irish culture.

Second, and partly overlaid on this intellectual dynamic, is the importance of Irish migration and the creation of Irish diaspora, evident both in Britain and its Empire and in the US. 'Emigration' as Foster (1988: 345), puts it, 'is the great fact of Irish social history from the early nineteenth century'. Between 1801 and 1921 when Ireland became independent, around eight million people emigrated, a far higher rate of outward movement than any other European country. Prior to the Famine, Britain was the primary destination, with large numbers of Irish moving to cities like London and Manchester with opportunities opened up by industrialization. After the Famine, the US and Canada took the lion's share, which contrary to stereotypes was almost equally divided between Catholics and Protestants (Inglis, 2008: 90). Significant numbers also left for Australia. After independence, with US immigration restrictions, Britain became the leading destination once more.

Empire and migration were connected in a number of positive and negative senses. Empire was both a source of opportunity and a structure of domination, from which escape was desired. But migration, outward and now inward, is a larger issue than Empire. This is partly through the forging of strong connections between Ireland and the US, an earlier example of republican independence. Although new forms of racial hostility were encountered in the US, where Irish fought to be regarded as 'whites' rather than 'blacks' (Ignatiev, 1995), over time recognition and upward social mobility was achieved. This was symbolized in the mid-20th century in the election of John F. Kennedy, from an Irish-American background to be the first Catholic president of the United States. The US connection also took other forms, including Irish involvement in working-class 'internationalism', with James Connolly, the trade union militant and participant in the Irish Rising of 1916 working in the US as an organizer for the syndicalist Industrial Workers of the World (IWW).

The advent of the Irish Free State in 1921 and complete independence by the 1930s severed political and legal ties with Empire. This helped but did not guarantee greater national autonomy in building a new nation-state. The new Irish state which emerged was in the first instance economically protectionist, culturally conservative and largely inward-looking. The spiritual vision of a rural 'Celtic' Ireland projected by its major political leader Eamon de Valera (born in the US, but taken back to Ireland as a young child), combined with economic and social protectionism, the latter guided by an austere puritanical Church. Censorship through the banning of many books and later films, together with strict control of sexuality and personal life, was a strong feature of the period until the last third of the 20th century. This climate encouraged a number of writers and intellectuals, such as Samuel Beckett (Cronin, 1997), to leave for cosmopolitan London or Paris, where career opportunities were in any case greater than in Ireland.

Research on Irish literature has noted the importance of the theme of wandering in the early 20th-century work of Joyce, W.B. Yeats, Lady Gregory and Synge (Rickard, 2001). This is taken to be a metaphor for Irishness, but one that is ambivalent, in that the wanderer, while identifying with Ireland, cannot find a resting place within it. However while Yeats and Synge associated Irishness with rural life, Joyce saw this connection as facile. Through alternative notions of wandering, as Rickard (*ibid*: 83), puts it, he sets out using the notion 'as a negative expression for paralysed Irishness', but ends with wandering being 'a positive sign of fluid identity and hybridity'. Within his work there is an Irish Joyce, but also a French Joyce, an Italian Joyce, and thus a European Joyce.

Such themes may be connected with ambivalence to the British connection, which render the Irish as both colonized in Ireland and part of the colonizing power externally (Valente, 1996). These give a hybrid character to what might be called the cosmopolitan element in his work. For Walkowitz (2006: 56), it is the tension in his work between the fixed everyday experiences, pleasures and objects of ordinary 'Irish' life, and the more transient 'cosmopolitan' emphasis on fluidity and rejection of conventions that matters most. She also notes that offensive aspects of his work were rightly interpreted by critics as directed at the pieties of national literary traditions, such as those associated with the late 19th- and early 20th-century Irish cultural revival.

Walkowitz also argues that the national and the cosmopolitan are brought together in Joyce. He wanted Ireland to have political and cultural self-determination so that its culture may change and diversify and thereby become less rather than more distinct. Other linkages between nation and the world beyond are evident in art. Herrero (2007), in her study of the making of modern art collections in Ireland, notes how in the early 20th century a positive intellectual reception was given by many to French impressionism (48–9). This was seen by some as a stimulus to the emergence of a distinct Irish school rather than a dilution of national artistic integrity.

It would be simplistic and inaccurate, therefore, to argue that the emergence of a more autonomous *and* more outward-looking society in Ireland occurred only from the 1960s onward. While the nationalist mobilizations that led to the Free State in the early 1920s and the subsequent decades of state-building represented a certain turn inwards, this was never absolute. Irish foreign policy and Irish migration provided bridges to the world beyond. Having said this the period from the 1960s is significant for a greater rapidity of economic and social change

(Tovey and Share, 2003). Change occurred during this period from a combination of (a) opportunities such as inward foreign investment created by economic globalization, coupled with (b) a more outward economically liberal policy revolution, accelerated by the urgent need to respond to deep financial crises in Ireland during the late 1980s, together with (c) re-distributive EU regional policies. These did much to prompt the radical economic revival known as the Celtic Tiger phenomenon of the 1990s, characterized by high rates of economic growth, the development of new industries in information technology and pharmaceuticals, and improved living standards (Fitzgerald, 2000), together with the onset of rapid immigration.

Immigration is now a major feature of contemporary Ireland. Between 1995 and 2004, Ireland experienced a net inflow of around 225,000 people bringing population levels back to four million for the first time since 1871 (Crowley, Gilmartin and Kitchin, 2006). While around 40% of these were returning members of the Irish diaspora, the remainder represent a culturally diverse pattern, with significant non-EU flows, including asylum seekers from Nigeria, Somalia, and Rumania. This new pattern brings Ireland more into line with the experience of other Western countries, but also brings with it similar challenges for social cohesion and the inclusion of incomers in the face of a certain degree of hostility from elements within the existing Irish population. How these challenges are met will reveal how far Ireland has developed a cosmopolitan polity and cultural framework.

A final aspect of the historical legacy, again with very recent ramifications, affects community relations between Catholic Nationalists and Protestant Unionists in the North. The legacies here of the original planting of a Protestant, largely Presbyterian, population in Northern counties during the 17th century, and subsequent discrimination against Catholics, together with partition in 1921 to protect the Unionist minority and the IRA campaign for re-unification provide a good deal of the backdrop to recent politico-cultural conflicts over the last 40 years. The shift from incipient civil war to the Good Friday peace process represents a further dimension to cosmopolitan trends in contemporary Ireland, requiring further scrutiny below.

Cosmopolitanism and Ireland: Some Contemporary Indicators

How far does contemporary Ireland display cosmopolitan characteristics, and what kind of evidence is there to determine reliable answers to this sort of question? In line with the general approach of this book, this question demands a multidimensional approach to cosmopolitanism which takes in economic and social as well as political and cultural indicators. It is also important to emphasize limits to cosmopolitanism as well as its scope. This question, as we have seen, needs to be approached cautiously, because one cannot treat cosmopolitan and national or local attitudes and orientations as mutually exclusive. Forms of national affiliation and cultural particularity may vary in their relations with others, from racist exclusion at one end of the spectrum to cosmopolitan hospitality and cultural inclusion on the other. Between the two ends, one may often find glocal features that partake of the global and the national. This not only reflects the variability of national/local orientations and institutions, but also the point that cosmopolitanism, in spite of its outward-looking stance, always has roots in time and across space.

There is another important distinction that needs to be made at the outset. This is between cosmopolitanism as a feature of Irish society, and cosmopolitan approaches by others towards Ireland. Put another way, the distinction is between Ireland as perceived by others, and Ireland as a lived experience for its inhabitants. While others may perceive Ireland as more or less cosmopolitan than it really is, residents of Ireland may equally find themselves repelled by or attracted to the various images of Ireland that are available. In pursuing this distinction, attention turns first of all to cosmopolitanism and consumption.

Ireland and the Consumption of Global Commodities

Two recent studies of contemporary Ireland by Kuhling and Keohane (2007) and Inglis (2008) both emphasize the significance of consumption for Irish identity and its relationship with globalization. The economic boom of the Celtic Tiger has not done away with social inequalities within Ireland (Allen, 2000), but it has created increases in incomes and new consumption patterns. This has helped Ireland move beyond the economic austerity and social disciplines of the post-independence period, but in so doing the power of the Church and traditional cultural controls over individualism and materialism have weakened. The Irish, one might say, have become a nation of consumers, very much like other particular segments of the globalized economy. In this sense lived experience is no longer of a rural society close to the rhythms of the land, drinking in the local pub, and singing traditional music.

This mythical sense of Irishness has in a sense never been the complete picture, given high historic levels of emigration as well as the formation of Irish cities and an urban class structure. Emigration, as Inglis points out (*ibid*: 86), gave the Irish the reputation of a world-leading and successful diaspora. This was reflected in the jubilant visit of President John F. Kennedy back to Ireland in July 1963. His comments on Ireland cited by Inglis (*ibid*: 87) are very interesting because they are far more than a recognition of the Kennedy family's roots. It is rather Ireland's achievements in the world that matter. 'No larger nation did more to keep Christianity and Western culture alive in their darkest centuries. No larger nation did more to spark independence in America and around the world. And no larger nation has ever provided the world with more literary and artistic genius.'

The comments, whether or not they are soundly based analytically, indicate a kind of cosmopolitan reputation for Ireland. This takes the form of an outward-looking orientation to the world, even while founded on a particular and distinctive nation. They fuse the global with the national, the cosmopolitan with the particular. But they are comments from a 'sympathetic' outsider looking in, dressed up in heroic language. They still matter in spite of this, in part because there are far more people with an Irish background living outside Ireland than within it. Some diasporic activities, as we have seen earlier in this study, seem rather introverted. The Irish case, in this respect, seems rather more outward. This is summed up in another speech cited by Inglis (*ibid*: 92), made in the US by the Irish President Mary McAleese, in which she describes the Irish as a 'connecting people. It is our strength, and our global Irish family is today one of our greatest resources, feeding our culture, expanding its imagination, opening doors, and keeping faith with our intriguing homeland'.

Ireland then has a symbolic identity, which is as much the property of the diaspora as those who live in Ireland. The construction of identity, in the two examples cited, also has outward-looking components at variance with rural stereotypes. Kuhling and Keohane (2007) take the analysis of symbols further into the specific arena of the selling of commodities. They look in detail at the branding of Irish identity in three major brands, Ballygowan mineral water, Guinness stout, and Jameson whisky. One theme here, in Ballygowan advertising campaigns between 2002–4 and some Guinness campaigns, does indeed evoke idealized images of a pure authentic natural rural Ireland unmarked by time. Other Guinness ads evoke the sociability of drinkers in pubs, reflecting broader community-like characteristics of friendliness, honesty, and native charm (*ibid*: 80–1). None of the advertisements in such genres depict Ireland's recent non-white migrants, and many suggest localized ideals that have no place for global modernity.

More recently, however, Kuhling and Keohane (*ibid*: 82–5) note the appearance of representations of what they term cosmopolitan Ireland, using images that move beyond nostalgia. Examples include the Ballygowan 'Bodies Never Lie' campaign which featured a variety of dance forms – ballet and hip-hop – as well as individuals from recognizably different ethnic groups. Another case features the Jameson 'Beyond the Obvious' campaign which used images of culturally specific individuals performing activities that challenged ethnic and other cultural stereotypes. These included a mixed-race man with dreadlocks playing the harp – an Irish symbol – and an elderly Chinese playing a drum kit loudly and vigorously. These images not only draw on a wider set of cultural images, but also challenge binary stereotypes of Irish/non-Irish, white/non-white.

There is of course no necessary or neat fit between the products of advertising images and the attitudes and worlds of those who consume images. Kuhling and Keohane do not indicate how far this array of images do in fact represent Irish attitudes and sustain a sense of development beyond traditional stereotypes of Irish ways of life towards a more multicultural awareness and acceptance of differences.

Cultural indicators of this kind are not of course indicators of politico-legal and what have been termed 'emancipatory' forms of cosmopolitanism, but they begin to suggest a sense of contemporary cultural change that bears on the assessment of cosmopolitanism in Ireland. While it is an ahistorical myth to depict Ireland as an introverted traditional society that only began to move outward in the late 20th century, most commentators recognize the 1970s and 1980s as crucial for processes of cultural change.

One important element of this was the coming of television and a greater opening up to political and cultural influences beyond Church and State. Ireland at this time still has significant elements of social restriction such as banning of the sale of contraceptives and of cultural products such as Joseph Strick's film of the life of James Joyce, deemed to be too salacious. Until 1973, the Gaelic Athletic Association (GAA), guardian of Ireland's distinctive national sports, hurling and Irish football, would not allow members to play other sports such as soccer (Inglis, 2008: 23). Cultural change was reflected in a new openness and a shift away from the Church's previous moral monopoly over so many matters of personal and family life (Inglis, 1998).

Trans-national Mobilities and National Responses in Economy and Culture

Within this context a number of trans-national initiatives are evident, the foremost of which has been a striking growth of inward capital investment. This has seen new manufacturing and research facilities within industries such as information technology and pharmaceuticals attracted to Ireland, involving multinational firms such as Intel, Hewlett-Packard and NEC (van der Bly, 2007; Inglis, 2008). Global financial services companies have meanwhile increased their presence, many with headquarters in Dublin's International Financial Services Centre (IFSC). Migrant labour, as in many other global cities (Sassen, 1994), is employed at varying skill levels whether as professional or skilled IT workers, the building trades, or in unskilled service employment in cleaning, catering and retail. While there are no clear figures of the proportion of (non-Irish) migrants in the labour force or population, the level has increased on one analysis from around 1.5% in the mid-1990s to around 5% today.

How far trends such as these make Ireland or any other globalized society a cosmopolitan society is however debatable. At its most superficial, the presence of young educated urbanites, referred to by McWilliams (2005: 215) as 'Hi-Cos' (i.e. Hibernian Cosmopolitans), working in professional and technical employment, consuming global products and living globally oriented lifestyles, is culturally relevant but equally compatible with narcissism as openness to others. This world has little in common with the low-paid migrants and asylum seekers who service their needs.

Within the world of consumption, all sections of the Irish population consume global products, but it is not clear what difference this makes to views about life and the future. Inglis (2008) studied the village of Ballivor in County Meath some 45 miles from Dublin, where the Japanese multinational electronics company NEC established a manufacturing plant in the 1970s. This expanded, contracted and then closed in 2006, the last of NEC's manufacturing plants in Europe, with production re-located to China and South East Asia. Inglis described the emergence of cultural tensions within the plant between Japanese management strategies to lift productivity and workers' resistance to intensification of the labour process. This occurred in spite of a decentralization of some decisions, such as the hiring of local female workers. This case study is an instance of a multicultural workforce, with a number of Nigerian workers employed in the factory alongside the predominantly Irish workforce.

Inglis regards the study of NEC in Ballivor as amenable to analysis in terms of glocalization. This is partly because global managerial strategies were locally adapted to meet corporate aims, and partly because Ballivor itself was like similar places at the intersection of global media and local gossip, whether about the economy, sport or politics. As I have argued throughout this study, glocalization in interactionist contexts such as these seems a better term to describe the processes at work than cosmopolitanization, not simply because there is no detectable normative aspect of cosmopolitanism at work, but also because of a lack of effective bridges between the parties involved, in this example between Japanese managers and workers. This may not be true of all instances of multinational location in Ireland (van der Bly, 2007), but it remains a warning against possibly misleading implications of the language of cosmopolitanism.

A final aspect of this case study of great interest to questions of ways of life in an epoch of globalization is provided by the stories told by 11–13-year-old school children in Ballivor on their lives. These blended local and global themes as in the following extracts:

> In my world, I love horse riding, football, hurling and swimming... In hurling I play for Killyon and in football for Ballivor... My favourite film is *Hotel Rwanda*, it is sad in the middle of the film, but happy at the end. My favourite programme is *Scrubs* (*ibid*: 239).

> My favourite thing to do on a Monday is to see my friends...on Tuesday is Tae Kwon Do...Ballivor is a great village. My favourite football team is Manchester United (*ibid*: 242).

> I go to my house, and then help my mother with the twin baby girls. I then play my X box for a hour.... I then play with my friends.... I like to listen to all sorts of music such as hip hop, dance music and rock, heavy metal...and others (*ibid*: 243).

These comments have been cited at some length because glocal evidence of this kind is hard to come by. It is strong on patterns of sociability and consumption, but for children of this age the wider world of work is largely absent. What is not clear is whether the glocal ambience of their lives would lead in their adult lives to a way of life or forms of identity that would differ markedly from their parents'.

Inglis' research into NEC in Ballivor is one of comparatively few Irish studies dealing with working for multinationals. It is thus very hard to determine whether the experience of working for multinationals has led, in and of itself, to more cosmopolitan perspectives. The world of work has often taken second place to the world of consumption in studies of cosmopolitanism. O'Riain (2000), has nonetheless provided insights into the nature of employment in such a setting. The firm is a small, largely US-owned software developer. The Irish operation was designed to provide software development services to the US company from which it was originally spun off. While the professional work involved autonomy and some creativity, the discipline was exerted through tight US deadlines conveyed through phone conversations or emails. Control of time was the key disciplinary mechanism, and this, while cross-border in nature, scarcely created conditions for cosmopolitan conversations.

Limits to Cosmopolitanism at an Inter-personal and Public Policy Level

Other limits on cosmopolitan encounters are set by hostility and sometimes racist violence to migrant workers and asylum seekers (Loyal, 2003). While themselves historical victims of racial and ethnic prejudice in both the UK and the US, some members of the Irish population have been perpetrators of racial hostility and exclusion in their own country. Data collected in a study by O'Mahony, Loyal, and Mulcahy (2001) for Amnesty International suggest the majority of respondents surveyed had experienced hostility, much of it in the street, shops or pubs, but some at the hands of public officials and employers. Lentin and McVeigh (2002) and Fanning (2002) link contemporary examples of racism with a longer exclusionary tradition in Ireland reflected in anti-semitism and hostility to travelling people (a distinct ethnocultural group). It may nonetheless be that contemporary social and economic conditions are more salient. The Celtic Tiger boom has been associated with growing social inequalities (Allen, 2000). This may feed both into a sense of insecurity among working-class communities who fear job competition and into the perception that asylum seekers have become privileged clients of the state in receipt of large welfare payments.

Such data conflicts with the self-image that many Irish have of themselves as being a welcoming, hospitable, even 'cosmopolitan' country. As Kuhling and Keohane (2007: 68) point out, 'when we say that Ireland is cosmopolitan often we are misrecognising that what we are celebrating is the exact opposite: it's not that we are celebrating what immigrants are bringing to us from our culture, but that from their presence we can see ourselves, our conceits of national identity in a refreshed and refreshing light'.

The interpretive difficulty in assessing the scope and limitations of racism in Ireland is nonetheless the lack of parallel evidence of positive inter-cultural engagement, anti-racism and positive or at least neutral provision of public services. Such interpretive problems are not unique to Ireland. However, comparative evidence for Ireland and elsewhere would also be necessary to assess whether Ireland is disproportionately intolerant.

Attitude data on individuals is of some help in pinning down such issues, but it may tell us more about how people like to think of them-selves rather than what they do in everyday interactions. We may like to appear more tolerant than we actually are. Within such limitations, evidence from the period between 1980 and 2000, drawn from the European and US sections of the World Values Surveys is of interest, because it compares the 1980s when immigration to Ireland was low with the 1990s when it surged (Rother and Medrano, 2006). Tolerance may be defined in different ways from a general life-skill (getting on with others) to a measure of attitudes towards other social and cultural groups, including 'foreigners'. Ireland is in the mid-range of 11 countries measured when it comes to general tolerance, with no detectable decline in the 1990s.

Tolerance towards foreigners within the 11 nations shows a more complex picture. Intolerance has generally increased over the period 1980–2000 for most countries, though not Sweden, the Netherlands, and West Germany. However individual patterns across the two decades vary considerably. Ireland became more tolerant in the 1980s, but less tolerant in the 1990s, a pattern rather similar to the UK which experienced immigration in both decades. By the year 2000 this put Ireland in the top third of countries in terms of intolerance to foreign-ers, still less than Italy, Belgium and Britain, but slightly greater than France and significantly more than Sweden (the most tolerant) and the Netherlands. Intolerance in Ireland since 2000, as indicated by negative public opinion polls (e.g. *Sunday Tribune*, 2005) and in the overwhelm-ingly support for a 2004 referendum restricting access of non-nationals to citizenship rights (Kuhling and Keohane, 2007: 58), is discussed further below.

As with other data on cosmopolitanism and tolerance, there are significant variations within each national case across the generations. Thus within Ireland, the youngest generation is the most tolerant and the oldest the least. Religion, employment status and gender explain very little of the variations involved.

These data suggest firstly that immigration since the early 1990s has strained levels of tolerance to foreigners, but that this is not a simple matter of strains in the labour market or community tensions. Rother and Medrano (2006: 167) argue that the impact of similar levels of immigration has different effects on attitudes in different countries. This suggests more attention needs to be given to the yardsticks by which such changes are judged, to the policies of institutions involved, and media representations of migrants. In the case of Ireland, the generations closest to the war of independence and to the inward-looking period of national consolidation lived in a country that was ethnically and culturally homogenous, and proudly so. The matter of cultural difference in the North is another matter, but within the Republic, homogeneity was a reality. From this yardstick foreigners are harder to tolerate, and religious affiliation may make little difference one way or another. In a historical context, as Fanning (2002: 16) points out, where Irish missionary publications projected views of black Africans as in serious need of civilizing in order to save their souls, the experience of such older generations was one in which ideas of racial difference and inferiority were incubated.

Greater tolerance in the younger generation may be both a function of greater education, more direct experience of globalization and exposure to information through the global media, processes discussed in previous chapters. While it might be expected that labour market competition with foreigners (real or perceived) might be a greater concern for this group, it does not seem this way according to the data reported. The yardsticks of the younger generation are then rather different from those of the post-independence monocultural Ireland.

Such generational contrasts do not however support Beck's theory of two modernities for several reasons. The first is that earlier Irish processes of economic modernization within the Imperial system (Tovey and Share, 2003) together with massive emigration, were not constrained within a bounded national framework. The second related point is that cosmopolitan connections are present through the *longue durée* of Irish history, rather than a recent phenomenon.

Another interesting issue arising from this discussion of tolerance is that high levels of culturally diverse immigration do not necessarily generate increased intolerance. The Swedish example of significant levels of African immigration during the 1990s is a case in point. Given Sweden has a more active policy of social inclusion than many other countries, it may be asked whether Ireland lacked the optimal policy environment to receive and settle new migrants with the minimum disruption to social cohesion. While committed to 'integration' rather than older kinds of wholesale assimilation, it is not clear that Ireland had a clearly articulated model of how existing notions of citizenship rights and obligations should be adapted to a new demographically multicultural population. As an Irish Centre for Migration Studies report for the EU published in 2002 points out, this reflects a greater policy concern with policing admission rather than with settlement and integration (Irish Centre for Migration Studies, 2002: 17).

Ireland like most other Western countries has enacted a range of equal opportunity and anti-discrimination policies, under which immigrants may be subsumed. Critics, however, regard these as largely unsuccessful. Once again yardsticks matter here. At a general level social cohesion and community relations have not broken down. This yardstick, however, is not sufficient for many commentators. A number have made the claim that public policy is contradictory, operating in practice if not in theory, in both anti-racist and racist ways (Fanning, 2002: 108; Crowley, Gilmartin and Kitchin, 2006: 17–19; Kuhling and Keohane, 2007: 55–6). An even more critical strand is evident in arguments that describe Ireland as a racial or racist state (Lentin and McVeigh, 2002, 2006). This point of view seems grossly over-stated in denying the variety and complexity of state policies, let alone by comparison with different historical examples like Nazi Germany.

A more subtle argument that recognized liberal-democratic elements in Irish state policy, as well as rational types of migrant exclusion linked with labour market planning, need not underplay racial exclusions and prejudices. Thus, in spite of equal opportunity and anti-racism initiatives, it is arguable that asylum seekers have been racialized as predominantly black, and then bundled together with migrants in elements of both the official imagination and popular opinion (Crowley, Gilmartin and Kitchin, 2006). This in turn has led to immigration being seen simply as a 'problem' rather than an 'opportunity', especially when political and media discourses about migrants and asylum seekers abandon analytical detachment for populist outrage and possible electoral advancement. Whether or not such sentiments are grounded in racism (a term widely used in a loose rhetorical fashion), or in emotive concerns about social tensions thought to be associated with cultural difference, their net effect is the same in terms of fostering social exclusion.

The limits to cosmopolitanism within Ireland came to a head in the anti-cosmopolitan verdict in the 2004 Citizenship Referendum (Kuhling and Keohane, 2007: 58–62). The verdict here, supported by a margin of four to one, scaled back rights to citizenship by virtue of residence and promoted a more ethno-cultural emphasis on 'blood ties', going very much against the grain of trends elsewhere in Europe. The context was the existence of incomers who were believed to have exploited rules allowing children born in the state to citizenship, and by extension allowing non-national parents the same rights. The Irish Government argued this had been exploited strategically by pregnant women deliberately coming to Ireland simply to benefit from the constitutional right. However comparatively few instances of this were adduced, and public debates were skewed once again to seeing all migrants as problems, in spite of the labour shortages that economic immigrants made up for, and the taxes many paid. The national courts subsequently became involved in deportation cases following the constitutional change, and a number of judgements ensued which rejected government attempts to deport parents of child-citizens on both Irish constitutional grounds in relation to children's rights and in relation to the European Convention on Human Rights. This testifies to a complexity in official responses rather than a thoroughgoing racism or exclusionism, once again undermining one-dimensional theories of Ireland as a 'racial' state.

But what of wider public attitudes? If public tolerance of foreigners and migrants has dissipated, has there perhaps been a revival of anti-cosmopolitan nationalism? Or is the position yet more complex?

Cosmopolitanism and Political Attitudes to Nation and the World

In an important survey of recent evidence on the scope and character-istics of the Irish sense of nation, Davis (2003) presents evidence suggesting the strength of Irish support for their nation. Rather than being overrun by globalization, or having shifted towards a post-national position (Garvin, 1996), where the rhetoric of the independence struggle has become eroded, the majority of Irish people still feel close to Ireland. This evidence is drawn from the International Social Science Program survey for 1995 carried out in two dozen mainly European countries. Here the Irish are somewhat more likely to feel 'very close' to their nation (53.8%), compared to the average figure for the 24 countries (45.5%). Even higher levels of support are found in the bi-annual Eurobarometer surveys conducted by the EU between 1994 and 2001, which measured the slightly different notion of 'pride' in one's nation. Here the rate for Ireland varied between 70 and 78%. Meanwhile Ireland ranked highest or joint highest on this measure among the EU countries involved, with only Greece ranking higher, and Great Britain and Finland coming next. These data suggest a strengthening of national feelings in a period of intensifying global-ization and increasing immigration into Ireland. They are also con-sistent with theories that see nationalism as one possible reaction to negative characterizations of globalization in terms of loss of national sovereignty or imposition of global cultural homogenization.

Yet a great deal also depends on the characteristics of the nationalism involved. How far is it ethno-cultural and inward-looking as distinct from outgoing and hospitable to others? Davis (2003), using the ISSP data, surveys the answers respondents gave to various possible characteristics of Irishness. When asked what it means to be truly Irish, 32.1% said it was very important to be Catholic, 58.1% strongly emphasized being born in Ireland, 49.3% to have lived in Ireland for most of one's life, but only 14.5% mentioned speaking the Irish language as important. These data indicate a considerable leeway for non-Catholics, those born elsewhere or who have lived elsewhere. This might suggest a significant civil element, rather than a predominantly ethno-cultural orientation, though this leeway could equally be to accommodate members of the Irish diaspora who have been born or lived elsewhere but who would be very welcome on their return. Having been carried out in the early years of the Celtic Tiger expansion before mass immigration had become a consistent feature of social change, these data do not however make clear whether or not Ireland will shift to the national profile of countries of mass migration. In such cases, as in Canada or Australia, having lived in a country before is regarded as less than half as important for national identity as in Ireland (*ibid*: 22).

Beyond this, it is important to discern how far Irish national identity is compatible with a sense of regional and global affiliation, for as emphasized throughout this study, there is considerable evidence of multiple combinations of identities and/or orientations rather than incompatibility. Davis (2003) uses the Eurobarometer data to see how far the Irish think of themselves as European as well as or instead of Irish. Here evidence from the 1980s and 1990s suggests both that a majority of Irish never think of themselves as European, and also that the Irish feel more strongly non-European than other EU populations. Finally this gap seems to be growing. Such national affiliations matter in spite of the fact that the Irish are more likely to think that they have benefited from EU membership than do many other nations within the EU. In addition, the combination 'both Irish and European' still appeals to a significant minority, though Davis does not explore their characteristics any further, except to note Laffan's (2002) argument that EU membership strongly resonates with Catholic Ireland.

Irish feelings of hostility to the EU reached their peak with the rejection in 2001 of the Treaty of Nice, which sought to facilitate the entry of new members from Central and Eastern Europe. In Ireland 54% of those voting rejected the Treaty. Whether this is unambiguous evidence of anti-cosmopolitanism is not all clear. This is partly because of the low turnout of 35% (Sinnott, 2001), and partly because of a second vote in 2002, with strong Government support for the Treaty securing 63% agreement, with turnout increasing to nearly 50%.

A further dimension to Irish national identity is of course partition of the island and the continuing support of the majority of the population in the South and of the Catholic population in the North for re-unification. Yet such historic sentiments have been significantly trans-formed by political developments in the last 15 years, with the Good Friday Agreement of 1998, and subsequent power-sharing in Northern Ireland. This is now regarded by many in the South as a solution to problems in the North, even though it falls short of re-unification (Davis, 2003). Yet it is by no means clear how far the agreement repres-ents any kind of conventional cosmopolitan standard. On the one hand formal political bridges and an increased degree of pragmatism are evid-ent at the level of power-sharing leaders. On the other hand the agree-ment represents a kind of bi-cultural 'parity of esteem' rather than a more thoroughgoing multicultural arrangement that would, for exam-ple, apply to Asian migrants in Northern Ireland. This recognizes only 'two communities' in terms of group rights of groups that are repre-sented as fixed and all-encompassing, rather than the citizenship rights of all. As such the arrangement may be seen as holding back multi-culturalism and cosmopolitan democracy in Ireland (Finlay, 2004).

Alternatively such moves may represent a kind of bicultural proto-cosmopolitanism that may lead to a stronger form of social cohesion. The prospects for this, however, depend on a loosening rather than tightening of nationalist and unionist ties. Ruane and Todd (2003) have drawn attention to other features of the Peace Agreement which create more flexible and individualized forms of citizenship. These include the individual right of those born in Northern Ireland to claim either British or Irish or both nationalities. This places some emphasis on the individual intentions of citizens as against the group focus, while also moving beyond narrow territorially bounded forms of iden-tity and nationality. This does not go as far as post-nationalism, and is more consistent with ideas of scalar complexity in identities and orientations carried on within and across soft borders.

Beyond these national and regional scales of activity, there remains the global prominence of Irish figures like Peter Sutherland, the corpo-rate lawyer and regulator, and Mary Robinson, former President of Ireland and subsequently UN High Commissioner for Refugees. What however can be said about Irish political attitudes or Government policies in relation to global issues and scales of activity that bear upon cosmopolitan issues?

In terms of attitudes, Norris (2006), using World Values data from the early 1980s to 2000, presents a complex that is typical of the complicated ways in which the national and the global intersect. One way of assessing attitudes is to ask about confidence in institutions such as the United Nations. On this measure, Ireland stands in the top third of countries whose populations were surveyed. The level of confidence of 62.5% was similar to many small countries like Denmark, Hungary and Malta, but also similar to very large ones such as China and Japan (*ibid*: 16). Norris nonetheless concludes that no clear pattern exists either between structural features of countries (e.g. levels of income or development) and confidence, nor more self-interested connections between sites of UN intervention and confidence.

In the Irish case, as we have seen, levels of orientation to nation are very high. In this respect it is interesting to consider how far this leaves any role for the UN either instead of or alongside nation-states in relation to world problems. The WVS data here on concrete issues such as human rights and refugees indicate some complexity. While Irish respondents saw a significant role for the UN on its own on refugee matters (44%), compared with the nation alone (34%), and a combination of both (22%), on the human rights issue the option of a combination of nation and UN was the view of the majority (54%), with the nation alone receiving the next highest figure (40%), and the UN alone only 6% (*ibid*: 22). These data indicate that the UN is supported as a significant world institution on these issues, but especially so in partnership with nation-states, a finding rather similar to respondents' views in many other countries. They also suggest a more pragmatic rather than ideological view of institutions, including a significant element of what might be termed practical cosmopolitanism.

This is partly borne out by the final set of data on national and cosmopolitan identities, identified in the survey with a sense of personal belonging. Here a scale of identities was constructed from information supplied by respondents on the two most important 'geographical' identifiers, from the locality at one end of the spectrum to the world as a whole at the other. They placed Ireland at a mid-point on the 'cosmopolitan identities scale' for 1981 and 1990, but at a lower point in 2001, consistent with earlier data reported on a stiffening of national feelings during the Celtic Tiger expansion. In this respect the Irish experience of declining cosmopolitan identity during the 1990s is consistent with some other countries like West Germany, Poland, Finland and Denmark, as well as Northern Ireland (measured separately), but divergent from the pattern of a continuing increase of cosmopolitan identity in Mexico, the US and Belgium. This suggests that increased economic globalization is unlikely to be directly responsible in some general sense for the decline, since it affects all countries during this period. The spread may better be explained, according to

Norris (*ibid*: 14), by feelings of greater insecurity in poorer countries, and post-Communist dislocation in Eastern Europe, where nationalism may remain as some kind of symbol for and bulwark against rapid de-stabilizing social change. This rapidity of change factor, rather than income levels, may also help to explain the Irish pattern.

Ireland and Human Rights

Another dimension to cosmopolitanism in any given country relates to commitments and actions relevant to human rights on a global as much as national basis. For Ward (2002), there are some interesting historical contrasts between domestic and foreign policy. While the former is seen as dominated by inward-looking 'social protectionism' until well into the second half of the 20th century, the latter was from the outset closely aligned with international institutions and causes. Ireland was both a strong supporter of the League of Nations and United Nations, and has more recently actively supported global human rights initiatives. This meant challenging the apartheid regime in South Africa and supporting intervention in East Timor in opposition to Indonesian occupation in favour of the rights to self-determination of the East Timorese people.

As a small country with little or no geo-political power, Ireland has conventionally taken a neutralist position in conflicts such as the Second World War and the subsequent Cold War. Behind this stands a commitment to the non-violent resolution of disputes within international relations. Ireland was indeed a key nation in the development of the League of Nations policies on non-violent conflict resolution (Kennedy, 1996: 19–29), as well as supporting multilateralism, international law, anti-colonialism and nuclear non-proliferation within the United Nations (Tonra, 2006). Membership of the EC, later EU, has of course created a further European level of policy-making. At this point, as Ward (2002: 156) indicates, Ireland pressed hard on international issues like South African apartheid, while only acknowledging human rights issues within its own domestic policies in the late 1980s.

By the 1990s, Ireland had formally recognized the importance of human rights in foreign policy by establishing a separate unit on this area within the Department of Foreign Affairs, as well as establishing an inter-departmental committee to examine human rights issues across all policy domains – foreign and domestic. Even so, the controversies of the last ten years over the rights of migrants and asylum seekers, together with the Constitutional Referendum of 2004, discussed above, do not suggest a consistent commitment to human rights, when more ethno-cultural considerations on citizenship rights are concerned.

How far does this record on internationalism and human rights stand out as distinctive and significant for cosmopolitanism? One of the difficult analytical issues here is in deciding whether Irish Government policy has simply been following national interest rather than pursuing a more cosmopolitan direction. Perhaps neutralism and multilateralism make most sense to small nations lacking geo-political power. This way of putting things, however, treats the national and the cosmopolitan as mutually exclusive, when in reality they may become interwoven in the largely pragmatic world of international relations. From this perspective it may be easier for smaller nations to be cosmopolitan since they have less to lose in supporting multilateralism and peace, compared with more powerful nations with extensive foreign interests.

Beyond this pragmatic point, it may also be argued that while patchy and uneven, Irish foreign policy has taken a stronger cosmopolitan line on some issues, in part through the pressure of outward-looking NGOs. Ward (2001) treats South African apartheid and the ending of the Indonesian occupation as two of these. In the former case the strong support of both the Catholic Church and trade union movement and the creation of a strong anti-apartheid movement led to Government support for the banning of imports of certain South African goods. In the latter case Ireland pursued a stronger and more consistent position on East Timorese independence within the UN and EU than most other countries. And beyond this, participation in the Northern Ireland peace-process, while it relates to Ireland as an island, may equally be seen as a human rights as well as nationalist issue.

Overall then there is concrete but not unambiguous evidence for the proposition that Ireland's global human rights record is a significant one, but not necessarily one that overrides other considerations. One way of getting at this is to emphasize the multiple discourses evident within foreign policy-making over the last few decades. As discussed by Tonra (2006: 188–95), these include Ireland as a global citizen and Ireland as a European Republic, but also feature the more inward-looking ethno-cultural sense of a distinctive Irish Nation, and finally, the more recent reaction against it, in terms of Ireland as an Anglo-American state located within the English-speaking world. Tonra's conclusion, based on interview evidence, is that none of these discourses occupies a position of hegemony over the others.

Conclusion

While cosmopolitanism is a cross-border phenomenon by its very nature, it is in practice tied up with particular histories, memories, institutions and places. This enables us to speak of cosmopolitanism as situated, even embedded, in time and across space. There are therefore multiple cosmopolitanisms, rather than a singular unitary flee-floating cosmopolitanism that transcends context and relations with particulars. This is no less true of Irish cosmopolitanism than any other.

A number of writers have referred to both paradox and ambivalence in relation to cosmopolitanism within Ireland. This is true both in relation to social and cultural evidence dealing with migrants or literature, as with political evidence on attitudes and institutions. Ireland is both a highly globalized country and one where nation and Irishness matter. The paradox is not however that between two separate entities facing each other in conflict, but one in which the global and the national, the cosmopolitan and the local inter-penetrate. This is as true when looking at the writings of James Joyce, the comments of school children of Ballivor writing about their worlds, the Irish diaspora, and the attitudes of Irish to their country, Europe and the world. When Inglis (2008), speaks of Global Ireland, it is this kind of glocal inter-connection he is getting at.

This argument in turn allows us to speak of Ireland as both highly globalized from an economic point of view, but simultaneously one in which nation and particularity matter. Inter-penetration of the global and local is a fundamental aspect of such inter-connections, but it has many modalities, a number of which involve boundary-drawing in contrast to openness. This limits cosmopolitan openness as seen in the more restrictive citizenship laws of 2004, and in resistance to completely open borders to all who would work and live in Ireland. Once again it seems that the idea of glocalization is a better way of getting at such bordering and closed modalities than Beck's cosmopolitanization.

8

Conclusion

This book began by naming some of the major challenges facing the contemporary world, and asked how far cosmopolitanism might be a potential solution. In order to take this question further, I have reviewed a wide-ranging set of analytical questions surrounding cosmopolitanism. The understanding of cosmopolitanism has been revolutionized over the last two decades. This book has been designed to explain how and why. It has covered a wide range of historical and contemporary ground, pursued across many branches of knowledge. It has also sought to combine theoretical discussion and empirical evidence in providing the interpretations offered.

The main grounds for the revolutionizing of the topic are twofold. Firstly there is the shift from seeing cosmopolitanism as a body of philosophical ideas, to a far broader concern with cosmopolitan activities and institutions as well as ideas. Secondly there is the displacement of cosmopolitanism from the moral high ground, upon which previous adherents had appeared to place it, to a more critical approach stressing multiple and often conflicting modalities rather than a unitary universalistic doctrine intrinsically superior to particular loyalties and commitments. The combined effect of these two trends has been to bring cosmopolitanism into society in its many manifestations, but equally to make the study of cosmopolitanism far more complex.

There are now multiple cosmopolitanisms being produced and announced at a bewilderingly rapid rate in this or that geographic or historical setting, pertaining to desires as well as values, bodies as much as institutions. This proliferation of cosmopolitanisms has not however finally established a boundaryless 'post-territorial', 'post-modern' or 'post-national' world of transient liquid connections. This is because continuities matter, as does the constant re-institutionalization of social relations. The national and the global, the local and the cosmopolitan co-exist, even if in dynamic inter-action with each other. In the modish sociological condition called 'postism', whose adherents rush to be the first to name another new social change that is 'post-' some characteristic that went before, there is a great danger of conceptual and historical superficiality. Concepts are elaborated too freely, undisciplined by careful scrutiny of social processes across time and space. How do we know if something is really 'post' some anterior phase if that phase is given only cursory examination?

A good example of this is that particular version of post-national thinking that assumes that the nation-state is in decline, whether because of the impact of globalization or cosmopolitanism. As we have seen, Beck's theory of the two modernities – the first national, the second cosmopolitanism – is especially vulnerable to this charge, resting as it does on a very selective and schematic representation of phase one, compounded by the sense of normative necessity surrounding phase two. Whether or not the world needs cosmopolitanism to save itself from autocratic geo-political tyranny and environmental crisis, the idea that cosmopolitanism – false or real, imagined or actually existing, emancipatory or unintended – now dominates everything is a profoundly misleading position. Resistance to all these modalities remains strong. Although Beck accepts a dialectic between the global and the national, his choice of methodological cosmopolitanism over Robertson's methodological glocalism underplays the national or local term in the dialectic. This is not a mere semantic point, but one that matters a great deal, both to analytical discussions of cosmopolitanism and its limits, and to normative questions about the complexity of scales of moral and political action within the global arena.

Beck is right that the nation-state is no longer adequate as an analytical framework for social analysis and that national politics is by itself inadequate for democratic politics. Adherents of methodological nationalism are on very weak ground in supposing that nationally focussed analysis remains adequate for any understanding of social change. If 'postism', as defined above, has any value in social analysis, it is for its diagnostic role in pointing to symptoms of social change. Beck is right to discern change, and his work is also an advance on 'postist' intimations of new trends, in that he has provided increasingly substantive clues into the dynamics and directionality of change. The Robertsonian position advanced in this study is nonetheless that such substantive analyses are not sufficient to do justice to the complexities of the contemporary world in which the global and the local co-exist, inter-penetrate, sometimes co-operatively, and sometimes conflictually, sometimes conscious of their mutual interdependence and sometimes not. This is the reason that methodological glocalization is preferred here to the idea of methodological cosmopolitanism.

The Empirical Research Agenda

Several comments are also required in relation to the coherence and helpfulness of the empirical research agenda proposed by Beck (2002a). This is certainly a step forward from previous highly speculative comments, though there remains a tendency in much scholarship to foreclose on empirical analysis in order to cut to the normative chase as to whether and if so, how, one might best choose a cosmopolitan position on global ethical and political challenges, or whether patriotism offers a sustainable alternative.

Beck's research agenda also contains within it ambiguities as to what the indicators signify. It is not clear, for example, whether they suggest the presence of the weaker state of 'cosmopolitanization', akin to living in a world of cross-border relationships and institutions, or the stronger notion of 'cosmopolitan outlook' which presumes a more explicit cosmopolitanism. In cases such as non-exclusionary citizenship rights or recognition of ethnicity within a nation-state, for example, it is not clear whether these necessarily signify cosmopolitanism in any sense, as distinct from social-democratic or liberal kinds of openness.

We have, in Chapters 5 and 6, already noted the incompleteness of Beck's valuable early formulation of a cosmopolitan research agenda (2002a), in particular its neglect of cosmopolitan law. This has been explored in more depth in Chapter 6 and stands as a crucial empirical indicator of the presence of cosmopolitanism with the institutional world of law and governance. Beyond this, there is some value in specifying more clearly exactly how far and in what senses Beck's indicators hold up as measures of cosmopolitanism, even allowing for the diffuse and wide-ranging character of the subject-matter. In the following section, the list of 13 is briefly reviewed, including both indicators which have been a major focus of this study, and those which have not.

Consumption of Global Cultural Commodities

This is an important indicator of socio-cultural aspects of cosmopolitanism, but conventionally of less direct significance for normative and political aspects. Economic globalization has penetrated many consumer markets, while products themselves have gained a sign-value as cultural commodities beyond any exchange-value they may have. It is certainly hard to conceive of market-based consumption any longer on a localized basis. What is less clear is how far the consumption of global commodities is of salience to broader cosmopolitan imaginings. Nava (2002, 2007) has made one of the most powerful cases for such a connection, indicating in the process not simply the gendering of global consumption, but also establishing connections between visceral cosmopolitanism, intimate social relations and the bodily politics of desire. In this way consumption and politics may be connected. At the same time, as with the Irish school-children studied by Inglis (2008), issues of the salience of wide-ranging cross-border connections to everyday life are not always clear. Meanwhile like all other indicators this one may be linked with others in Beck's agenda, such as cross-border mobility, international travel and trans-national ways of life.

Dual Citizenship

Dual citizenship in a technical sense means the holding of citizenship rights in two or more jurisdictions. It is distinct from multiple kinds of citizenship that invoke human rights or regional forms of citizenship. Dual citizenship in this restricted sense might function as an indicator of cosmopolitan citizenship rights, where immigrants gain the rights to citizenship in countries of destination, while retaining citizenship in their country of origin. Faist (2007: 1) observes that around half the countries in the world now tolerate some element of dual citizenship. In countries like Australia with a commitment to a liberal-democratic conception of multiculturalism, or social-democratic Sweden, full rights to dual citizenship are possible. Dual citizenship recognizes multiple cross-border loyalties within a population. Nonetheless, it is not all clear that countries who accept some element of dual citizenship are necessarily more cosmopolitan in relation to human rights in general.

Conversely, in countries where joint citizenship is denied, this generally represents an official refusal to countenance two parallel loyalties. This may occur in settings characterized in terms of civil nationalism but with a strong sense of the need for loyalty within strong borders (e.g. the US), as in locations where ethno-cultural senses of nationalism are stronger (e.g. Greece). Such a refusal suggests an inward-looking standpoint, but is not a definitive marker of it, since a good deal also depends on government policies on questions such as human rights and rights of immigrants. Apparent contradictions may therefore ensue, as in Germany where recent liberalization of immigration law including a strong *ius soli* element was combined with a strict refusal to accept dual citizenship (Gerdes and Faist, 2007).

Beyond this it is not clear whether migrants who are able to retain the old citizenship, while adding a new one, become more cosmopolitan in attitude or practice, or indeed whether this increases integration in some sense into the new country. Overall the study of dual citizenship and its relationship with cosmopolitanism is still in its infancy (Kivisto, 2007: 285).

Beck (2002a) treats dual citizenship in a wider non-technical sense to include 'the legal basis and official practice in dealing with migrants, asylum seekers...[as well as]...how are foreigners defined statistically in the media and everyday life' (79–80). These are relevant considerations to empirical research into cosmopolitanism, but subject to problems of ambiguity. Various types of exclusion of migrants or asylum seekers from any given national polity are not consistent with complete cosmopolitanism openness, though it is interesting that Kant saw cosmopolitan obligations to those coming from other countries in terms of hospitality rather than unambiguous rights of residence. Where national immigration policies limit entry, however, this may be compatible with cosmopolitanism, provided such limitations are not on grounds of race or inconsistent with human rights.

Cosmopolitan Law

This key indicator, strangely absent from Beck's original list, might well be added at this point as a way of elaborating political and legal indicators of cosmopolitanism that have often surfaced in discussions of dual citizenship. The idea of multiple citizenship, indicative to claims to membership in more than one polity, is in a sense a half-way house between national citizenship and the intrinsically cosmopolitan notion of human rights.

Cosmopolitan law is of enormous significance for cosmopolitanism and may well be its most crucial indicator. This is because it involves a limitation to national state sovereignty in the name of human rights rather than national citizenship rights. This incorporates elements such as crimes against humanity as well as making individuals parties to cross-border public legal processes, contrasted with the state-based character of international law.

There remain nonetheless very significant limitations to the scope of cosmopolitan law, since many powerful nation-states including China and the US, have the capability to defy it. Cosmopolitan law we might say is an incomplete normative project. And even when 'protection of human rights' is invoked during international conflicts and interventions by some states into the territory of others, there remain moral dilemmas to do with justification for war in order to prevent human rights violations.

Nor is cosmopolitan law strictly accountable to democratic institutions, partly because a global representative polity does not exist, and partly because of separation of legal powers from democratic determination. Human rights are nonetheless a key element in global public spaces of deliberative democracy, a sphere where NGOs are extremely active as a normative force bearing considerable social legitimacy, even if not elected through representative procedures.

Political Representation for Cultural Minorities

For Beck, this indicator includes questions as to the extent to which 'ethnic groups' are represented in 'centres of national power, parties, parliaments, governments, trade unions'. Such issues have not received much attention in the body of this book. This is largely because of fundamental ambiguities in how such indicators relate to cosmopolitanism. A key distinction here is between group rights and individual rights. The presence of members from ethnic groups in political institutions is not at all the same thing as representation of ethnic groups as a group. It may simply signify the personal achievement of individuals, though such individual instances may be far harder to achieve where racial or ethnic exclusion is practised. A further problem exists with the idea of unitary ethnic groups. This presumes a homogeneity that somehow rises above divisions by class, gender, ethnicity and age. It is hard to see groups acting in this way, and even if they do, it is not clear that the presence of exclusive ethnic groups within a polity is consistent with cosmopolitan openness. Where multiculturalism takes the form of political support for the cultural maintenance of the ways of life of particular groups (as dictated by powerful interests within such groups), this is a poor indicator of cosmopolitanism in any expansive intercultural sense. However, it should equally be emphasized that formally liberal polities that espouse equal rights and seem more explicitly cosmopolitan may in practice be dominated by existing cultural groups, such as white Anglo-Saxon Protestants (WASPS), in the United States for much of the 20th century. In this sense apparent cosmopolitan openness always requires to be tested for its effectiveness in practice.

Formal political representation based on group rights is not a widespread feature of national political systems, though there are clearly regional arrangements, such as the special recognition of French-speaking citizens in the Canadian province of Quebec that remain significant for national patterns of minority inclusion. This is not by itself a strong or explicit indicator of cosmopolitan openness to the world, however, since openness to all others matters too, as does demonstration that group rights do not create exclusionary vested interests.

Language Diversity

Language diversity among individuals may or may not represent a cosmopolitan standpoint. Such diversity may be a voluntary product of individual choice to broaden skills and perspectives that may be carried into the world. It may also represent mixed marriages, where children learn the languages of both parents. Mixed marriages are themselves an important indicator of inter-cultural engagement, though in the resulting situation cultural arrangements may be skewed to one background or the other, rather than being an open cosmopolitan experiment. What have been termed 'inter-racial' marriages are particularly salient measures for the decline of racial thinking, since such relationships are generally regarded as anathema by racists. The language diversity of individuals is therefore hard to separate out from other factors in assessing cosmopolitan attitudes.

Language diversity within a given nation-state may be consistent with multicultural and cosmopolitan policy formation. National policies which mandate more than one official language in a given territory, may be justified for a number of reasons. In Canada, use of English and French recognizes cultural and political traditions and is built into multiculturalism. In Ireland, use of the minority language Irish as well as English is very much about cultural maintenance and an ethno-cultural sense of what being Irish signifies in the post-colonial setting. Language diversity in these varied settings is again a rather weak indicator, in that it may represent policy settings that are inward-looking.

Language diversity in a global context is generally seen as a way of combating the threat of cultural uniformity created by globalization and the growing dominance of English. Many late 19th- and early 20th-century cosmopolitans espoused the artificial world language Esperanto, but this project has all but disappeared. International organizations such as the UN or EU use several official languages but it is not clear whether this makes them more or less cosmopolitan than if they used Esperanto alone. While the total stock of world languages is in decline, the co-existence of a number of languages is once again ambiguous in what it says about cosmopolitanism. Are such languages particularistic limits to cosmopolitanism? Or are such languages, and the cultural repertoires that are expressed within them, part of the stuff through which particular sources of cosmopolitanism are constructed? Provided languages can be shared through translation and interpretation, they would seem not to disrupt cosmopolitanism. Translators themselves may be seen very much as agents of cosmopolitanism. This line of argument is also consistent with ideas of glocalization discussed above.

Cross-border Mobility

This has been discussed extensively throughout this study. Cross-border mobility is a necessary though not a sufficient condition for the presence of cosmopolitanism. This is because exposure to and involvement in an open stance able to cross political and cultural borders and boundaries is essential to cosmopolitanism on any definition. At the same time, the concept of mobility requires further conceptual elaboration.

In the first place the idea of mobility has recently been extended beyond the very important notion of physical or corporeal mobility, to wider forms of visual mobility through communications media, and imaginative mobility through a range of possibilities, including religious commitment, inter-cultural solidarity and desire. The conventional emphasis on migration – both short and long term – and travel, is included under mobility, but so too are virtual mobility through the internet, visual mobility through television, as well as the various kinds of imaginative mobility, whether through public performance of religious devotion or the more internalized processes of book-reading or engagement with film.

Secondly, attention needs to be given to the problem of transforming mobility from a necessary to a sufficient condition of cosmopolitanism. The considerable analytical challenge here is that cross-border mobility is a better indicator of trans-nationality than of cosmopolitanism. We have encountered this problem at many points in the book, notably when analysing migrant mobility and diaspora populations. These may move, but in what sense are they cosmopolitan? Movement may after all produce populations or sections of populations that are embedded in an inward-looking sense, within particular cultural milieux. Migrants, as Hannerz (1990) hypothesized at the outset of the recent revival of interest in cosmopolitanism, are not in and of themselves cosmopolitans. Nor, from the other end of the mobility spectrum, are the physically settled and immobile necessarily non-cosmopolitans, especially if they somehow maintain active sympathy, hospitality and solidarity with others.

The analytical implications here are that each instance of migrant mobility needs considerable and sensitive empirical scrutiny before issues of openness and closure can be determined. Even then, as we have also seen, one is generally talking about conditional 'glocal' forms of openness, which may often be implicitly rather than overtly cosmopolitan. And beyond the issue of migrants, there are other forms of mobility, such as tourism and travel, which require consideration in their own right. Similarly there are what might be called the sedentary cosmopolitans, physically but not virtually or imaginatively immobile. Research on this group within the cosmopolitan research agenda is again still in its infancy.

Global Communication Patterns

There are a number of debates here, many of them focussing on contemporary changes in global media industries and communications technologies.

The emergence of powerful media conglomerates, coupled with technological convergence of transmission and content provision, has given a top-down character to many global communications patterns. Companies that once focussed on telecommunications (BT or Telstra) or internet provision (AOL) are now involved – whether through merger or internal expansion – in the more extensive development of content, while former content providers, such as print publishers Newscorp, have become heavily involved in transmission technologies. Such processes are certainly relevant to the consumption of global commodities and visceral or aesthetic modes of cosmopolitanism, as well as the construction and supply of global news, considered below. But in another sense, older discrete technologies such as the telephone are still enormously important for inter-personal communication in the conduct of trans-national ways of life, but these as we have seen are not necessarily synonymous with cosmopolitanism. Lonely global professionals ringing the home country for news of family, kin and friends are at best reluctant cosmopolitans.

From a bottom-up as well as top-down perspective, the internet has often come to dominate discussions of global communications. Research here has emphasized its multiple rather than singular uses. These include business transactions and data transmission and mundane searches for information, as much as lateral democratic linkages across borders. Used for the transmission of hate as well as cosmopolitan love of others, this technology is very far from being a necessary enhancement to the building of a cosmopolitan world in any normative or political sense. Inter-personal networks still seem to matter more than electronic ones in this respect (see Holton, 2008).

International Travel

International travel is a rapidly expanding feature of the global economy. Recent debates about the relationship between travel and cosmopolitanism have broadened this area beyond conventional ideas of travel as physical mobility, to include imaginative travel, sometimes linked with communications media like the TV or internet.

A simple equation between 'more travel' and 'more cosmopolitanism' is however hard to make. While willingness to travel to experience other peoples and places may seem to represent a kind of openness, it is equally possible that the cultural frameworks involved deploy rather stereotypical notions of 'others', whether as exotic and very different from us, or as nobly 'authentic' as distinct from our own mundane lives. There is some difficulty or ambivalence therefore in determining whether travel opens up active cosmopolitan engagement or simply represents a passive gaze on the part of the traveller, locked within stereotypes. Where travel is overlaid with greater power and/or wealth on the part of travellers, this may tend to distort engagement through the unequal position of participants.

On the other hand engagement is possible, especially if notions of culture are freed from the grip of essentialism. This treats cultures as both distinct and unitary entities. Most anthropologists, as we have seen earlier in this study, now reject this approach, replacing this with a sensitivity to the shifting and pluralistic character of cultural practices. This does not do away with global inequalities, but it does suggest the possibility of cross-cultural openings to mutual understanding if not agreement, as occurs within inter-faith dialogues and cross-border linkages within civil society organizations. These require more than physical travel, though they may indeed draw on imaginative travel. An under-researched issue here is the world as an 'imagined community', how this comes about, and (linking this theme with global communications patterns) what it is that stimulates imaginative travel amongst imagined world citizens.

Trans-national Initiatives and Organizations

This is a vast theme. Initiatives and organizations span the full range of economic, social, political, and cultural life, and embrace both formal organizations and informal networks, states, markets and civil society. One of the critical and unresolved analytical questions here remains the problem of multiple and intersecting scales of initiative and organization. Cross-border activities are one thing, but whether they are international or trans-national, trans-local or supra-local matters a good deal to the indicative presence of cosmopolitanism. This is NOT because the national and trans-national designate separate non-cosmopolitan and cosmopolitan spheres. Nor is it because trans-local links, such as those evident between cities or villages in different countries tied together by migrant diaspora, are necessarily inward-looking.

The glocal methodology applied throughout this study requires that closer empirical scrutiny is required in all such cases. This is necessary to determine the terms of interaction between the global and the local and the sense in which these are more or less open and outward-looking. This in turn stems from recent and radical revisions in the understanding of cosmopolitanism that see it as situated in time and space, rather than abstract universalism. On this basis, the global and the local may be interlinked in ways that are more or less cosmopolitan. This argument has been sustained with examples at a number of points in Chapters 3, 5, 6, and in particular depth with Irish evidence in Chapter 7. Overall this indicator is important but methodologically problematic.

Criminal Activity

This indicator has not been discussed in the body of the book. It seems to be better thought of as a measure of trans-nationality than cosmopolitanism. Organized crime certainly operates across borders, but seems inimical to human rights activities, especially where people are trafficked, or laws evaded or spurned in pursuit of material gain. Complications nonetheless arise where activities such as human rights campaigns may be branded illegal by particular states. The increased securitization of states in an epoch of terrorism also raises the possibility that attributions of terrorist connections may be made more liberally than before, catching in the criminal net those who simply belong to certain mobile ethnic groups.

In a broader socio-cultural sense it may be that organized crime involves many in trans-national ways of life as well as elements of inter-cultural openness in the exchange of illegal global commodities such as drugs or arms. However it is also clear that ethno-cultural ties undergird many global criminal operations, offering a measure of trust in a world of great uncertainty, competition and personal danger.

Trans-national Ways of Life

This indicator is hard to separate out from several other indicators such as cross-border mobility or international travel. It is perhaps most helpful to treat trans-national ways of life in terms of activities and relationships that have an on-going rather than very occasional trans-national character. Migration and travel are ambiguous in this respect, creating possibilities for trans-national ways of life rather than requiring them. Individuals and groups may migrate only to settle in a new location and become integrated into it, abandoning the past. This would not count as a trans-national way of life, but cases where activities continue to be conducted across two or more countries would do so. Similarly, employment outside the country of origin on a one-off contract basis scarcely counts as a trans-national way of life, whilst continuing employment in occupations such as Hannerz's (2004b) foreign correspondents would do so.

But even where one may suppose a trans-national way of life to be present, there still remains the question of how far this way of life is a cosmopolitan one. The problem of treating any trans-national way of life as intrinsically cosmopolitan, is that little or no openness to others may be present. If diasporic communities conduct their affairs behind exclusive cultural boundaries, as in Diouf's (1999) Senegalese trading diaspora, then there seems no warrant for describing them as cosmopolitan. The same variability in relation to inter-cultural openness applies to those employed outside the country of origin.

Once these limitations are acknowledged, however, it is important not to lose sight of the significant extent to which trans-national mobility creates openings for cosmopolitanism. This may exist in some kind of tension with continuing emotional links with, or nostalgia for the country of origin, as with Nowicka's (2006) professionals working in international organizations. Such tensions do not however rule out cosmopolitan elements within such settings, if cosmopolitanism is seen as emerging from particular contexts rather than an abstract context-free commitment to a universalist philosophy.

A final point here is the importance of trans-national ways of life that may depend on a trans-national imagination rather than mobility. To stay in one place, whether through limits of poverty or through choice, does not necessarily entail a closed mind to the rest of the world, especially where access to global media and communications channels are open. An example, which falls under the heading of working-class internationalism, is the formation in the 1920s and 1930s of what were called 'Little Moscows' in radical mining villages in England and Scotland, under the impact of the Communist Party (McIntyre, 1981). Most miners had never been to Moscow and had lives very much focussed on locality, but this did not preclude involvement in a wider kind of Communist cosmopolitanism. This pre-internet example warns us once again as to the facile ahistorical difficulties with Beck's theory of the two modernities.

Trans-national News Coverage

This is clearly a significant feature of global communications patterns and is crucial to global inter-dependence and a sense of the world as a single place. The development of non-Western news providers like al Jazeera alongside sources such as the BBC, CNN and Reuters also extends the range of coverage and perspective further than in the colonial period. The transmission of virtually simultaneous news stories permits stories to do with war, human rights violations or environmental crisis to circulate more widely and more quickly than in the past, giving an immediacy to cosmopolitan awareness that was lacking in the past. These provide institutional underpinnings to the sense of a global cosmopolitan sympathy that Kant postulated in general terms in the late 18th century.

National Identities and their Relationship to Cosmopolitanism

Some of the hardest questions about the scope and limits of cosmopolitanism appear under this heading, which remains one of the most significant indicators in Beck's list. One of the strongest objections to cosmopolitanism is that particular loyalties to nation or locality mean more than any kind of supra-national loyalty or identity. Many still regard this as fatal to both the possibility and desirability of cosmopolitanism. Research into cosmopolitanism over the last two decades has nonetheless challenged this assumption in a very fundamental way. There is now a very strong evidence-based argument against this objection, but it is a subtle rather than simplistic argument.

The argument is not that people are cosmopolitan rather than nationalist. It is rather that the two are not necessarily incompatible. This is partly because types of cosmopolitanism are situated in particular locations in time and space – an insight developed by anthropologists and sociologists who have prised the study of cosmopolitanism away from the previous monopoly of philosophers. It is also because cosmopolitanism and national attachment or patriotism are often perfectly compatible. The one does not necessarily preclude the other. This still applies, as was seen in the case study of Ireland, which is both highly globalized in an economic sense but culturally more nationally focussed.

Globalization has not destroyed the nation-state or nationalism. Economic globalization relies on the institutional frameworks, stability and infrastructure provided by many nation-states, while nationalism has been stimulated in part as a response to threats of homogenization associated with globalization. This is sometimes inward-looking but increasingly has to come to terms with global inter-dependence, in which national autarky 'going it alone' is no longer a feasible option, and in which national sovereignty is insufficient. Regionalism, as seen within the EU, is one half-way house as it were, between globalization and the nation. Even here, regional tensions with nationalism remain, but normatively speaking Europe is capable of standing for enhanced human and citizenship rights that recognize but also cross borders.

Ecological Crisis Responses

Conditions of life under the impact of economic and technological globalization may have undermined the feasibility of purely national solutions to contemporary challenges. This is nowhere more true than with the environmental and ecological challenges facing the planet. Global warming, atmospheric and marine pollution and species destruction are all issues which are cross-border and demand global solutions that are both locally and globally effective. Environmental movements are well described as cosmopolitan, insofar as they are open to the peoples of the world who share the planet, its resources and its challenges. Consciousness of the world as a single place has been enhanced both by the norm of human rights and that of

environmental sustainability. 'Think globally, act locally' is a slogan
that both fits sources of environmental consciousness and one that
captures the glocal character of much cosmopolitan thought and
action.

There are however analytical difficulties with this indicator in determining the relationship between norms of environmental justice and
cosmopolitan democracy. These stem from a disconnect between
norms and institutions. Progress towards institutions of cosmopolitan
democracy have not matched the progression of cosmopolitan norms.
This is one reason to be sceptical that with the environmental crises,
the hour of cosmopolitanism has come.

Normative Considerations: Ten Theses on Cosmopolitanism

What implications do all these have for the suitability of cosmopolitanism as a contribution to solving the problems of the age? At
best, this contribution will clearly never cover everything. And since
there are many strands of cosmopolitanism, the potential ways in
which global problems might be addressed are manifold. This may be
illustrated with two examples.

The first involves cosmopolitan law as a means to securing more
effective human rights. Here cosmopolitanism has the potential to
decrease war and conflict and increase peace, but not to provide a
detailed guide to how the personal lives of individuals should be
conducted. Cosmopolitan law may also need to draw upon violence to
challenge systematic opponents of human rights, which raises the
possibility that apparent cosmopolitan solutions may generate
cosmopolitan-induced problems.

The second example is cosmopolitan consumption. Here those who
can afford to travel or consume global products may develop greater
sensitivity and tolerance towards others, without in any way lessening
inequality or enhancing the democratic character of political institutions. Consumption activity may do nothing to alleviate world poverty
or environmental crisis and may simply feed the stomachs and prejudices of those whose lives are not blighted by poverty or hunger. Yet
cosmopolitan consumption has the capacity to address the larger problems. This is evident through campaigns like the fair trade movement
or support for environmental sustainability.

Such examples sketch different kinds of connections, one centred on
state institutions, the other on civil society. The two may become linked

where consumption gains a political salience, but this seems to occur in a contingent rather than necessary manner, influenced in part by pressure from NGOs. The cosmopolitanism of civil society is too multiform to be limited by political processes and vocabularies, in part because there are limits to what states can do as states. They may remove obstacles to the good life as imagined by cosmopolitans, but cannot create positive inter-personal and inter-cultural relations.

Another very diffuse contribution that cosmopolitanism can make to problems of the age is perhaps to suggest that there is hope beyond the litany of crises and problems that seem to beset us. To sustain hope, however, cosmopolitanism of the old philosophical kind is not enough. In the following theses on cosmopolitanism, a guide is given to how a more research-based understanding of cosmopolitanism can inform questions about its desirability and feasibility, as well as identify its limitations.

Ten Theses on Cosmopolitanism:

1. Cosmopolitanism arises in multiple settings across time and space, embracing a range of economic, political, cultural, and ethical objectives and institutions. There are multiple cosmopolitanisms, but no overarching and unitary cosmopolitanism.

2. There is no necessary relationship between cosmopolitanism and projects of political or ethical emancipation. Indifference to questions of emancipation is clearest in cosmopolitanisms that focus on experiencing and enjoying inter-cultural ways of life.

3. The existence of patriotism, nationalism, racism and war around the world may represent serious limits to cosmopolitanism. But they are not in themselves sufficient reason for writing it off either as a way of life or as a source of values and norms aiming at global justice, human rights or trans-national democracy.

4. Emancipatory cosmopolitanisms nonetheless need fundamentally re-casting if they are to be of any normative value in addressing the problems faced by a globalizing post-colonial world. Class-based and Euro-centric conceptions of cosmopolitanism are too implicated in structures of power and domination to act as legitimate bases for a global cosmopolitan ethics or democratic polity.

5. For many of the world's populations it is religious cosmopolitanism and salvation that matter most rather than emancipation as defined by secular rationalism. Ecumenism and other forms of

inter-faith dialogue may nonetheless help to bridge institutional divides between religious institutions.

6. The Western legacy is of great significance for the development of human rights and democracy, but notions of justice, inter-cultural co-operation, tolerance and good governance have a multiplicity of roots that do not depend on cosmopolitan gifts from the West.

7. Re-casting also requires a balance to be struck between universalism and particularism. An excessive universalism that downplays particularism has now become politically fruitless with the continuing rejection of a world government and world language. But excessive particularism that rules out universal or at least trans-contextual norms and values fails as a model of 'living with strangers' through neglect of inter-cultural ties and failure to accept mutually binding obligations.

8. Ideas of glocalism and glocalization offer ways of understanding the inter-penetration of the global and the local and its ambivalences, thus by-passing fruitless rhetorical wars between those who are for or against cosmopolitanism and nationalism.

9. Supporters of cosmopolitanism may hope for the simultaneous construction of a more just and democratic world, but it is not clear that the two are necessarily connected in the world of institutions and activists. The top-down delivery of forms of 'justice' and 'human rights' through so-called cosmopolitan military interventions, is very far from representing a democratic mode of cosmopolitan governance.

10. As a utopia, cosmopolitanism is a very fertile one. As practical politics and as a way of life, its place in history has however proven episodic rather than unfolding from early beginnings to some kind of contemporary fruition. Cosmopolitans should therefore be sceptical both of their opponents' arguments, and of their own cosmopolitan rhetoric. They should also beware of the false assurances built on philosophies of history that assume the time is now ripe for cosmopolitanism in a global world. History is not on anyone's side.

This book is intended not simply as a dispassionate intellectual mapping of cosmopolitanism. The analytical insights contained in these ten theses matter because they challenge the excess of speculation and rhetoric that surrounds claims and counter-claims made for and against cosmopolitanism. And this challenge matters, in turn, because the war of claims and counter-claims engages with some of the most fundamental issues and problems affecting the contemporary world. These include the question of whether it is possible to end war, dismantle racism and transcend the walls and fences that divide rather than unite the world's peoples and cultural groups.

There is no simple yes/no answer to this set of questions. What scholarly analysis can offer is ways of understanding social change and the dilemmas facing those who seek to shape it in particular ways to meet their particular objectives. Those who seek to construct 'one world' will continually face the reality of social difference, inequality and multiple cultural yardsticks by which institutions are judged. Difference cannot be obliterated by military action, religious funda- mentalism or through the standardized marketing of homogenized commodities. A single highly integrated world in any of these senses is a sociological impossibility.

Cosmopolitan projects may either ignore this, blinded by an opti- mistic rhetoric, or will have to take difference and particularism on board in some kind of 'glocal' re-casting. Ideas of human rights, justice or simply tolerance of others may or may not turn out to be amenable to re-casting to achieve this. But attempts at re-casting will require a greater understanding of the multiple sources and modalities of cosmo- politan thought and practice identified and elaborated in this study and the wider literature it draws upon. Scholarship matters, in the end, not simply as a way of disciplining the over-vaunting rhetorical ambitions of would-be cosmopolitans and their anti-cosmopolitan opponents. It also matters because greater theoretical rigour and confrontation with bodies of evidence may help clarify the conditions under which an enlargement of the scope of feasible cosmopolitanism is possible.

Appendix 1:
Cosmopolitanism, Cosmopolitan, Cosmopolitans, Cosmopolitics

This appendix provides detailed background material to support the argument in Chapter 2 of this book. In particular it provides a full listing of types of cosmopolitanism together with the sources in which they appear. It is not comprehensive, referring mainly to English language uses (as written or translated). The instances cited may be explicitly tied to theoretically elaborated arguments, may be descriptive, or may be innocent of any direct connection with specific debates around cosmopolitanism. Widely used examples are not accompanied by a definitive list of citations. Where citations occur in many places within a source, a lengthy list of page citations is not provided. Page references are used where sources used these terms sparingly, or to draw attention to a particularly striking usage.

Within these limitations the appendix provides, at the very least, a sense of the recent explosion of usages, and some initial indications of the substance of variations in these terms. An exercise of this kind has not to my knowledge been attempted on this scale before.

Instances of Cosmopolitanism

Abject: Nyers, 2003
Aboriginal: Connelly, 2000: 602
Academic: Robbins, 1999: 30
Actually Existing: Malcolmson, 1998: 238; Calhoun, 2003: 86–116
Aesthetic: Urry, 1995
Affective: Gandhi, 2000
African: Strongman, 2002: 128–32; Hoad, 2006
Analytical–Empirical: Beck and Sznaider, 2006a: 13
Ancient: Kristeva, 1993; Douzinas, 2007
Anti-Colonial: van der Veer, 2002

Anti-Imperial: Malcolmson, 1998: 238
Anti-Proprietary: Posnock, 2000: 809
Archaic: Lonsdale, 2002: 198–9
Aural: Szerszynski and Urry, 2002
Banal: Beck, 2006
Black: Posnock, 2000: 804; Nwankwo, 2005
Borges: Abbas, 2000: 769
Bourgeois: Levenson, 1971: 19–55
Catholic: Beck, 2006 speaking of Oskar Maria Graf
Cautious: Stevenson, 2000
Christian: Kristeva, 1993: 26–7; Sennett, 1994; Connelly, 2000: 602
Colonial: van der Veer, 2002
Communist: Levenson, 1971: 1–18
Complex: Binney, 2006
Consumer: Purdy, 1998
Corporate: Connelly, 2000: 602
Critical: Mignolo, 2000; Delanty, 2006b; Walkowitz, 2006: 5
Cultural: Levinson, 1971: 7–8; Kleingeld, 1999: 515–18; Delanty, 2006b:
    31–6; Gilbert and Lo, 2007: 8–11
Deep: Beck, 2006: 161
Deformed: Beck and Sznaider, 2006a: 8; Beck, 2006: 20
Democratic: Honig, 1998: 193
Despotic: Beck, 2006: 44–5, 151–2
Discrepant: Robbins, 1992: 181; Clifford, 1998
Dogmatic: Connelly, 2000: 614
Domestic: Nava, 2007: 12–15
Eccentric: Radhakrishnan, 1995
Ecological: Connelly, 2000: 602
Economic: Beck, 2006: 108
Emancipatory: Beck, 2006: 45ff
Embedded: Erskine, 2000
Embodied: Mellor, 2006
Empirical: Beck and Sznaider, 2006a: 8
Enlightenment: Kymlicka, 2001
Environmental: Clark, 2002
Ethical: Giri, 2006
(as) Ethical Glocalism: Tomlinson, 1999: 194–6
Evangelical: van der Veer, 2002: 173
Exclusionary and Inclusionary: Anderson, 1998: 268–78
Export and Import: Pollock *et al.*, 2000: 587
Fake: Beck, 2005: 18
False: Beck, 2005: 17–18
Feminist: Connelly, 2000: 602

Forced: Malcolmson, 1998: 240
Fraternal: Harland-Jacobs, 2007
French: Kleingeld, 1999: 506
From Above: Kaldor, 1996
From Below: Kaldor, 1996; Kurasawa, 2004; Nwnakwo, 2005: 14
Genuine: Beck, 2005: 17–18
German: Kleingeld, 1999
German-Jewish: Beck, 2006, speaking of Lyon Feuchtwanger
Hegemonic: Nwankwo, 2005
Imagined: Schein, 1999
Institutional: Pojman, 2004
Institutionalized: Beck and Sznaider, 2006a: 11
Internalized: Beck and Sznaider, 2006a: 9; Beck, 2006: 21ff
International: Rennella, 2008: 194–5
International Federative: Kleingeld, 1999: 509–13
Instinctive: Nava, 2007: 69–70
Intimate: Mitchell, 2007
Islamic: Connelly, 2000: 602; Euben, 2006: 174–97
Laissez-faire: Reich, 1992: 315
Left: Beck, 2005: 270–6
Liberal: van der Veer, 2002: 173
Lost: Robbins, 1999: 100
Managed: Mignolo, 2000: 741
Marginal: Bhabha, 1996: 195
Market: Kleingeld, 1999: 518–21
Merchant: Malcolmson, 1998: 239
Mediterranean: Larguèche *et al.*, 2001
Methodological: Beck, 2002; Beck, 2005: 23–4; Beck and Sznaider, 2006a
Middle Eastern: Zubaida, 1999: 33
Migrant: Beck, 2006: 106
Military: Connelly, 2000: 602
Minority: Beck, 2006: 106
Modern: Douzinas, 2007
Moral: Kleingeld, 1999: 507–9; Dallmayr, 2006; Delanty, 2006b: 28–9; Jones, 2007
More-or-Less: Beck, 2006: 105
Mundane: Hebdige, 1990
National: Mignolo, 2000: 727; Beck, 2006: 11 (speaking of Thomas Mann)
Neo-: Beck and Sznaider, 2006a: 2
New: Fine, 2007
New Liberal: Gowan, 2003
Nineteenth Century: Rennella, 2008: 198–204
NGO: Beck, 2006: 107

Non-Elite: Robbins, 1999: 100
Non-Universalist: Posnock, 2000: 807
Normative: Beck and Sznaider, 2006a: 8
Normative-Political: Beck and Sznaider, 2006a: 13
Of Dependency: Abbas, 2000: 778
Of Extraterritoriality: Abbas, 2000: 778
Oppositional: Schein, 1998
Organizational: Robertson and Wind, 1983
Passive: Beck, 2006: 19
Philosophical: Beck, 2006: 17ff
Political: Dallmayr, 2003, *passim*; Delanty, 2006b: 29–31
Popular Non-Western: Robbins, 1999: 100
Post-Colonial: Parry, 1991: 41
Post-Enlightenment: Venn, 2002
Post-Identity: Posnock, 2000: 807
Post-Universalistic: Delanty, 2006
Postmodern: Garnham, 1992; Douzinas, 2007
Principled: Mahoney, 2007: 184–7
Providential: Connelly, 2000: 599
Real: Beck, 2006: 77
Realistic: Beck and Sznaider, 2006a: 2, 19
Reflexive: Beck and Sznaider, 2006a: 6
Representative: Binney, 2006
Republican: Bohman, 2004
Religious: Mignolo, 2000: 727
Restricted: Tan, 2005: 167, 177–182
Risk: Beck, 2006: 33
Romantic: Kleingeld, 1999: 521–4
Rooted: Cohen, 1992; Ackerman, 1994; Hollinger, 1995: 5
Rural: Gidwani and Sivaramakrishnan, 2004
Sartorial: Bayly, 2002: 47–8
Self-Critical: Beck, 2005: 280; Beck, 2006: 160
Shallow: Beck, 2006: 161
Social-scientific: Beck, 2006: 17
South Asian: Desai, 2006: 116
South Asian Diasporic: Desai, 2006
Spiritual: Malcolmson, 1998: 238; van der Veer, 2002: 177
Stoic: Nussbaum, 1997; Giri, 2006
Symbolic: Beck, 2005: 17–18
Syncretic: Walkowitz, 2006: 12
Thick: Dobson, 2006
Thin: Gilbert and Lo, 2007: 9–10
Traditional: Walkowitz, 2006: 5

Transgenerational: Nava, 2007: 135
Upper Class: Dehija, 2006: 113
Unconscious: Beck, 2006: 19
Vernacular: Bhabha, 1996; Diouf, 2000; Werbner, 2006
Visceral: Nava, 2007
Western: Euben, 2006: 174–97
Working Class: Werbner, 1999: 23; Waxer, 2001: 223

Types of Cosmopolitanisms

In general: Pollock *et al.*, 2000

Specific:
Discrepant: Robbins, 1992: 181
Indian Ocean: Hawley, 2008
New: Rajan and Sharma, 2006
Ordinary: Lamont and Aksartova, 2002

Types of Cosmopolitans

Anti-: Appiah, 2006
Asian and Pacific: Robinson, 2005
Boston: Rennella, 2008
Chinese: Ong, 1998
Counter-: Appiah, 2006
Hibernian: McWilliams, 2005
Intimate: Mitchell, 2007
Minoritarian: Pollock *et al.*, 2000: 582–3
Nationalist: Malachuk, 2007: 142–3
Nativist: Kaufmann, 2001
New: Malcolmson, 1998: 237; Rajan and Sharma, 2006a
Newport: Rennella, 2008: 103–4
Patrican: Gidwani and Sivaramakrishnan, 2004: 341
Plebeian: Gidwani and Sivaramakrishnan, 2004: 341
Reluctant: Swetschinski, 2000
Subaltern: Barucha, 2006: 119–23
Working Class: Werbner, 1999

Cosmopolitan (as a characteristic of institutions, social groups, processes, bodies of knowledge)

Advocacy: Beck, 2006: 106
Americans: Malcolmson, 1998: 234
Anthropology: Kuper, 1994
Anxieties: Mandel, 2008
Art: Chaney, 2002
Borders: Rumford, 2007
Brotherhood: Harland-Jacobs, 2007: 6
Capital: Harris, 2002
Capitalism: Beck, 2005: 59
Capitalists: Hamilton, 1999
Cities: Zubaida, 1999: 15
Cosmopolitanism: Douzinas, 2007
Community: Beck and Sznaider, 2006a: 13
Competence: Beck, 2006: 89
Condition: Beck and Sznaider, 2006a: 3
Connections: Falzon, 2004
Consciousness: Beck and Sznaider, 2006a: 14
Contamination: Appiah, 2006: 101–14
Culture: Smith, 2008
Democracy: Held, 1997; Archibugi, 1998, *passim*; Archibugi, 2003; Calhoun, 2003
Desire: Foster, 2006
Dream: Calhoun, 2007
Empathy: Beck, 2006: 5–10
Ethics: Beck and Sznaider, 2006a: 13
Ethnicity: Werbner, 2002
Europe: Delanty, 2005
Fictions: Stanton, 2006
Gaze: Beck, 2002a: 61
Geographies: Dhawadker, 2001
Global Fluids: Urry, 2002: 133
Governance: Held, 1995
Idealism: Beck and Sznaider, 2006a: 19
Ideologies: Zubaida, 1999: 16
Imagination: Delanty, 2006b
Impartiality: Tan, 2005
Individuals: Zubaida, 1999: 15
Interdependence: Beck and Sznaider, 2006a: 12; Beck, 2006: 23

Vernacular: Pollock, 1998
Virtue: Turner, 2002
Vision: Beck, 2006
Working Class: Werbner, 1999
World Order: Beck, 2002a: 65

Instances of Cosmopolitics

In general:
Archibugi, 2003
Arnopoulos, 1998
Cheah and Robbins, 1998

Specific:
Nationalist: Malachuk, 2007
Performing: Gilbert and Lo, 2007
Cosmopolitics and the Emergence of a Future: Morgan and Banham, 2006
Cosmopolitics of Dress and Language: Barucha, 2006: 130–8

Cosmopolitical as a Quality:
Claims: Mani, 2007
Freedom: Cheah, 1998

Instances of Cosmofeminism

In general: Pollock, 2000: 584

Bibliography

The following is a general bibliography for the theoretical and empirical contents of this book. It is not intended as a detailed bibliography on cosmopolitanism *per se*. But it does augment the initial foray into bibliography provided in U. Beck and N. Sznaider (2006b) with particular respect to empirical and historical work, as well as items published in the last two years.

Abu-Lughod, J. (1989) *Before European Hegemony: The World System A.D. 1250–1350*, New York: Oxford University Press.

Abbas, A. (2000) 'Cosmopolitan De-scriptions: Shanghai and Hong Kong', *Public Culture*, 12(3), 769–86.

Ackerman, B. (1994) 'Rooted Cosmopolitanism', *Ethics*, 104(3), 516–35.

Ake, C. (1991) 'Rethinking African Democracy', *Journal of Democracy*, 2(1), 32–44.

Alexander, J. (1982) *Theoretical Logic in Sociology, Vol. 1, Positivism, Presuppositions and Current Controversies*, London: Routledge.

Allen, K. (2000) *The Celtic Tiger: The Myth of Social Partnership in Ireland*, Manchester: Manchester University Press.

Anderson, A. (1998) 'Cosmopolitanism, Universalism, and the Divided Legacies of Modernity', in P. Cheah and B. Robbins (eds) *Cosmopolitics: Thinking and Feeling Beyond the Nation*, Minneapolis: Minneapolis UP, 265–89.

Anderson, B. (1983) *Imagined Communities*, London: Verso.

Anderson, E., S. Brooks, R. Gunn and N. Jones (2004) 'Being Here and Being There: Fieldwork Encounters and Ethnographic Discoveries', *Annals of the American Academy of Political and Social Science*, 595(4), 14–31.

Appadurai, A. (1996) *Modernity at Large: Cultural Dimensions of Globalization*, Minneapolis: University of Minneapolis Press.

Appelbaum, R., W.L. Felstiner and V. Gessner (eds) (2001) *Rules and Networks: The Legal Culture of Global Business Transactions*, Oxford and Portland Oregon: Hart Publishing.

Appiah, K.A. (1996) 'Cosmopolitan Patriots', in M. Nussbaum and J. Cohen (eds) *For Love of Country*, Boston: Beacon Press, 21–9.

Appiah, K.A. (2006) *Cosmopolitanism. Ethics in a World of Strangers*, London: Penguin.

Archibugi, D. (1998) 'Principles of Cosmopolitan Democracy', in D. Archibugi, D. Held and M. Köhler (eds) *Re-imagining Political Community*, Cambridge: Polity Press, 198–230.

Archibugi, D. (ed.) (2003) *Debating Cosmopolitics*, London: Verso.

Arnopoulos, P. (1998) *Cosmopolitics: Public Policy of Outer Space*, Toronto: Guernica.

Assmann, J. (1991) 'Die Katastophe des Vergessen', in J. Assmann and D. Harth (eds) *Mnemosyne. Formen und Functionnen der Kulturellen Erinnerung*, Frankfurt: Fischer, 337–55.

Australian Council on Population and Ethnic Affairs (1982) *Multiculturalism for All Australians*, Canberra: AGPS.

Axford, B. (2006) 'The Dialectic of Borders and Networks in Europe: Reviewing "Topological Presuppositions"', *Comparative European Politics*, 4, 160–82.

Balibar, E. (1994) *Masses, Classes, and Ideas: Studies on Politics and Philosophy Before and After Marx*, London: Routledge.

Bamyeh, M. (2000) *The Ends of Globalization*, Minneapolis: University of Minnesota Press.

Bamyeh, M. (2004) 'Global Order and the Historical Structures of dar al-Islam', in M. Steger (ed.) *Rethinking Globalism*, Lanham MD: Rowan and Littlefield, 217–29.

Banks, R. (2001) 'Introduction', *Autodafe*, 2, fall, 2–3.

Barucha, R. (2006) *Another Asia: Rabindranath Tagore and Okakura Tenshin*, Delhi: Oxford University Press.

Batnitzky, A., L. McDowell and S. Dyer (2008) 'A Middle-class Global Mobility? The Working Lives of Indian Men in A West London Hotel', *Global Networks*, 8(1), 51–70.

Bauman, Z. (2003) *Liquid Love: On the Frailty of Human Bonds*, Cambridge: Polity Press.

Bayly, C. (2002) '"Archaic" and Modern Globalization in the Eurasian and African Arena: 1750–1850', in A.G. Hopkins (ed.) *Globalization in World History*, London: Pimlico, 47–73.

Beck, U. (1998) 'The Cosmopolitan Manifesto', *New Statesman*, March 20th, 28–30.

Beck, U. (2000) 'The Cosmopolitan Perspective: Sociology in the Second Age of Modernity', *British Journal of Sociology*, 15(1), 79–105.

Beck, U. (2002a) 'The Cosmopolitan Perspective: Sociology in the Second Age of Modernity', in S. Vertovec and R. Cohen (eds) *Conceiving Cosmopolitanism*, Oxford: Oxford University Press, 61–85.

Beck, U. (2002b) 'The Cosmopolitan Society and Its Enemies', *Theory, Culture and Society*, 19(1–2), 17–44.

Beck, U. (2005) *Power in the Global Age*, Cambridge: Polity Press.

Beck, U. (2006) [2004] *Cosmopolitan Vision*, Cambridge: Polity Press.

Beck, U., A. Giddens and S. Lash (1994) *Reflexive Modernization*, Cambridge: Polity Press.

Beck, U. and E. Grande (2006) *Cosmopolitan Europe*, Cambridge: Polity Press.

Beck, U. and N. Sznaider (2006a) 'Unpacking Cosmopolitanism for the Social Sciences: A Research Agenda', *British Journal of Sociology*, 57(1), 1–23.

Beck, U. and N. Sznaider (2006b) 'A Literature on Cosmopolitanism: An Overview', *British Journal of Sociology*, 57(1), 153–64.

Beck-Gernsheim, E. (2007) 'Transnational Lives, Transnational Marriages: A Review of the Evidence from Migrant Communities in Europe', *Global Networks*, 7(3), 271–88.

Bellamy, R. and D. Castigleone (1998) 'Between Cosmopolis and Community: Three Models of Rights and Democracy within the European Union', in D. Archibugi, D. Held and M. Köhler (eds) *Re-imagining Political Community*, Cambridge: Polity Press, 152–78.

Benhabib, S. (2007) 'Twilight of Sovereignty or the Emergence of Cosmopolitan Norms? Rethinking Citizenship in Volatile Terms', in T. Faist and P. Kivisto, *Dual Citizenship in Global Perspective: From Unitary to Multiple Citizenship*, Basingstoke: Palgrave Macmillan, 247–71.

Benton, T., C. Benton and G. Wood (2003) *Art-Deco, 1910–39*, London: Victoria and Albert Museum.

Berlin, I. (1998) *Many Thousands Gone: The First Two Centuries of Slavery in North America*, Cambridge, Mass: Harvard University Press.

Berman, P.S. (2004–5) 'From International Law to Law and Globalization', *Columbia Journal of Transnational Law*, 43, 484–556.

Bhabha, H. (1996) 'Unsatisfied: Notes on Vernacular Cosmopolitanism', in L. García-Morena and P.C. Pfeiffer (eds) *Text and Nation*, London: Camden House, 191–207.

Bhebe, N. and T. Ranger (2001) 'Introduction to Volume 1', in N. Bhebe and T. Ranger (eds) *The Historical Dimensions of Democracy and Human Rights in Zimbabwe, Volume One: Pre-colonial and Colonial Legacies*, Harare: University of Zimbabwe Publications, xxi–xlvii.

Biao, X. (2005) 'Gender, Dowry, and the Migration System of Indian Information Technology Professionals', *Indian Journal of Gender Studies*, 12(2&3), 357–80.

Billig, M. (1995) *Banal Nationalism*, London: Sage.

Binney, M. (2006) *The Cosmopolitan Evolution: Travel, Travel Narratives, and the Revolution of the Eighteenth Century European Consciousness*, Lanham: University Press of America.

Binnie, J., J. Holloway, S. Millington and C. Young (2006) *Cosmopolitan Urbanism*, London: Routledge.

Bohman, J. (1997) 'The Public Spheres of the World Citizen', in J. Bohman and M. Lutz-Bachmann (eds) *Perpetual Peace: Essays on Kant's Cosmopolitan Ideal*, Cambridge Mass: MIT Press, 179–200.

Bohman, J. (2004) 'Republican Cosmopolitanism', *Journal of Political Philosophy* 12(3), 336–52.

Bohman, J. (2005) 'Constituting Humanity: Democracy, Human Rights, and Political Community', in D. Weinstock (ed.) *Global Justice, Global Institutions*, Calgary: University of Calgary Press, 227–52.

Boli, J. and G. Thomas (1999) *Constructing World Culture: International Non-governmental Organizations since 1875*, Stanford: Stanford University Press.

Bottomley, G. (1992) *From Another Place: Migration and the Politics of Culture*, Cambridge: Cambridge University Press.

Boucher, D. (1998) *Political Theories of International Relations*, Oxford: Oxford University Press.

Bowden, B. (2003) 'Nationalism and Cosmopolitanism. Irreconcilable Differences or Possible Bedfellows?', *National Identities*, 5(3), 235–49.

Braithwaite, J. and P. Drahos (2000) *Global Business Regulation*, Cambridge: Cambridge University Press.

Breckenridge, C., S. Pollock, H. Bhabha and D. Chakrabaty (eds) (2002) *Cosmopolitanism*, Durham: Duke University Press.

Brenner, N. (1998) 'Global Cities, Glocal States: Global City Formation and State Territorial Restructuring in Contemporary Europe', *Review of International Political economy*, 5(1), 1–37.

Brenner, N. (2003) *Merchants and Revolution: Commercial Change, Political Conflict, and London's Overseas Traders, 1550–1653*, London: Verso.

Bull, H. (1977) *The Anarchical Society: A Study of Order in World Politics*, London: Macmillan.

Caldwell, L. (1988) 'Beyond Environmental Diplomacy: The Changing Institutional Structure of International Co-operation', in J. Carroll (ed.) *International Environmental Diplomacy*, Cambridge: Cambridge University Press, 13–28.

Calhoun, C. (2003) 'The Class Consciousness of Frequent Travellers: Towards a Critique of Actually Existing Cosmopolitanism', in D. Archibugi (ed.) (2003) *Debating Cosmopolitics*, London: Verso, 86–116.

Calhoun, C. (2004) 'A World of Emergencies: Fear, Intervention and the Limits of Cosmopolitan Order', the 2004 Sorokin Lecture, *Canadian Review of Sociology and Anthropology*, 41(4), 373–95.

Calhoun, C. (2007) *Nations Matter: Culture, History and the Cosmopolitan Dream*, London: Routledge.

Caney, S. (2005) 'Cosmopolitanism, Democracy, and Distributive Justice', in D. Weinstock (ed.) *Global Justice, Global Institutions*, Calgary: University of Calgary Press, 29–63.

Canovan, M. (2000) 'Patriotism is Not Enough', *British Journal of Political Science*, 30, 413–32.

Carenti, L. (2006) 'Perpetual War for Perpetual Peace? Reflections on the Realist Critique of the Kantian Project', *Journal of Human Rights*, 5, 341–53.

Castells, M. (1996) *The Rise of the Network Society*, Oxford: Blackwell.

Castells, M. (2000) *The End of the Millennium*, Oxford: Blackwell.

Castells, M. (2001) *The Internet Galaxy: Reflections on the Internet, Business, and Society*, Oxford: Oxford University Press.

Castles, S. (ed.) (1992) *Australia's Italians: Culture and Community in a Changing Society*, North Sydney: Allen and Unwin.

Chaney, D. (2002) 'Cosmopolitan Art and Cultural Citizenship', *Theory, Culture, and Society*, 19(1–2), 157–74.

Charnovitz, S. (2002) 'WTO Cosmopolitics', *International Law and Politics*, 34, 299–354.

Charnovitz, S. (2004) 'The WTO and Cosmopolitics', *Journal of International Economic Law*, 675–82.

Cheah, P. (1998) 'The Cosmopolitan Today', in P. Cheah and B. Robbins (eds) *Cosmopolitics: Thinking and Feeling Beyond the Nation*, Minneapolis: Minneapolis UP, 20–41.

Cheah, P. and B. Robbins (1998) (eds) *Cosmopolitics: Thinking and Feeling Beyond the Nation*, Minneapolis: Minneapolis UP.

Cheah, P. (2001) 'Chinese Cosmopolitanism in Two Senses and Postcolonial Memory', in *Cosmopolitan Geographies: New Locations in Literature and Culture*: London: Routledge, 133–70.

Chen, W., J. Boase and B. Wellman (2002) '"The Global Villagers": Comparing Internet Users and Uses Around the World', in B. Wellman and C. Haythornthwaite (eds) *The Internet in Everyday Life*, Oxford: Blackwell, 74–113.

Clark, N. (2002) 'The Demon-Seed: Bioinvasion as the Unsettling of Environmental Cosmopolitanism', *Theory, Culture, and Society*, 19(1–2), 101–25.

Clifford, J. (1992) 'Travelling Cultures', in L. Grossberg, C. Nelson and P. Treichler (eds) *Cultural Studies*, London: Routledge, 96–116.

Clifford, J. (1998) 'Mixed Feelings', in P. Cheah and B. Robbins (eds) *Cosmopolitics: Thinking and Feeling Beyond the Nation*, Minneapolis: Minneapolis UP, 362–70.

Cohen, M. (1992) 'Rooted Cosmopolitanism: Thoughts on the Left, Nationalism and Multiculturalism', *Dissent*, Fall, 478–83.

Collins, R. (1998) *The Sociology of Philosophies. A Global Theory of Intellectual Change*, Cambridge, Mass: Harvard University Press.

Concannon, B. (2000) 'Beyond Complementarity: The International Criminal Court and National Prosecutions: A View from Haiti', *Columbia Human Rights Law Review*, 32, 201–50.

Connelly, W.E. (2000) 'Speed, Concentric Cultures and Cosmopolitanism', *Political Theory*, 28(5), 596–618.

Conversi, D. (2000) 'Cosmopolitanism and Nationalism', in A. Leoussi and A.D. Smith (eds) *Encyclopaedia of Nationalism*, Oxford: Transaction Books, 34–9.

Cosgrove, D. (1994) 'Contested Global Visions: One-World, Whole-Earth and the Apollo Space Photographs', *Annals of the Association of American Geographers*, 84(2), 270–94.

Cover, R. (1992) 'The Folktales of Justice: Tales of Jurisdiction', in M. Minow, M. Ryan and A. Sarat (eds) *Narrative, Violence, and the Law: The Essays of Robert Cover*, Ann Arbor: University of Michigan Press, 173–201.

Cronin, A. (1997) *Samuel Beckett. The Last Modernist*, London: Flamingo.

Crowley, U., M. Gilmartin and R. Kitchin (2006) 'Vote Yes for Commonsense Citizenship: Paradoxes at the Heart of Ireland's *Caid Mile Failte*', NIRSA Working Paper Series, http://www.nuim.ie/nirsa/research/documents/WPS.30.pdf (accessed 25th September 2007).

Dallmayr, F. (2003) 'Cosmopolitanism: Moral and Political', *Political Theory*, 31(3), 421–42.

Davis, M.C. (ed.) (1995) *Human Rights and Chinese Values: Legal, Philosophical, and Political Perspectives*, Hong Kong: Oxford University Press.

Davis, T.C. (2003) 'The Irish and Their Nation: A Survey of Recent Attitudes', *Global Review of Ethnopolitics*, 2(2), 17–36.

Dehija, V. (2006) 'Identity and Visibility: Reflections on Museum Displays in South Asian Art', G. Rajan and S. Sharma (eds) *New Cosmopolitans: South Asians in the US*, Stanford: Stanford University Press, 71–90.

Delanty, G. (2003) 'Conceptions of Europe. A Review of Recent Trends', *European Journal of Social Theory*, 6(4), 471–88.

Delanty, G. (2005) 'The Idea of a Cosmopolitan Europe: On the Cultural Significance of Europeanization', *International Review of Sociology*, 15(3), 405–21.

Delanty, G. (2006a) 'Borders in a Changing Europe', *Comparative European Politics*, 4, 183–202.

Delanty, G. (2006b) 'The Cosmopolitan Imagination Critical Cosmopolitanism and Social Theory', *British Journal of Sociology*, 57(1), 25–47.

Delanty, G. (ed.) (2006c) *Europe and Asia Beyond East and West: Towards a New Cosmopolitanism*, London: Routledge.

Derrida, J. (2001) *Cosmopolitanism and Forgiveness*, London: Routledge.

Desai, J. (2006) 'Bollywood Abroad: South Asian Diasporic Cosmopolitanism and Indian Cinema', in G. Rajan and S. Sharma (eds) *New Cosmopolitans: South Asians in the US*, Stanford: Stanford University Press, 115–37.

Dharwadker, V. (ed.) (2001) *Cosmopolitan Geographies: New Locations in Literature and Culture*, London: Routledge.

Diawara, M. (1998) *In Search of Africa*, Cambridge, Mass: Harvard University Press.

Dinwoodie, G. (2000) 'A New Copyright Order: Why National Courts Should Create Global Norms', *University of Pennsylvania Law Review*, 469.

Diouf, M. (1999) 'The Senegalese Murid Trade Diaspora and the Making of a Vernacular Cosmopolitanism', *Public Culture*, 12(3), 679–702.

Dobson, A. (2006) 'Thick Cosmopolitanism', *Political Studies*, 54(1), 165–84.

Donia, R. (2006) *Sarajevo: A Biography*, London: Hurst.

Douzinas, C. (2007) *Human Rights and Empire: The Political Philosophy of Cosmopolitanism*, Abingdon: Routledge.

Doyle, D. (2002) *Nations Divided: America, Italy, and the Southern Question*, Athens: University of Georgia Press.

Doyle, M. (1983) 'Kant, Liberal Legacies and Foreign Affairs', *Philosophy and Public Affairs*, 12, 205–35, 323–53.

Doyle, M. (1986) 'Liberalism and World Politics', *American Political Science Review*, 80(4), 1151–69.

Doyle, M. (1993) 'Liberalism and International Relations', in R. Beiner and W. Booth (eds) *Kant and Political Philosophy*, Newhaven: Yale University Press, 173–206.

Eder, K. and B. Giesen (2001) 'Conclusion: Citizenship and the Making of a European Society: From the Political to the Social Integration of Europe', in K. Eder and B. Giesen (eds) *European Citizenship*, Oxford: Oxford University Press, 245–69.

Edwards, R. (2001) '"The Metropol and the Mayster-Toun", Cosmopolitanism and Late Medieval Literature', in V. Dharwadker (ed.) *Cosmopolitan Geographies: New Locations in Literature and Culture*, London: Routledge, 33–62.

Elliott, L. and G. Cheeseman (eds) (2004) *Forces for Good: Cosmopolitan Militaries in the Twentieth Century*, Manchester: Manchester University Press.

Erskine, T. (2000) 'Embedded Cosmopolitanism and the Case of War: Restraint, Discrimination and Overlapping Communities', *Global Society*, 14(4), 569–90.

Euben, R. (2006) *Journeys to the Other Shore: Muslim and Western Travelers in Search of Knowledge*, Princeton: Princeton UP.

Faist, T. (2007) 'Introduction: The Shifting Boundaries of the Political', in T. Faist and P. Kivisto (eds) *Dual Citizenship in Global Perspective: From Unitary to Multiple Citizenship*, Basingstoke: Palgrave Macmillan, 1–23.

Faist, T. and P. Kivisto (eds) (2007) *Dual Citizenship in Global Perspective: From Unitary to Multiple Citizenship*, Basingstoke: Palgrave Macmillan.

Falk, R. (1996) 'Revisioning Cosmopolitanism', in M. Nussbaum and J. Cohen (eds) (1996) *For Love of Country*, Boston: Beacon Press, 53–60.

Falzon, M-A. (2004) *Cosmopolitan Connections: The Sindhi Diaspora, 1860–2000*, Leiden: Brill.

Fanning, B. (2002) *Racism and Social Change in the Republic of Ireland*, Manchester: Manchester University Press.

Featherstone, D. (2007) 'The Spatial Politics of the Past Unbound: Transnational Networks and the Making of Political Identities, *Global Networks*, 7(4), 430–52.

Featherstone, M. (2002) 'Cosmopolis: An Introduction', *Theory, Culture, and Society*, 19(1–2), 1–16.

Ferguson, J. (2003) 'Stillborn Chrysalis: Reflections on the Fate of National Culture in Neoliberal Zambia', *Global Networks*, 3(3), 271–98.

Feyerabend, P. (1993) *Against Method*, London: Verso.

Fine, R. (2003) 'Taking the "Ism" Out of Cosmopolitanism: An Essay in Reconstruction', *European Journal of Social Theory*, 6(4), 451–70.

Fine, R. (2007) *Cosmopolitanism*, London: Routledge.

Fine, R. and D. Chernilo (2004) 'Between the Past and Future: The Equivocations of the New Cosmopolitanism', *Studies in Law, Politics, and Society*, 31, 25–44.

Finlay, A. (2004) 'Introduction', in A. Finlay (ed.) *Nationalism and Multiculturalism: Irish Identity, Citizenship and the Peace Process*, Munster: Lit Verlag, 1–32.

Fitzgerald, J. (2000) 'The Story of Ireland's Failure and Belated Success', in B. Nolan, P. O'Connell and C. Whelan (eds) *Bust to Boom? The Irish Experience of Growth and Inequality*, Dublin: Institute of Public Affairs, 27–57.

Fojas, C. (2001) 'Cosmopolitan Topographies of Paris: Citing Balzac', in M.P. Smith and T. Bender (eds), 'City and Nation: Rethinking Place and Identity', *Comparative Urban and Community Research*, 7, Edison, NJ: Transaction Publishers, 181–205.

Foster, R. (1988) *Modern Ireland, 1600–1972*, Harmondsworth: Penguin.

Foster, S.W. (2006) *Cosmopolitan Desire: Transnational Dialogues and Terrorism in Morocco*, Lanham, MD: Rowman and Littlefield.

Frank, A. and B. Gills (1993) *The World System: Five Hundred Years or Five Thousand?* London: Routledge.

Franklin, S., C. Lury and J. Stacey (2000) *Global Nature, Global Culture*, London: Sage.

Friedman, J. (1997) 'Global Crises, the Struggle for Identity and Intellectual Pork-barreling: Cosmopolitans versus Locals, Ethnics, and Nationals, in an Era of Dehegemonisation', in T. Modood and P. Werbner (eds) *Debating Cultural Hybridity. Multi-Cultural Identities and the Politics of Anti-Racism*, London: Zed Books, 70–89.

Friedman, J. (1998) 'Transnationalization, Socio-political Disorder and Ethnification as Expressions of Declining Global Hegemony', *International Political Science Review*, 19(3), 233–50.

Frost, C. (2006) 'Is Post-nationalism or Liberal-Culturalism behind the Transformation of Irish Nationalism?', *Irish Political Studies*, 21(3), 277–95.

Gandhi, L. (2000) 'Affective Cosmopolitanism: A Pathway of Multi-culturalism', in M. Seixo, J. Noyes, G. Abreu and I. Moutinho (eds) *The Paths of Multi-culturalism: Travel Writing and Multiculturalism*, Lisbon: Cosmo, 31–47.

Gangjian, D. and S. Gang (1995) 'Relating Human Rights to Chinese Culture: The Four Paths of the Confucian Analects and the Four Principles of the New Theory of Benevolence', in M.C. Davis (ed.) *Human Rights and Chinese Values: Legal, Philosophical, and Political Perspectives*, Hong Kong: Oxford University Press, 35–56.

Gans, H. (1979) 'Symbolic Ethnicity: The Future of Ethnic Groups in America', *Ethnic and Racial Studies*, 2(1), 1–20.

Garnham, N. (1992) 'The Media and the Public Sphere', in C. Calhoun (ed.) *Habermas and the Public Sphere*, Cambridge, Mass: MIT Press, 359–76.

Garsten, C. (2003) 'The Cosmopolitan Organization: An Essay on Corporate Accountability', *Global Networks*, 3(3): 355–70.

Garvin, T. (1996) 'Hibernian Endgame? Nationalism in Divided Ireland', in R. Caplan and J. Feffer (eds) *Europe's New Nationalism: States and Minorities in Conflict*, New York: Oxford University Press, 184–94.

Gerdes, J. and T. Faist (2007) 'Varying Views on Democracy, Rights, and Duties, and Membership: The Politics of Dual Citizenship in European Immigration States', in T. Faist and P. Kivisto (eds) *Dual Citizenship in Global Perspective: From Unitary to Multiple Citizenship*, Basingstoke: Palgrave Macmillan, 135–58.

Geras, N. (1995) *Solidarity in the Conversation of Humankind: The Ungroundable Liberalism of Richard Rorty*, London: Verso.

Gerholm, L. (2003) 'Overcoming Temptation: On Masculinity and Sexuality among Muslims in Stockholm', *Global Networks*, 3(3), 355–70.

Gheorghiu, C. (2007) *Globalisation, Christian Churches and Ecumenism*, Unpublished PhD thesis, Department of Sociology, Trinity College, Dublin

Ghosh, A. (1992) *In an Antique Land*, New York: Knopf.

Gidwani, V. and K. Sivaramakrishnan (2004) 'Circular Migration and Rural Cosmopolitanism in India', in F. Osella and K. Gardner (eds) *Migration, Modernity, and Social Transformation in South Asia*, New Delhi/London: Sage, 339–67.

Gilbert, H. and J. Lo (2007) *Performance and Cosmopolitics: Cross-cultural Transactions in Australia*, Basingstoke: Palgrave Macmillan.

Gilroy, P. (1993) *The Black Atlantic*, London: Verso.

Giri, A. (2006) 'Cosmopolitanism and Beyond', *Development and Change*, 37(6), 1277–92.

Glaser, B.G. (1963) The Cosmopolitan-Local Scientist', *American Journal of Sociology*, 69(3), 249–59.

Glazer, N. (1996) 'Limits of Loyalty', in M. Nussbaum and J. Cohen (eds) (1996) *For Love of Country*, Boston: Beacon Press, 61–5.

The Global Gastronomer (2008) http://www.cs.yale.edu/homes/hupfer/global/gastronomer.html (accessed 7th Jan 2008).

Görg, C. and J. Hirsch (1998) 'Is International Democracy Possible?', *Review of International Political Economy*, 5(4), 585–615.

Gouldner, A.W. (1957–8) 'Cosmopolitans and Locals: Towards an Analysis of Latent Social Roles', *Administrative Science Quarterly*, II, 281–306 and 444–80.

Gowan, P. (2003) 'The New Liberal Cosmopolitanism', in D. Archibugi (ed.) (2003) *Debating Cosmopolitics*, London: Verso, 51–66.

Guillén, M. and S. Suárez (2005) 'Explaining the Global Digital Divide: Economic, Political and Sociological Drivers of Cross-National Internet Use', *Social Forces*, 84(2), 681–708.

Gürner, R. (2006) 'Nietzsche, the 'Good European'? Or: The Praise of Prejudice in Beyond Good and Evil and the Will to Power', in M. Perkins and M. Liebscher (eds) *Nationalism versus Internationalism: German Thought and Culture, 1789–1914*, Lewiston NY: Edwin Mellen Press, 243–56.

Habermas, J. (1976) *Legitimation Crisis*, London: Heinemann.

Habermas, J. (1996) *Between Facts and Norms: Contributions to a Discourse Theory of Law and Democracy*, Cambridge, Mass: MIT Press.

Habermas, J. (1997) 'Kant's Idea of Perpetual Peace, with the Benefit of Two Hundred Years Hindsight', in J. Bohman and M. Lutz-Bachmann (eds) *Perpetual Peace: Essays on Kant's Cosmopolitan Ideal*, Cambridge Mass: MIT Press, 113–54.

Habermas, J. (2001) *The Postnational Constellation*, Cambridge, Mass: Harvard University Press.

Habermas, J. (2003) 'Interpreting the Fall of a Monument', *Constellations*, 10(3), 364–70.

Haines, R. (2004) *Charles Trevelyan and the Great Irish Famine*, Dublin: Four Courts.

Hamilton, G.G. (1999) *Cosmopolitan Capitalists: Hong Kong and the Chinese Diaspora at the End of the Twentieth Century*, University of Washington Press.

Hannerz, U. (1990) 'Cosmopolitans and Locals in World Culture', in M. Featherstone (ed.) *Global Culture*, London: Sage, 237–51.

Hannerz, U. (1992) *Global Complexity*, New York: Columbia University Press.

Hannerz, U. (1996) *Transnational Connections*, London: Routledge.

Hannerz, U. (2004a) 'Cosmopolitanism', in D. Nugent and J. Vincent (eds) *A Companion to the Anthropology of Politics*, Oxford: Blackwell, 69–85.

Hannerz, U. (2004b) *Foreign News. Exploring the World of Foreign Correspondents*, Chicago: University of Chicago Press.

Hardt, M. and A. Negri (2000) *Empire*, Cambridge, Mass: Harvard University Press.

Harland-Jacobs, J. (2007) *Builders of Empire: Freemasons and British Imperialism, 1717–1927*, Chapel Hill: University of North Carolina Press.

Harper, T.N. (2002) 'Empire, Diaspora, and the Languages of Globalism: 1850–1914', in A.G. Hopkins (ed.) (2002a) *Globalization in World History*, London: Pimlico, 141–66.

Harris, N. (2002) *The Return of Cosmopolitan Capital: Globalization, the State and War*, London: Tauris.

Hart, R. (2006) 'Universals of Yesteryear: Hegel's Modernity in an Age of Globalization', in A.G. Hopkins (ed.) *Global History: Interactions between the Global and the Local*, Basingstoke: Palgrave, 66–97.

Hashmi, S.H. (2003) 'The Qu'ran and Tolerance: An Interpretive Essay on Verse 5:48', *Journal Of Human Rights*, 2(1), March, 81–103.

Hawley, J.C. (2008) *India in Africa, Africa in India: Indian Ocean Cosmopolitanisms*, Bloomington, Ind: Indiana University Press.

Hebdige, D. (1990) 'Fax to the Future', *Marxism Today*, Jan, 18–23.

Hegel, G. (1956) [1837] *Lectures on The Philosophy of History*, New York: Dover.

Heilman, S.C. and S. Cohen (1989) *Cosmopolitans and Parochials: Modern Orthodox Jews in America*, Chicago: University of Chicago Press.

Held, D. (1995) *Democracy and the Global Order: From the Modern State to Cosmopolitan Governance*, Cambridge: Polity Press.

Held, D. (1997) 'Cosmopolitan Democracy and the Global Order: A New Agenda', in J. Bohman and M. Lutz-Bachmann (eds) *Perpetual Peace: Essays on Kant's Cosmopolitan Ideal*, Cambridge Mass: MIT Press, 235–51.

Held, D. (2002) 'Cosmopolitanism: Ideas, Realities, and Deficits', in D. Held and A. McGrew (eds) *Governing Globalization*, Cambridge: Polity, 305–24.

Held, D. (2005) 'Principles of Cosmopolitan Order', in G. Brock and H. Brighouse (eds) *The Political Philosophy of Cosmopolitanism*, Cambridge: Cambridge University Press, 10–27.

Held, D., A. McGrew, D. Goldblatt and J. Perraton (1999) *Global Transformations, Politics, Economics, and Culture*, Cambridge: Polity Press.

Herrero, M. (2007) *Irish Intellectuals and Aesthetics: The Making of a Modern Art Collection*, Dublin: Irish Academic Press.

Hiebert, D. (2002) 'Cosmopolitanism at the Local level: The Development of Transnational Neighbourhoods', in S. Vertovec and R. Cohen (eds) *Conceiving Cosmopolitanism*, Oxford: Oxford University Press, 209–23.

Himmelfarb, G. (1996) 'The Illusions of Cosmopolitanism', in M. Nussbaum and J. Cohen (eds) (1996) *For Love of Country*, Boston: Beacon Press, 72–7.

Hirst, P. and G. Thompson (1996) *Globalization in Question*, Cambridge: Polity Press.

Hoad, N. (2006) *African Intimacies: Race, Homosexuality, and Globalization*, Minneapolis: University of Minnesota Press.

Hogan, E. (1990) *The Irish Missionary Movement: A Historical Survey 1830–1980*, Dublin: Gill and MacMillan.

Hollinger, D. (1995) *Postethnic America: Beyond Multiculturalism*, New York: Basic Books.

Hollinger, D. (2002) 'Not Universalists, Not Pluralists: The New Cosmopolitans Find Their Own Way', in S. Vertovec and R. Cohen (eds) *Conceiving Cosmopolitanism*, Oxford: Oxford University Press, 227–39.

Holton, R. (1986) *Cities, Capitalism, and Civilization*, London: Allen and Unwin.

Holton, R. (1998) *Globalization and the Nation-State*, Basingstoke: Macmillan.

Holton, R. (2003) 'Max Weber and the Interpretative Tradition', in G. Delanty and E. Isin (eds) *Handbook of Historical Sociology*, London: Sage, 27–38.

Holton, R. (2005) *Making Globalization*, Basingstoke: Palgrave Macmillan.

Holton, R. (2008) *Global Networks*, Basingstoke: Palgrave Macmillan.

Honneth, A. (1997) 'Is Universalism a Moral Trap?', in J. Bohman and M. Lutz-Bachmann (eds) *Perpetual Peace: Essays on Kant's Cosmopolitan Ideal*, Cambridge Mass: MIT Press, 155–78.

Honig, B. (1998) 'Ruth the Model Emigré: Mourning and the Symbolic Politics of Immigration', in P. Cheah and B. Robbins (eds) *Cosmopolitics: Thinking and Feeling Beyond the Nation*, Minneapolis: Minneapolis UP, 192–215.

Hopkins, A.G. (ed.) (2002a) *Globalization in World History*, London: Pimlico.

Howe, R. (1978) Max Weber's Elective Affinities: Sociology Within the Bounds of Pure Reason', *American Journal of Sociology*, 84(2), 366–85.

Huntington, S. (1996) *The Clash of Civilisations and the Remaking of the World Order*, New York: Simon and Schuster.

Ignatiev, N. (1995) *How the Irish became White*, London: Routledge.

Inglehart, R. (1997) *Modernization and Post-Modernization*, Princeton: Princeton University Press.

Inglis, D. and R. Robertson (2004) 'Beyond the Gates of the Polis: Reconfiguring Sociology's Ancient Inheritance', *Journal of Classical Sociology*, 4(2), 165–89.

Inglis, D and R. Robertson (2005) 'The Ecumenical Analytic: "Globalization", Reflexivity and the Revolution in Greek Historiography', *European Journal of Social Theory*, 8(2), 99–122.

Inglis, T. (1998) *Moral Monopoly: The Rise and Fall of the Catholic Church in Ireland*, 2nd edition, Dublin: University College Dublin Press.

Inglis, T. (2008) *Global Ireland*, Abingdon: Routledge.

Ingold, T. (2000) *The Perception of the Environment: Essays in Livelihood, Dwelling, and Skill*, London: Routledge.

Irish Centre for Migration Studies (2002) 'Governance Models and New Migration Patterns: Local Strategies to Foster Social Cohesion', http://www.iprs.it/docs/SocialQualityFinal%20Report%20(governance%20models%20...).doc accessed 9th April 2007.

Jackson, R. (2006) *Fifty Key Figures in Islam*, London: Routledge.

James, C.L.R. (1988) [1938] *The Black Jacobins: Toussaint L'Ouverture and the San Domingo Revolution*, New York: Vintage Books.

Jelin, E. (2000) 'Towards a Global Environmental Citizenship?', *Citizenship Studies*, 4(1), 47–63.

Jones, C. (1999) *Global Justice: Defending Cosmopolitanism*, Oxford: Oxford University Press.

Jones, C. (2007) ' Institutions with Global Scope: Moral Cosmopolitanism and Political Practice', in D. Weinstock (ed.), *Global Justice, Global Institutions*, Calgary: University of Calgary Press, 1–28.

Juris, J. (2005) 'The New Digital Media and Activist Networking within Anti-Corporate Globalization Movements', *Annals of the American Academy of Political and Social Science*, 597, 189–208.

Kaldor, M. (1996) 'Cosmopolitanism Versus Nationalism: The New Divide', in R. Caplan and J. Feffer (eds) *Europe's New Nationalism*, Oxford: Oxford University Press, 42–58.

Kant, I. (1960) [1764] *Observations on the Feelings of the Beautiful and the Sublime*, Berkeley: University of California Press.

Kant, I. (1991) [1784], 'Perpetual Peace. A Philosophical Sketch', in I. Kant, *Political Writings*, Cambridge: Cambridge University Press, 93–130.

Karim, K. (2002) 'Muslim Encounters with New Media: Towards an Inter-Civilizational Discourse on Globality', in A. Mohammadi (ed.) *Islam Encountering Globalization*, New York: Routledge, 36–60.

Katz, J.E., R. Rice and P. Aspden (2001) 'The Internet, 1995–2000', *American Behavioural Scientist*, 45(3), 405–19.

Kaufmann, E. (2001) 'Nativist Cosmopolitans: Institutional Reflexivity and the Decline of "Double-Consciousness" in American Nationalist Thought', *Journal of Historical Sociology*, 14(1), 47–78.

Keane, J. (2003) *Global Civil Society?*, Cambridge: Cambridge University Press.

Keane, J. (2006) 'Introduction, Cities and Civil Society', in J. Keane (ed.) *Civil Society. Berlin Perspectives*, New York: Berghahn Books, 1–36.

Kearns, G. (2003) 'Nation, Empire, Cosmopolis: Ireland and the Break with Britain', in D. Gilbert, D. Matless and Brian Short (eds) *Geographies of British Modernity: Space and Society in the 20th Century*, Oxford: Blackwell, 204–28.

Keck, M.E. and K. Sikkink (1998) *Activists Beyond Borders. Advocacy Networks in International Politics*, Ithaca: Cornell University Press.

Kennedy, M. (1996) *Ireland and the League of Nations, 1919–46: International Relations, Diplomacy and Politics*, Dublin: Academic Press.

Kennedy, P. (2004) 'Making Global Society: Friendship Networks Among Transnational Professionals in the Building Design Industry', *Global Networks*, 4(2), 157–79.

Keohane, R., P. Haas and M. Levy (1993) 'The Effectiveness of International Environmental Institutions', in P. Haas, R. Keohane and M. Levy (eds) *Institutions for the Earth: Sources of Effective International Environmental Protection*, Cambridge, Mass: MIT Press, 3–24.

Kigongo, J.K. (2002) 'The Relevance of African Ethics to Contemporary African Society', in A. Dalfovo (ed.) *Ethics, Human Rights and Development in Africa*, Washington DC: CRVP, consulted on line at http://www.crvp.org/book/ Series02/11-8/contents.htm.

Kivisto, P. (2007) 'Conclusion. The Boundaries of Citizenship in a Transitional Age', in T. Faist and P. Kivisto (eds) *Dual Citizenship in Global Perspective: From Unitary to Multiple Citizenship*, Basingstoke: Palgrave Macmillan, 272–87.

Klein, N. (1999) *No Logo*, London: Flamingo.

Kleingeld, P. (1999) 'Six Varieties of Cosmopolitanism in Late 18th Century Germany', *Journal of the History of Ideas*, 60(3), 505–24.

Köhler, M. (1998) 'From the National to the Cosmopolitan Public Sphere', in D. Archibugi, D. Held and M. Köhler (eds) *Re-imagining Political Community*, Cambridge: Polity Press, 231–51.

Kokaz, N. (2005) 'Institutions for Global Justice', in D. Weinstock (ed.) *Global Justice, Global Institutions*, Calgary: University of Calgary Press, 65–108.

Kristeva, J. (1993) *Nations without Nationalism*, New York: Columbia Press.

Kuhling, C. and K. Keohane (2007) *Cosmopolitan Ireland: Globalisation and Quality of Life*, London: Pluto Press.

Kuper, A. (1994) 'Culture, Identity, and the Project of Anthropology', *Man*, 29(3), 537–54.

Kurasawa, F. (2004) 'A Cosmopolitanism from Below: Anti-Globalization and the Creation of a Solidarity without Bounds', *European Journal of Sociology*, 45, 233–55.

Kymlicka, W. (2001) 'From Enlightenment Cosmopolitanism to Liberal Nationalism', in W. Kymlicka (ed.) *Politics in the Vernacular: Nationalism, Multiculturalism, and Citizenship*, Oxford: Oxford University Press, 203–20.

Laffan, B. (2002) 'Ireland and the European Union', in W. Crotty and D. Schmitt (eds) *Ireland on the World Stage*, Harlow: Pearson Educational, 83–94.

Lakatos, I. (1978) *The Methodology of Scientific Research Programmes*, Cambridge: Cambridge University Press.

Lamont, M. and S. Aksartova (2002) 'Ordinary Cosmopolitanisms: Strategies for Bridging Racial Boundaries amongst Working-Class Men', *Theory, Culture and Society*, 19(4), 1–25.

Lapidus, I. (1975) 'Hierarchies and Social Networks; A Comparison of Chinese and Islamic Societies', in F.J. Wakeman (ed.) *Conflict and Control in Late Imperial China*, Berkeley: University of California Press, 26–42.

Larguèche, A., J. Clancy-Smith and C. Audet (2001) 'The City and the Sea: Evolving Forms of Mediterranean Cosmopolitanism in Tunis, 1700–1881', *Journal of North African Studies*, 6(1), 117–28.

Lee, D. and B.S. Turner (eds) (1996) *Controversies about Class: Debating Inequalities in Late Industrialism*, London: Longman.

Lentin, R. and R. McVeigh (2002) 'Situated Racisms: A Theoretical Introduction', in R. Lentin and R. McVeigh (eds) *Racism and Anti-Racism in Ireland*, Dublin: Beyond the Pale Publishers, 1–48.

Lentin, R. and R. McVeigh (2006) *After Optimism? Ireland, Racism, and Globalisation*, Dublin: Metro Éireann Publications.

Levenson, J. (1971) *Revolution and Cosmopolitanism*, Berkeley: University of California Press.

Levy, D. and N. Sznaider (2002) 'Memory Unbound: The Holocaust and the Formation of Cosmopolitan Memory', *European Journal of Social Theory*, 5(1), 87–106.

Lockwood, D. (1964) 'Social Integration and System Integration', in G. Zollschan and F. Hirsch (eds) *Explorations in Social Change*, London: Routledge, 244–57.

Lonsdale, J. (2002) 'Globalization, Ethnicity and Democracy: A View from the "Hopeless Continent"', in A.G. Hopkins (ed.) *Globalization in World History*, London: Pimlico, 194–219.

Loyal, S. (2003) 'Welcome to the Celtic Tiger: Racism, Immigration and the State', in C. Coulter and S. Coleman (eds) *The End of Irish History? Critical Reflections on the Celtic Tiger*, Manchester: Manchester University Press, 74–94.

Lyons, F.S.L. (1963) *Internationalism, 1815–1914*, Leiden: Sythoff.

Lyotard, J-F. (1984) *Le Tombeau de l'intellectual et autres papiers*, Paris: Galilée.

Lyotard, J-F. (1985) 'Histoire Universelle et Difference Culturelle', *Critique*, 41 (May) translated into English in A. Benjamin (ed.) *The Lyotard Reader*, Oxford: Blackwell, 314–23.

MacIntyre, A. (1981) *After Virtue*, London: Duckworth.

MacIntyre, S. (1980) *Little Moscows*, London: Croom Helm.

McWilliams, D. (2005) *The Pope's Children: Ireland's New Elite*, Dublin: Gill and Macmillan.

Mahoney, J. (2007) *The Challenge of Human Rights*, Oxford: Blackwell.

Malachuk, D. (2007) 'Nationalist Cosmopolitics in the Nineteenth Century', in D. Morgan and G. Banham (eds) *Cosmopolitics and the Emergence of a Future*, Basingstoke: Palgrave Macmillan, 139–62.

Malcolmson, S. (1998) 'The Varieties of Cosmopolitan Experience', in P. Cheah and B. Robbins (eds) *Cosmopolitics: Thinking and Feeling Beyond the Nation*, Minneapolis: Minneapolis UP, 233–45.

Mandaville, P. (2002) 'Reimagining the Ummah? Information Technology and the Changing Boundaries of Political Islam', in A. Mohammadi (ed.) *Islam Encountering Globalization*, New York: Routledge, 61–90.

Mandel, R.E. (2008) *Cosmopolitan Anxieties: Turkish Challenges to Citizenship and Belonging in Germany*, Durham, NC: Duke University Press.

Mani, M.V. (2007) *Cosmopolitical Claims: Turkish-German Literatures from Nadolny to Pamuk*, Iowa City: Iowa University Press.

Mann, M. (1986) *The Sources of Social Power, Vol. 1*, Cambridge: Cambridge University Press.

Mann, M. (1993) 'Nation-states in Europe and Other Continents: Diversifying, Developing not Dying', *Daedalus* (Summer), 115–40.

Mann, M. (1997) 'Has Globalization Ended the Rise and Rise of the Nation-state?', *Review of International Political Economy*, 4(3), 472–96.

Maris, V. (2005) 'The Convention on Bio-Diversity: From Realism to Cosmopolitanism', in D. Weinstock (ed.) *Global Justice, Global Institutions*, Calgary: University of Calgary Press, 335–62.

Marx, K. and F. Engels (1962) [1848] 'Manifesto of the Communist Party', in K. Marx and F. Engels, *Selected Works*, vol 1, Moscow: Foreign Languages Publishing House, 34–65.

Mbiti, J.S. (1990) *African Religions and Philosophy*, second edition, London: Heinemann.

Mellor, A. (2006) 'Embodied Cosmopolitanism and the British Romantic Woman Writer', *European Romantic Review*, 17(3), 289–300.

Menocal, M.R. (2002) *The Ornament of the World: How Muslims, Jews and Christians Created a Culture of Tolerance in Medieval Spain*, Boston: Little Brown.

Mercer, K. (ed.) (2005) *Cosmopolitan Modernisms*, Cambridge MA: MIT Press.

Merton, R.K. (1968) *Social Theory and Social Structure, Enlarged Edition*, Glencoe: Free Press.

Mignolo, W. (2000) 'The Many Faces of Cosmo-polis: Border Thinking and Critical Cosmopolitanism', *Public Culture*, 12(3), 721–48.

Miller, D. (1988) 'On the Ethical Significance of Nationality', *Ethics*, 98(4), 647–62.

Mitchell, K. (2007) 'Geographies of Identity: The Intimate Cosmopolitan', *Progress in Human Geography*, 31(5), 706–20.

Morgan, D. and G. Banham (2007) (eds) *Cosmopolitics and the Emergence of a Future*, Basingstoke: Palgrave Macmillan.

Morgenthau, H. (1992) *Politics among Nations*, New York: McGraw Hill.

Mumford, L. (1966) *The City in History*, Harmondsworth: Pelican.

Murphy, D. (2000) *A History of Irish Emigrant and Missionary Education*, Dublin: Four Courts Press.

Nagle, J. (2004) 'Is "Everybody Irish on St. Paddy's?"' Ambivalence and Conflict on St Patrick's Day: A Research Report into People's Attitudes into St Patrick's Day, Belfast: Institute of Irish Studies.

Nava, M. (2002) 'Cosmopolitan Modernity: Everyday Imaginaries and the Register of Difference', *Theory, Culture and Society*, 19(1–2), 81–99.

Nava, M. (2007) *Visceral Cosmopolitanism*, Oxford: Berg.

Nielsen, K. (2000) 'Cosmopolitan Nationalism', in H. Miscevic (ed.) *Nationalism and Ethnic Conflict*, Chicago: Open Court, 299–320.

Njoroge, R. and G. Bennars (1986) *Philosophy and Education in Africa*, Nairobi: Transworld Press.

Norris, P. (2000) 'Global Governance and Cosmopolitan Citizens', in J.S. Nye and J.D. Donoghue (eds) *Governance in a Globalizing World*, Washington DC: Brookings Institute Press, 155–77.

Norris, P. (2006) 'Confidence in the United Nations: Cosmopolitan and Nationalistic Attitudes', paper presented to the World Values Conference Society, *Politics and Values, 1981–2006*, Istanbul 3–4 Nov 2006 http:// ksghome.harvard.edu.au/'~pnorris/Acrobat/Cosmopolitan%20and %20nationalistic%20attitudes%20towards%20the%20United%Nations.pdf

Nowicka, M. (2006) *Transnational Professionals and their Cosmopolitan Universes*, Frankfurt: Campus Verlag.

Nussbaum, M. and J. Cohen (eds) (1996) *For Love of Country*, Boston: Beacon Press.

Nussbaum, M. (1997) 'Kant and Stoic Cosmopolitanism', *Journal of Political Philosophy*, 5(1), 1–25.

Nwankwo, I.K. (2005) *Black Cosmopolitanism: Racial Consciousness and Transnational Identity in the Nineteenth Century Americas*, Philadelphia: University of Pennsylvania Press.

Nyers, P. (2003) 'Abject Cosmopolitanism: The Politics of Protection in the Anti-Deportation Movement', *Third World Quarterly*, 24(6), 1069–93.

O'Dowd, L. (2002) 'The Changing Significance of European Borders', *Regional and Federal Studies*, 12(4), 13–36.

Gráda, C.Ó. (1999) *Black 47 and Beyond: The Great Irish Famine in History, Economy and Memory*, Princeton: Princeton University Press.

Ohmae, K. (1990) *The Borderless World*, London: Collins.

Ohmae, K. (1995) *The End of the Nation State*, London: Harper Collins.

O'Mahony, E., S. Loyal and A. Mulcahy (2001) *Racism in Ireland: The Views of Black and Ethnic Minorities*, Dublin: Amnesty.

Ong, A. (1998) 'Flexible Citizenship among Chinese Cosmopolitans', in P. Cheah and B. Robbins (eds) *Cosmopolitics: Thinking and Feeling Beyond the Nation*, Minneapolis: Minneapolis UP, 134–62.

O'Riain, S. (2000) 'Net-working for a Living: Irish Software Developers in the Global Workplace', in M. Burawoy *et al.* (eds) *Global Ethnography: Forces, Connections and Imaginations in a Global World*, Berkeley: University of California Press, 175–202.

Osiander, A. (2001) 'Sovereignty, International Relations and the Westphalian Myth', *International Organization*, 55(2), 251–87.

Osterdahl, J. (2003) 'The Surprising Originality of the African Charter on Human and Peoples' Rights', in J. Petman and J. Klabbers (eds) *Nordic Cosmopolitanism: Essays in International Law*, Leiden: Markus Nijhoff, 5–32.

Parry, B. (1991) 'The Contradictions of Cultural Studies', *Transitions*, 53, 37–45.

Parsons, T. (1937) *The Structure of Social Action*, New York: McGraw-Hill.

Pécoud, A. (2000) 'Cosmopolitanism and Business: Entrepreneurship and Identity among German-Turks in Berlin', *ESRC Transnational Communities Working Paper Series* WPTC-2K-05, Oxford.

Perkins, M. (2006) 'Introduction', in M. Perkins and M. Liebscher (eds) *Nationalism versus Internationalism: German Thought and Culture, 1789–1914*, Lewiston NY: Edwin Mellen Press, 1–34.

Pettit, P. (1997) *Republicanism: A Theory of Freedom and Government*, Oxford: Oxford University Press.

Phillips, A. (2000) *Promises, Promises: Essays on Literature and Psychoanalysis*, London: Faber.

Phillips, T. (2002) 'Imagined Communities and Self-Identity: An Exploratory Quantitative Analysis', *Sociology*, 36(3), 597–617.

Phillips, T. and P. Smith (2008) 'Cosmopolitan Beliefs and Cosmopolitan Practises: An Empirical Investigation', *Journal of Sociology*, 44(4), 391–9.

Pogge, T. (2008) *World Poverty and Human Rights: Cosmopolitan Responsibilities and Reforms*, Cambridge: Polity Press.

Polanyi, K. (1957) [1944] *The Great Transformation*, Boston: Beacon Press.

Pollard, C.W. (2001) 'Travelling with Joyce: Derek Walcott's Discrepant Cosmopolitan Modernism', *Twentieth Century Literature*, 47(2), 197–216.

Pollock, S. (1998) 'The Cosmopolitan Vernacular', *Journal of Asian Studies*, 57(1), 6–37.

Pollock, S. (2000) 'Cosmopolitanism and Vernacular in History', *Public Culture*, 12(3), 6–37.

Pollock, S., H. Bhabha, C. Breckenridge and D. Chakrabaty (2000) 'Cosmopolitanisms', *Public Culture*, 12(3), 577–89.

Posnock, R. (2000) 'The Dream of Deracination: The Uses of Cosmopolitanism', *American Literary Review*, 12(4), 802–18.

Pojman, L. (2004) 'The Moral Case for Institutional Cosmopolitanism', *Croatian Journal of Philosophy*, 1(10), 3–28.

Powell, W.W. (1990) 'Neither Market nor Hierarchy: Network Forms of Organization', *Research in Organizational Behaviour*, 12, 295–335.

Prodi, R. (2001) 'The European Union and its Citizens: A Matter of Democracy', Speech to the European Parliament, Strasbourg, 4 September. Weblink cited Rumford (2007) 17, but broken when attempted to access 17th April 2008.

Purdy, D.L. (1998) *The Tyranny of Elegance: Consumer Cosmopolitanism in the Era of Goethe*, Baltimore: Johns Hopkins University Press.

Rabinow, P. (1986) 'Representations are Social Facts: Modernity and Post-modernity in Anthropology', in J. Clifford and G. Marcus (eds) *Writing Culture: The Poetics and Politics of Ethnography*, Berkeley: University of California Press, 234–61.

Radhakrishnan, R. (1995) 'Towards an Eccentric Cosmopolitanism', *Positions*, 3, 814–21.

Rajan, G. and S. Sharma (2006) 'New Cosmopolitanisms: South Asians in the United States at the Turn of the Twenty-First Century', in G. Rajan and S. Sharma (eds) *New Cosmopolitanisms: South Asians in the US*, Stanford: Stanford University Press, 1–36.

Rediker, M. (1987) *Between the Devil and the Deep Blue Sea, Merchant Seamen, Pirates and the Anglo-American Maritime World, 1700–50*, Cambridge: Cambridge University Press.

Reich, R. (1991) *The Work of Nations*, London: Simon and Schuster.

Reiss, H. (1991) 'Introduction', in I. Kant, *Political Writings*, Cambridge: Cambridge University Press, 1–40.

Rennella, M. (2008) *The Boston Cosmopolitans: International Travel and American Arts and Letters*, Basingstoke: Palgrave Macmillan.

Rickard, J. (2001) '"A Quaking Sod". Hybridity, Identity, and Wandering Irishness', in M.P. Gillespie (ed.) *James Joyce and the Fabrication of an Irish Identity*, Amsterdam: Rodopi, 83–110.

Ritzer, G. (1998) *The McDonaldization Thesis*, London: Sage.

Robbins, B. (1992) 'Comparative Cosmopolitanism', *Social Text*, 31/2, 169–86.

Robbins, B. (1998a) 'Introduction Part 1: Actually Existing Cosmopolitanism', in P. Cheah and B. Robbins (eds) *Cosmopolitics: Thinking and Feeling Beyond the Nation*, Minneapolis: Minneapolis UP, 1–19.

Robbins, B. (1998b) 'Comparative Cosmopolitans', in P. Cheah and B. Robbins (eds) *Cosmopolitics: Thinking and Feeling Beyond the Nation*, Minneapolis: Minneapolis UP, 246–64.

Robbins, B. (1999) *Feeling Global: Internationalism in Distress*, New York: New York University Press.

Robertson, R. (1992) *Globalization: Social Theory and Global Culture*, London: Sage.

Robertson, R. (1995) 'Glocalization, Time-Space and Homogeneity-Homogeneity', in M. Featherstone, S. Lash and R. Robertson (eds) *Global Modernities*, London: Sage, 25–44.

Robinson, F. (1997) 'Ottomans-Saffayids-Mughals: Shared Knowledge and Connective Systems', *Journal of Islamic Studies*, 8, 151–84.

Robinson, J. (2006) *Ordinary Cities: Between Modernity and Development*, London: Routledge.

Robinson, J.P., K. Meyer, A. Neustadt and A. Alvarez (2002) 'The Internet and Other Uses of Time', in B. Wellman and C. Haythornthwaite (eds) *The Internet in Everyday Life*, Oxford: Blackwell, 224–62.

Robinson, K. (ed.) (2005) *Asian and Pacific Cosmopolitans: Self and Subject in Motion*, Basingstoke: Palgrave Macmillan.

Robertson, T. and Y. Wind (1983) 'Organizational Cosmopolitanism and Innovativeness', *The Academy of Management Journal*, 26(2), 332–8.

Rodrigues, M.G.M. (2004) *Global Environmentalism and Local Politics: Transnational Advocacy Networks in Brazil, Ecuador, and India*, Albany: SUNY Press.

Rorty, R. (1992) 'Cosmopolitanism Without Emancipation: A Response to Lyotard', in S. Lash and J. Friedman (eds) *Modernity and Identity*, Oxford: Blackwell, 59–72.

Rose, D. (1997) 'State Policy, Immigrant Women's Support Networks and the Question of Integration in Montreal', in J. Fairhurst, I. Booysens and P. Hattingh (eds) *Migration and Gender: Place, Time and People Specific*, Pretoria: University of Pretoria, Department of Geography, 403–24.

Rosenau, J. (1990) *Turbulence in World Politics: A Theory of Change and Continuity*, Princeton: Princeton University Press.

Rother, N. and J.D. Medrano (2006) 'Is the West Becoming More Tolerant?', in P. Ester, M. Braun and P. Mohler (eds) *Globalization, Value Change and Generations: A Cross-National and Intergenerational Perspective*, Leiden: Brill, 151–78.

Ruane, J. and J. Todd (2003) 'A Changed Irish Nationalism? The Significance of the Good Friday Agreement of 1998', in J. Ruane, J. Todd and A. Mandeville (eds) *Europe's Old States in the New World Order*, Dublin: UCD Press, 121–45.

Rumford, C. (2002) *The European Union: A Political Sociology*, Oxford: Blackwell.

Rumford, C. (2007) 'Does Europe have Cosmopolitan Borders?', *Globalizations*, 4(3), 1–13.

Rumford, C. (2008) *Cosmopolitan Spaces*, London: Routledge.

Rushbrook, D. (2002) 'Cities, Queer Space, and the Cosmopolitan Tourist', *GLQ: A Journal of Lesbian and Gay Studies*, 8(1–2), 183–206.

Said, E. (1978) *Orientalism*, New York: Pantheon Books.

Santos, B. and C. Rodríguez-Garavito (2005) (eds) *Law and Globalization from Below: Towards a Cosmopolitan Legality*, Cambridge: Cambridge University Press.

Sassen, S. (1994) *Cities in a World Economy*, Thousand Oaks: Pine Forge Press.

Sassen, S. (1996) *Losing Control? Sovereignty in an Age of Globalization*, New York: Columbia University Press.

Sassen, S. (2002) 'Digitization: Its Variability as a Variable in the Reshaping of Cross-Border Relations', paper delivered at the LSE April 2002 cited B. Axford (2003) 'Editorial: Towards a Political Sociology of the Internet and Local Governance', *Telematics and Informatics*, 20, 185–92.

Scheffler, S. (1999) 'Conceptions of Cosmopolitanism', *Utilitas*, 11(3), 255–76.

Schein, L. (1998) 'Forged Transnationality and Oppositional Cosmopolitanism', in M.P. Smith and L.E. Guranizo, *Transnationalism from Below*, New Brunswick: Transaction, 291–313.

Schein, L. (1999) 'Of Cargo and Satellites: Imagined Cosmopolitanism', *Postcolonial Studies*, 2(3), 345–75.

Schiller, H. (1976) *Communication and Cultural Domination*, New York: International Arts and Sciences Press.

Schindler, S. and L. Koepnick (eds) (2008) *The Cosmopolitan Screen: German Cinema and the Global Imaginary, 1945 to the Present*, Ann Arbor: University of Michigan Press.

Scholte, J-A. (2005) *Globalization: Critical Perspectives*, Basingstoke: Palgrave Macmillan.

Sen, A. (2005) *The Argumentative Indian*, London: Penguin.

Sennett, R. (1994) 'Christian Cosmopolitanism', *The Boston Review*, xix, 5, Oct/Nov.

Shore, C. (2000) *Building Europe: The Cultural Politics of European Integration*, London: Routledge.

Simmel, G. (1950) [1903] 'The Metropolis and Mental Life', in K. Wolff (ed.) *The Sociology of George Simmel*, Glencoe, Ill: Free Press, 409–23.

Sinnott, R. (2001) *Attitudes and Behaviour of the Irish Electorate in the Referendum on the Treaty of Nice*, Dublin: European Commission Representative in Ireland.

Skrbis, Z. and I. Woodward (2007) 'The Ambivalence of Ordinary Cosmopolitanism: Investigating the Limits of Cosmopolitan Openness', *Sociological Review*, 55(4), 730–47.

Skrbis, Z., G. Kendall and I. Woodward (2004) 'Locating Cosmopolitanism: Between Humanist Ideal and Grounded Social Category', *Theory, Culture, and Society*, 21(6), 115–36.

Smith, A. (2002) [1781] *The Theory of Moral Sentiments*, Cambridge: Cambridge University Press.

Smith, A.D. (1980) *The Ethnic Revival*, Cambridge: Cambridge University Press.

Smith, A.D. (1990) 'Towards a Global Culture?', in M. Featherstone (ed.) *Global Culture: Nationalism, Globalization and Modernity*, London: Sage, 171–91.

Smith, C. (2008) *Cosmopolitan Culture and Consumerism in Chick Lit*, London: Routledge.

Soysal, Y. (2001) 'Changing Boundaries of Participation in European Public Spheres: Reflections on Citizenship and Civil Society', in K. Eder and B. Giesen (eds) *European Citizenship between National Legacies and Postnational Projects*, Oxford: Oxford University Press, 159–79.

Stanton, K. (2006) *Cosmopolitan Fictions: Ethics, Politics, and Global Change in the Works of Kazuo Ishiguro, Michael Ondaatje, Jamaica Kincaid and J.M. Coetzee*, London: Routledge.

Stevenson, N. (2000) 'The Future of Public Media Cultures', *Information, Communication, and Society*, 3/2, 192–214.

Strongman, L. (2002) *The Booker Prize and the Legacy of Empire*, Amsterdam/ New York: Rodopi, 128–32.

Sunday Tribune (2005) 'Irish Marketing Survey', 1 May.

Swetschinski, D. (2000) *Reluctant Cosmopolitans: The Portuguese Jews of Seventeenth Century Amsterdam*, Oxford: Littman Library of Jewish Civilization.

Szerszynski, B. and J. Urry (2002) 'Cultures of Cosmopolitanism', *Sociological Review*, 50(4), 461–81.

Szerszynski, B. and J. Urry (2006) 'Visuality, Mobility, and the Cosmopolitan: Inhabiting the World from Afar', *British Journal of Sociology*, 57(1), 113–31.

Taylor, R. (1986) *Franz Lizst: The Man and the Musician*, London: Grafton.

Tai, T.V. (1988) *The Vietnamese Tradition of Human Rights*, Berkeley: Institute of East Asian Studies.

Tan, K-C. (2005) 'Cosmopolitan Impartiality and Patriotic Partiality', in D. Weinstock (ed.) *Global Justice, Global Institutions*, Calgary: University of Calgary Press, 165–92.

Teubner, G. (ed.) (1997) *Global Law Without a State. Studies in Modern Law and Policy*, Aldershot: Dartmouth Publishing.

Thompson, C.J. and S.K. Tambyah (1999) 'Trying to be Cosmopolitan', *Journal of Consumer Research*, 26, 214–41.

Thompson, E.P. (1963) *The Making of the English Working Class*, London: Gollancz.

Thompson, G. (2003) *Between Hierarchies and Markets: The Logic and Limits of Network Forms of Organisation*, Oxford: Oxford University Press.

Tomlinson, J. (1999) *Globalization and Culture*, Cambridge: Polity Press.

Tonra, B. (2006) *Global Citizen and European Republic*, Manchester: Manchester University Press.

Tovey, H. and P. Share (2003) *A Sociology of Ireland*, second edition, Dublin: Gill and Macmillan.

Trubek, D., J. Mosher and J. Rothstein (2000) 'Transnationalism in the Regulation of Labour Relations: International Regimes and Transnational Advocacy Networks', *Law and Social Enquiry*, 25, 1187–212.

Turner, B.S. (2001) 'The Erosion of Citizenship', *British Journal of Sociology*, 52(2), 189–209.

Turner, B.S. (2002) 'Cosmopolitan Virtue, Globalization, and Patriotism', *Theory, Culture, and Society*, 19(1–2), 45–63.

Urbinati, N. (2003) 'Can Cosmopolitan Democracy be Democratic?', in D. Archibugi (ed.) (2003) *Debating Cosmopolitics*, London: Verso, 67–85.

Urry, J. (1990) *The Tourist Gaze*, London: Sage.

Urry, J. (1995) *Consuming Places*, London: Routledge.

Urry, J. (2000) *Sociology beyond Societies*, London: Routledge.

Urry, J. (2002) *Global Fluids*, Cambridge: Polity.

Valente, J. (1996) 'James Joyce and the Cosmopolitan Sublime', in M. Wollaeger *et al.*, *Joyce and the Subject of History*, Ann Arbor: University of Michigan Press, 59–82.

van der Bly, M. (2007) *The Universal Surname: A Theoretical-Empirical Enquiry into the Relationship Between Globalization and Sameness*, Unpublished PhD thesis, Department of Sociology, Trinity College, Dublin.

van der Veer, P. (2002) 'Colonial Cosmopolitanism', in S. Vertovec and R. Cohen (eds) *Conceiving Cosmopolitanism*, Oxford: Oxford University Press, 167–79.

Vansina, J. (1991) *Paths in the Rainforests, Towards a History of Political Tradition in Equatorial Africa*, London: James Currey.

Venn, C. (2002) 'Altered States: Post-Enlightenment Cosmopolitanism and Transmodern Socialities', *Theory, Culture and Society*, 19(1–2), 65–80.

Vertovec, S. and R. Cohen (2002) 'Introduction', in S. Vertovec and R. Cohen (eds) *Conceiving Cosmopolitanism*, Oxford: Oxford University Press, 1–22.

Vertovec, S. (2006) 'Fostering Cosmopolitanisms: A Conceptual Survey and Experiment in Berlin', in G. Lenz, F. Ulfers and A. Dallmann (eds) *Towards a New Metropolitanism: Reconstituting Public Culture, Urban Citizenship, and the Multicultural Imaginary in New York and Berlin*, Winter: Heidelberg, 277–98.

Waldron, J. (1995) 'Minority Cultures and the Cosmopolitan Alternative', in W. Kymlicka (ed.) *The Rights of Minority Cultures*, Oxford: Oxford University Press, 93–122.

Walkowitz, R. (2003) 'The "Vision of Salome": Cosmopolitanism and Erotic Dancing in Central London 1908–1918', *American Historical Review*, 108(2), 337–96.

Walkowitz, R. (2006) *Cosmopolitan Style. Modernism Beyond the Nation*, New York: Columbia University Press.

Wallerstein, I. (1974) *The Modern World System: Capitalist Agriculture and the Origins of the European Economy in the 17th Century*, New York: Academic Press.

Wallerstein, I. (1976) 'A World System Perspective on the Social Sciences', *British Journal of Sociology*, 27(2), 343–52.

Wallerstein, I. (1990) 'Culture as the Ideological Battle Ground of the World System', in M. Featherstone (ed.) *Global Culture: Nationalism, Globalization and Modernity*, London: Sage, 31–56.

Wallerstein, I. (1991) *Geopolitics and Geoculture*, Cambridge: Cambridge University Press.

Walters, W (2006) 'Border/Control', *European Journal of Social Theory*, 9(2), 187–203.

Waltz, K. (1959) *Man, the State, and War*, New York: Columbia University Press.

Waltz, K. (1979) *The Theory of International Politics*, Reading, Mass: Addison Wesley.

Watenpaugh, K. (2005) 'Cleansing the Cosmopolitan City: Historicism, Journalism, and the Arab Nation in the Post-Ottoman Eastern Mediterranean', *Social History*, 30(1), 1–24.

Ward, E. (2002) 'Ireland and Human Rights', in W. Crotty and D. Schmitt (eds) *Ireland on the World Stage*, Harlow: Longman, 153–67.

Waxer, L. (2001) 'Llegó la Salsa: The Rise of Salsa in Columbia and Venezuela', in L. Waxer (ed.) *Situating Salsa: Global Markets and Local Meanings in Latin Popular Music*, 219–46.

Weber, E. (1977) *Peasants into Frenchman: The Modernization of Rural France 1870–1914*, London: Chatto and Windus.

Weber, M. (1949) 'Objectivity in Social Science', in M. Weber, *The Methodology of the Social Sciences*, New York: Free Press, 50–112.

Weber, M. (1961) [1904] *The Protestant Ethic and the Spirit of Capitalism*, London: Allen and Unwin.

Weber, M. (1978) *Economy and Society*, 2 vols, Berkeley: University of California Press.

Werbner, P. (1999) 'Global Pathways and Working Class Cosmopolitans: The Creation of Transnational Worlds', *Social Anthropology*, 7(1), 17–35.

Werbner, P. (2006) 'Vernacular Cosmopolitanism', *Theory, Culture and Society*, 23(2–3), 496–8.

Werbner, R. (2002) 'Cosmopolitan Ethnicity, Entrepreneurship and the Nation: Minority Elites in Botswana', *Journal of South African Studies*, 28(4), 731–53.

Williams, B. (1995) *Making Sense of Humanity*, Cambridge: Cambridge University Press.

Wimmer, A. and N. Glick Schiller (2003) 'Methodological Nationalism, the Social Sciences, and the Study of Migration: An Essay in Historical Epistemology', *International Migration Review*, 37(3), 576–610.

Wood, F. (2002) *The Silk Road*, London: Folio Society.

Woodward, I., Z. Skrbis and C. Bean (2008) 'Attitudes Towards Globalization and Cosmopolitanism: Cultural Attitudes, Personal Consumption, and the National Economy', *British Journal of Sociology*, 59(2), 208–26.

Yue Meng (2006) *Shanghai and the Edges of Empires*, Minneapolis: University of Minnesota Press.

Zangwill, I. (1914) *The Melting Pot*, London: Heinemann.

Zubaida, S. (1999) 'Cosmopolitanism and the Middle East', in R. Meijer (ed.) *Cosmopolitanism, Identity and Authenticity in the Middle East*, London: Curzon, 15–34.

Zubrzycki, G. (1986) *Multiculturalism and the Search for Roots*, Adelaide: Centre for Multicultural Studies, Flinders University.

Index